Financialisation and Macroeconomics

Financialisation has become a widely discussed and debated term leading to a plurality of perspectives, but no fixed definition or single reading. This book presents a critical exploration and review of the current literature on financialisation, focussing on the financialisation of NFCs and its possible implications for the macroeconomic and financial stability of advanced countries.

Starting from this critical analysis, it proposes some new readings of the process of financialisation, linking it directly, on the one hand, to the evolution of interest-bearing capital and the credit system, and, on the other hand, to the historical tendencies of monopoly capital towards financial arrangements to manage corporate control. Finally, a conceptual scheme for interpretation and a mathematical model of corporate portfolio choice is developed to explain how the tendency in developed countries to place growing shares of social surplus in speculative financial channels can contribute to their long-term real stagnation. The book also underlines the excessive attention usually being paid to some micro-epiphenomena that show a fallacy of composition at the macroeconomic level and can lead to some misunderstandings of the general trends in capitalist evolution. Moreover, some doubts are raised about the extent to which financialisation actually represents a change to the present regime of accumulation.

The book targets all the scholars who are interested in better understanding whether financialisation constitutes a profound change in the functioning of capitalist economic systems and what effects it can produce in social welfare in the advanced countries.

Giovanni Scarano is Professor of Economics at Roma Tre University and a member of STOREP (Italian Association for the History of Political Economy).

Routledge Critical Studies in Finance and Stability

Edited by ***Jan Toporowski****, School of Oriental and African Studies, University of London, UK*

The 2007–8 Banking Crash has induced a major and wide-ranging discussion on the subject of financial (in)stability and a need to revaluate theory and policy. The response of policy-makers to the crisis has been to refocus fiscal and monetary policy on financial stabilisation and reconstruction. However, this has been done with only vague ideas of bank recapitalisation and 'Keynesian' reflation aroused by the exigencies of the crisis, rather than the application of any systematic theory or theories of financial instability.

Routledge Critical Studies in Finance and Stability covers a range of issues in the area of finance including instability, systemic failure, financial macroeconomics in the vein of Hyman P. Minsky, Ben Bernanke and Mark Gertler, central bank operations, financial regulation, developing countries and financial crises, new portfolio theory and New International Monetary and Financial Architecture.

Financialisation in the European Periphery
Work and Social Reproduction in Portugal
Edited by Ana Cordeiro Santos and Nuno Teles

Emerging Economies and the Global Financial System
Post-Keynesian Analysis
Edited by Bruno Bonizzi, Annina Kaltenbrunner and Raquel A. Ramos

Financialisation in Emerging Economies
Changes in Central Banking
Juan Pablo Painceira

Financialisation and Macroeconomics
The Impact on Social Welfare in Advanced Economies
Giovanni Scarano

For more information about this series, please visit: www.routledge.com/series/RCSFS

Financialisation and Macroeconomics

The Impact on Social Welfare in Advanced Economies

Giovanni Scarano

Routledge
Taylor & Francis Group
LONDON AND NEW YORK

First published 2023
by Routledge
4 Park Square, Milton Park, Abingdon, Oxon OX14 4RN

and by Routledge
605 Third Avenue, New York, NY 10158

Routledge is an imprint of the Taylor & Francis Group, an informa business

British Library Cataloguing-in-Publication Data
A catalogue record for this book is available from the British Library

Library of Congress Cataloging-in-Publication Data
Names: Scarano, Giovanni (Professor of economics), author.
Title: Financialization and macroeconomics : the impact on social welfare in advanced economies / Giovanni Scarano.
Description: Abingdon, Oxon ; New York, NY : Routledge, 2023. | Series: Routledge critical studies in finance and stability | Includes bibliographical references and index. |
Identifiers: LCCN 2022035389 (print) | LCCN 2022035390 (ebook) | ISBN 9781032121307 (hardback) | ISBN 9781032121321 (paperback) | ISBN 9781003223221 (ebook)
Subjects: LCSH: Financialization—Case studies. | Financial services industry—Case studies. | Macroeconomics—Case studies.
Classification: LCC HG173 .S263 2023 (print) | LCC HG173 (ebook) | DDC 332—dc23/eng/20220923
LC record available at https://lccn.loc.gov/2022035389
LC ebook record available at https://lccn.loc.gov/2022035390

ISBN: 978-1-032-12130-7 (hbk)
ISBN: 978-1-032-12132-1 (pbk)
ISBN: 978-1-003-22322-1 (ebk)

DOI: 10.4324/9781003223221

Typeset in Bembo
By codeMantra

To my wife Valeria, who supports my life and work with her love and patience, and to my parents, who taught me to be myself in every circumstance.

Contents

Illustrations

Figures

Table

Introduction

During the last three decades, the world economy has undergone profound changes leading many heterodox economists to speak of a new phase of capitalist development, often named *neoliberal era*, characterised by a diminishing role for governments, financial deregulation and liberalisation, globalisation and financialisation. Moreover, in most advanced countries, the "rentier share" – i.e. the share of national income accruing to financial institutions and holders of financial wealth – has seen steady increase over the same period.

Of course, all these different phenomena are probably closely interconnected and none could exist without the others. However, in some respects, financialisation has frequently been perceived as the synthesis of all the other transformations.

The term *financialisation* began to appear in economic literature only in the early 1990s and it has often been used to refer to three different, even though interconnected, phenomena. The first is the reduction of reliance on bank loans by large non-financial corporations (NFCs) and their growing autonomous ability to raise funds in financial markets. The second is the expansion of banks' mediating activities in financial markets and their tendency to lend mainly to households. The third is the increasing involvement of households in the financial markets, as both debtors and asset holders (see Orhangazi, 2008; Lapavitsas, 2011).

In some respects, therefore, financialisation seems simply to refer to "the increasing role of financial motives, financial markets, financial actors and financial institutions in the operation of the domestic and international economies" (Epstein, 2005). However, the word *finance*, strictly speaking, refers solely to financial markets, which are only a part of modern financial systems, alongside the more traditional credit channels, like banking and issue of bonds, as well as forms of direct finance such as self-financing or providing capital by purchasing shares in corporations. From this viewpoint, finance is certainly broader than credit as it also relates to mobilisation of idle money through the capital market in the form of joint-stock capital (see Mavroudeas and Lapavitsas, 1999), but at the same time, it is only part of the channelling of funds in the financial system as a whole. So what do heterodox economists really mean when they speak of growing finance? Are they simply detecting

DOI: 10.4324/9781003223221-1

a structural change in the functioning of the economy and sectoral composition or are they rather fearing the rise of new financial oligarchies, which can create new economic powers, able to dominate the way capitalist economies work, even outside the financial markets?

Unfortunately, the concept has long remained very basic and undeveloped, and even now there is no common agreement about its meaning, with a consequent proliferation of definitions. Some scholars focus on the pursuit of "shareholder value" as a new mode of corporate governance. Others refer to the increasing role of the financial markets relative to the traditional bank-based financial systems. Some people, following Hilferding's approach, refer to the growing political and economic power of the rentier class. Others refer to the explosion of financial trading with a myriad of new financial instruments. Moreover, different authors focus on the different effects on the economy that the expansion of financial markets can produce, even though many emphasise the way changes in finance channels have affected income distribution and the level of effective demand.

Nevertheless, all these different focuses probably capture only some specific aspects of a more general phenomenon and the developments in financial dimension depend very much on how the capitalist economy is evolving as a whole. In fact, the expansion of financial markets follows different paths in time and space, affecting different aspects of economic and social life and ranging from mortgages through pension management to futures markets in carbon emissions, with multifarious effects on the rest of the economic system (see Fine, 2014).

Thus, today *financialisation* appears as an interpretative scheme emerging in the context of radical political economy, which, in turn, usually involves a critique of capitalism and rejection of neoclassical analysis and orthodox theory, favouring analysis of economic and power structures with a view to changing them and promoting more equitable economic outcomes (see Kim, 2018). Consequently, the fact that it is confined to heterodox approaches depends mainly on its being both a systemic and dynamic approach that is not easily reducible to optimisation behaviours and efficiency criteria typical of orthodox mainstream (see Fine, 2014), even though it draws attention to some phenomena, such as increasing liquidity holding and financial use of corporate savings, that today are a brainteaser for many mainstream economists, too.

Of course, the radical political economists are by no means a homogeneous group and there are a number of different readings of the way capitalism evolves. Thus, financialisation has undergone so many different readings over time that sometimes it is hard to understand what it really means.

According to some social scientists, like Krippner, the term financialisation really identifies a new "pattern of accumulation" in which "profit making occurs increasingly through financial channels rather than through trade and commodity production" (Krippner, 2004). This kind of reading has prompted several studies on financialisation to revive the interpretative schemes of the *French Regulation School* and the *Social Structures of Accumulation Approach*, in turn, developed in the United States.

The scholars who have contributed most to developing this strand of analysis follow a post-Keynesian approach and closely link the analysis of financialisation to macroeconomic problems such as those of capital accumulation and growth, focusing on the role of financial interest groups in the evolution of capitalism and in the determination and distribution of income.

However, a shift from real towards financial investment in the industrialised countries was already being highlighted as from the late 1960s by Marxist economists like Magdoff and Sweezy, who systematically began to explore this tendency in the pages of the *Monthly Review* (see Foster, 2007). The increasing role played by the financial institutions was, in this case, closely connected to corporate control strategies, which are a typical development of monopoly capital.

According to Marxist approaches, moreover, in the capitalist economies, interest, financial fees and speculative trading profits are types of income that simply arise as parts of the surplus value generated only in production processes and are appropriated through assertion of various property rights (see Foley, 2013). Therefore, according to many Marxists, national income accounting conventions create a distorted and misleading picture of value production and growth in the advanced capitalist economies because they impute a fictitious output as a counterpart to incomes generated in sectors such as finance, where there are no market-based measures of output. Consequently, a redistribution of surplus value between profits and financial rents can only be a side effect of the traditional conflict between *interest-bearing capital* and *industrial capital* and not a sign of a deeper change in the accumulation regime.

In the last 30 years, in the context of globalisation, the advanced capitalist countries have been de-industrialising and entering a "post-industrial" phase. In this context, there has been very rapid growth in financial assets and liabilities, as well as financial sector incomes, but not in financial sector employment (see Basu and Foley, 2013), showing that this is no simple change in sectoral structure. In this period, wages have stagnated despite continuing increases in labour productivity, and the personal and household distributions of income and wealth have become more unequal, showing, in turn, that a deeper process of income redistribution is underway.

Moreover, Marxist economists usually pay considerable attention to how industrial capital is accumulated and dynamically restructured. From this viewpoint, the interaction of internationally organised productive and financial capital and a more nationally confined labour force has probably played a major role in bringing about new restructuring forms of capital. And there is also a major role of the state, as a prominent agent of both economic and social restructuring, played by means of financial deregulation and liberalisation. Consequently, the real challenge is to understand how all the developments in the world of finance are connected to the present evolution of the capitalist mode of production.

Thus, in the context of Marxist approaches, financialisation is mainly viewed as an increasing role played by *interest-bearing capital* in real, as opposed to fictitious, accumulation of capital (see Fine, 2014). Of course, the expanding role of interest-bearing capital occurs in both intensive and extensive forms. The former manifests itself as an increase in financial assets without direct connection to production and exchange of commodities, while the latter involves the penetration of interest-bearing capital into new areas of economic and social life.

In any case, in the first decade of the 2000s, a growing part of the literature on financialisation focused on increasing rates of return on financial capital over those on fixed capital and at the same time increasing acquisition of short-term financial assets by NFCs in high-income OECD countries, providing empirical evidence of a structural change in their portfolio decisions (see Stockhammer, 2004; Crotty, 2005; Duménil and Lévy, 2005; Epstein and Jayadev, 2005). Thus, some scholars hold that financialisation affects the real investment of NFCs through two channels. The first involves the increase in financial assets of NFCs, which at the microeconomic level are by nature alternative to real investments in the same companies, while the second is connected to growing transfers of profits to financial rentiers, which leads to lower retention ratios and fewer funds for long-term investment projects.

Thus, financialisation of NFCs can constitute a radical change in corporate management behaviour in the advanced countries that produces major changes in investment demand for single firms, with direct effects on domestic aggregate demand.

However, even though financial investment can be alternative to physical investment at the level of the single corporation, at the macroeconomic level, the phenomenon shows a clear *fallacy of composition*. Indeed, financial investment only transfers liquidity from one agent to another one. Thus, it could transfer financial resources from firms with bad investment opportunities to others with better profitability prospects. From this point of view, it should have no global macroeconomic effect, apart from increasing efficiency.

The purpose of this book is to critically explore and review the literature on financialisation and its possible implications for the macroeconomic and financial stability of the advanced countries, proposing some alternative readings of the phenomena highlighted by it. In fact, even though we recognise the relevance to the macroeconomic and financial stability of the advanced countries of many phenomena highlighted by the economic literature on financialisation, we believe that too much attention is being paid to some micro-epiphenomena that show a fallacy of composition at the macroeconomic level and can lead to some misunderstandings of the general trends in capitalist evolution.

Consequently, in Chapter 1, we summarise the main features of the literature on financialisation produced in the context of the post-Keynesian theoretical approaches and critically analyse the origin and subsequent evolutions of this concept, pointing out their strengths and weaknesses. In particular, we discuss the idea of the shareholder revolution and the role played by some new financial intermediaries in the financialisation of NFCs.

Chapter 2 examines the theoretical apparatus of both the *French Regulation School* and the *Social Structure of Accumulation Approach*, considering their common elements and looking into their theoretical differences. In the last part of this chapter, some doubts are voiced about the idea that, considering these analytical approaches, neoliberal capitalism can actually be seen as a new *accumulation regime*.

In Chapter 3, we analyse some traditional topics of classical Marxism and the Neo-Marxists in order to highlight a series of financial aspects that already described, or anticipated, many of the features that are now emphasised as turning points in the new phase of capitalist development in the recent literature on financialisation. Specifically, we analyse the historical tendencies of monopoly capital towards financial arrangements in order to manage corporate control and the role played in this context by financial oligarchies and rentiers.

Chapter 4 deals with the structural relationship between *interest-bearing capital* and *industrial capital* on the basis of Marxian analysis, showing how certain current trends are inherent in the evolution of the credit system, regardless of the forms of regulation applied to it. The final part of this chapter analyses the reshaping of these basic tendencies in the context of the *shadow banking system* that has been developed as a result of the financial deregulation processes of the last 30 years.

Chapter 5, starting from analysis of the relationship between rents and profit and its effects on capital accumulation in classical political economy, applies this analysis to the relationship between financial rents and profit, aiming to identify its possible effects on growth rates and possible stagnation trends.

In Chapter 6, we provide an overview of phenomena like the corporate saving glut and corporate liquidity holding and their possible relevance in defining the nature of financial crises and the economic crises that follow them. We also show how these phenomena, which today seem to be a brainteaser for mainstream economics, had already been identified around the great depression of the 1930s and had only temporarily been countered during the "Golden Age" by the mode of regulation that emerged from the experience of the depression itself.

Chapter 7 provides a review of some contributions, both mainstream and heterodox, that analyse the portfolio management and investment decisions in big corporations, seeking to determine how they might play a major role in producing growing liquidity holdings and financialisation of NFCs, and how they can be influenced by the new opportunities created by the free movements of capital and the economic dynamics of the emerging countries. Then, starting from the critical analysis carried out in the previous chapters, we go on to propose an analytical framework in which the growing financialisation of big corporations, interacting with financial globalisation, can play a major role in timing the rhythms of real investment, at least in a part of the world economic system. Furthermore, we show how, besides the rates of return, the liquidity degree of the assets can also be a very important determinant in corporations' portfolio choices, in close connection with business fluctuations. Finally, a conceptual scheme for interpretation and a mathematical model will be proposed to explain how the tendency in developed countries to place growing shares of social surplus in speculative financial channels can contribute to their long-term real stagnation.

The book concludes with some general remarks on the possible effects produced on social welfare in the advanced countries by the financialisation of NFCs.

References

Basu, D. and Foley, D. K. (2013). "Dynamics of Output and Employment in the U.S. Economy". *Cambridge Journal of Economics*, 37 (5): 1077–1106.

Crotty J. (2005). "The Neoliberal Paradox: The Impact of Destructive Product market Competition and 'Modern' Financial Markets on Nonfinancial Corporation Performance in the Neoliberal Era". In: Epstein, G. A. (ed.), *Financialization and the World Economy*. Cheltenham and Northampton, MA: Edward Elgar Publishing Ltd, pp. 77–110.

Duménil, G. and Lévy, D. (2005), "Costs and Benefits of Neoliberalism: A Class Analysis". In: Epstein, G. A. (ed.), *Financialization and the World Economy*. Cheltenham and Northampton, MA: Edward Elgar Publishing Ltd, pp. 17–45.

Epstein, G. A. (2005), "Introduction: Financialization and the World Economy". In: Epstein G. A. (ed.), *Financialization and the World Economy*. Cheltenham and Northampton, MA: Edward Elgar Publishing Ltd, pp. 3–16.

Epstein, G. A. and Jayadev, A. (2005). "The Rise of Rentier Incomes in OECD Countries". In: Epstein, G. (ed.), *Financialization and the World Economy*. Cheltenham and Northampton, MA: Edward Elgar Publishing, pp. 46–74.

Fine, B. (2014). "Financialization from a Marxist Perspective". *International Journal of Political Economy*, 42 (4): 47–66.

Foley, D. K. (2013). "Rethinking Financial Capitalism and the 'Information' Economy". *Review of Radical Political Economics*, 45 (3): 257–268.

Foster, J. B. (2007), "The Financialization of Capitalism." *Monthly Review*, 58 (11), https://monthlyreview.org/2007/04/01/the-financialization-of-capitalism/.

Kim, M. (2018). "What Is Radical Political Economics?". *Review of Radical Political Economics*, 50 (3): 576–581.

Krippner, G. (2004). "What Is Financialization?". Mimeo. Department of Sociology, UCLA.

Lapavitsas, C. (2011). "Theorizing Financialization". *Work, Employment and Society*, 25 (4): 611–626.

Mavroudeas, S. and Lapavitsas, C. (1999). "Financial Systems and Capital Markets: An Alternative View". In: Siriopoulos, C. (ed), *Topics in Financial Economics and Risk Management Analysis*. Thessaloniki: Paratiritis, pp. 62–82.

Orhangazi, Ö. (2008). "Financialisation and Capital Accumulation in the Non-Financial Corporate Sector: A Theoretical and Empirical Investigation on the US Economy: 1973–2003". *Cambridge Journal of Economics*, 32 (6): 863–886.

Stockhammer. E. (2004). "Financialisation and the Slowdown of Accumulation". *Cambridge Journal of Economics*, 28 (5): 719–741.

1 Post-Keynesian approaches

The rise of finance in neoliberal era

Post-Keynesian literature is the theoretical research field where the economic concept of financialisation has found its major applications. As was aptly pointed out by Sawyer (2014), the origins of this concept are uncertain, although it has been increasingly utilised since the early 1990s. However, the scholars who have contributed most to developing it actually follow a post-Keynesian approach, which is usually characterised by the attempt to extend the scope of Keynes' analysis to the long run and is, consequently, interested above all in growth problems. This implies that their analysis of financialisation is closely linked to macroeconomic problems such as those of capital accumulation and growth.

This strand of analysis has had the major merit to bring new attention to the role of financial interest groups in the evolution of capitalism and in the determination and distribution of income (see Hein and van Treeck, 2010). In fact, as Minsky observed more than 40 years ago, if a theory of income and price determination is to explain the aggregate behaviour of economic systems, financial relations must be fully integrated into it (see Minsky, 1982).

Of course, there have been a number of attempts to define the role played by finance and financial markets in growth processes, also by mainstream economists (see McKinnon, 1973, 1988, 1989, 1991; Shaw, 1973; King and Levine, 1993a, 1993b; Pagano, 1993; Miller, 1998; Cecchetti and Kharroubi, 2012, 2015). In this kind of analysis, however, the main focus is on the efficiency contribution to growth rate trends in the developed and developing countries with the different forms of financing, whether bank- or market-oriented. Moreover, unfortunately, in all of today's neo-Keynesian, monetarist and *new consensus* macroeconomic approaches – all ultimately based on the neoclassical synthesis – instability and severe depressions are totally excluded as a possible normal outcome of the economic process, basically because they treat the complex system of financial institutions and instruments in an extremely simplified way and the financial structure of economic systems is represented simply by "money" – which, in turn, is treated as an exogenous variable, under the control of the central banks. Thus, any detailed analysis of

DOI: 10.4324/9781003223221-2

the behaviour of the financial institutions is usually removed from the core of the mainstream macroeconomic models (see Minsky, 1982).

However, in today's capitalist economic systems, money is created when banks acquire some peculiar assets, which are themselves only promises of future payments, based on expectations for future income. In other words, money is created to the extent that some peculiar financial assets are. And the financial system in contemporary capitalist economies is a complex one whose structure is given by the network of a wide range of contracts between lenders and borrowers. Just as the stability of any financial structure depends on the mix of the three main financial postures of its financing units: hedge, speculative and "Ponzi" ones (see Minsky, 1982).

Many post-Keynesian economists, therefore, have tried to explore the internal link between the evolution of financial systems, on the one hand, and economic growth and income distribution in the developed countries on the other. They focus on the kind of income – seen as part of social surplus – financiers can obtain through the actual evolution of their political power (see Epstein, 2005), and, in particular, analyse the effects of the rise of modern finance forms on inequality, which is, in turn, seen as one of the major factors involved in determining growth rates (see Phillips, 2002; Krippner, 2005; Tridico, 2017; Arestis and Sawyer, 2018; Tridico and Pariboni, 2018; Pariboni et al., 2020).

The United States is naturally the main reference for this kind of analysis since it is the country where market finance has seen the greatest expansion. Other countries are often only analysed in counterpoint (see Aglietta and Reberioux, 2005). However, according to many observers, most countries in Europe and Asia seem to have undergone similar processes, albeit at slower rates (see Crotty, 2005; Hein, 2013; Ferreiro and Gómez, 2016; Barradas, 2017).

In any case, what exactly is meant by the term financialisation and what are its effects on economic and social performance? Of course, post-Keynesian scholars bring out different facets, albeit on the basis of a common theoretical paradigm.

Most authors agree that financialisation is simply "the increasing role of financial motives, financial markets, financial actors and financial institutions in the operation of the domestic and international economies" (Epstein, 2005) – i.e. an increasing relative size of the financial sector in the developed economic systems (see Aglietta and Reberioux, 2005; Krippner, 2005; Arestis, 2016). In fact, some empirical analyses, carried out utilising the sum of profits made by financial firms and the interest realised by all private non-financial units as a proxy of "rentier income" – i.e. the income of money capitalists – show that in most OECD countries, the rentiers' share of national income dramatically increased in the 1980s and 1990s relative to its proportion in value in the 1960s and 1970s, in both nominal and real terms (see Epstein and Power, 2003; Power et al., 2003; Epstein and Jayadev, 2005). Yet, why does this relative size really matter?

According to the mainstream viewpoint, finance is concerned with how individuals and firms allocate resources through time (see Fama and Miller, 1972). Thus, it is concerned with the decisions made by owners of wealth to optimise the returns on their assets. This optimisation process is achieved, thanks to the possibility of exchanging goods available at different times, which is effectively provided by the existence of capital markets. Thus, the more developed capital markets are, the more efficient is the process of intertemporal allocation.

From this mainstream viewpoint, the financial sector is simply seen as a peculiar service sector, which provides services to savers for the best management of their savings. Thus, if aggregate saving grows faster than the national income, then one might expect that financial services would have to increase their relative size. The relative size of savings in income management, in turn, can simply be the outcome of changes in saving propensity, which can again, in turn, be closely connected to changes in the demographic structure of the population (see Summers, 2014a, 2014b; Bernanke, 2015). Moreover, even if the propensity to save had not increased, the relative expansion of the financial sector could only be the result of the need for more sophisticated services to manage the growing savings more efficiently.

However, the increasing alarm over the relative growth of financial activities shown by post-Keynesian economists is justified by the fact that it has led to a change in the power relations between different interest groups within society (see Palley, 2007, 2013). According to some post-Keynesian authors, in fact, the increase in the *rentier share* in national income suggests that in the late 1980s, there was a structural shift in the balance of power between financial interests and other economic interests, such as those of non-financial enterprises and workers (see Duménil and Levy 2004; Epstein and Jayadev, 2005).

The growth of finance power, according to many post-Keynesian economists, was initially enhanced by expansion of the financial markets and products, but the growing political influence of the rentier class successively made it possible to change economic policies in their own interest. Thus, the shift in the balance of power first prompted and was subsequently supported by policies characterised by a shift towards fiscal austerity, restrictive monetary policies, political pressures for independence for the central banks, inflation targeting, financial deregulation and international capital mobility. All these new political trends, often labelled "neoliberal", dramatically replaced the Keynesian regulations that had characterised the previous "Bretton Woods era" and, according to most post-Keynesians, radically altered the characteristic traits of contemporary capitalism (see Aglietta and Reberioux, 2005; Epstein and Jayadev, 2005). In this respect, therefore, financialisation is substantially identified with a rise to power of the main actors in market finance, which has radically changed the way capitalism works (see Crotty, 2005).

All post-Keynesian economists are, of course, keen supporters of Keynesian policies and consequently consider neoliberal policies extremely dangerous for potential growth and increase in the prosperity of nations (see Palley, 2012). Neoliberal economic policies, in fact, are seen merely as a way to transfer income from the real sector – which is the real basis of social welfare – to the financial sector, which has an essentially parasitic role (see Palley, 2007). They are also considered the main cause of wage and mass consumption stagnation, with increasing risk of debt deflation and prolonged phases of recession (see Hein, 2013; Sawyer, 2018).

Financial liberalisation, in particular – seen as one of the main political outcomes of the rise of financial interests – is considered by post-Keynesians to have been the main cause of increases in real interest rates in the 1990s, which, in turn, enhanced a further dramatic expansion in the amount of financial assets and financial profits (see Epstein and Jayadev, 2005). It is also seen as the main cause of the increasing macroeconomic instability and financial fragility that produced the major financial crises over the last three decades (see Arestis and Sawyer, 2005; Sawyer, 2017). Finally, the international liberalisation of capital mobility is seen as a way of weakening the bargaining power of the workers, with further benefits for the profitability of financial investments.

However, even if they can be influenced by the profitability of investments, which, in turn, can be improved by free movements of capital, market interest rates are, as we shall see in Chapter 4, essentially the result of the balance of power between lenders and borrowers. Thus, a rise in them may have quite other explanations than an arbitrary change in monetary policies induced by financial interests. Just as – although the international liberalisation of capital mobility has certainly helped to reduce the share of labour in national incomes in OECD countries – this relative decline has favoured the interests of capital in general and not only the financial interests.

In this kind of analysis, moreover, the final effects of financialisation on non-financial corporations (NFCs) are not at all clear. Indeed, these companies have, on the one hand, certainly benefited from a reduction in the bargaining power of the workers but, on the other hand, they have suffered from increased international competition and – at least in an initial stage – higher interest rates. Thus, the NFCs ultimately faced a more difficult environment unless they became increasingly like financial firms (see Epstein and Jayadev, 2005). Consequently, according to Crotty (2005), their ultimate attitude towards the growing power of finance can be effectively summarised by the slogan "if you can't beat them, join them".

In practice, most post-Keynesian literature on financialisation shows evident nostalgia for the so-called *Golden Age* – i.e. the period between the end of Second World War and the early 1970s – when the "Keynesian revolution" prevailed in formulating economic policies and the economies of the developed countries were brought under the ultimate control of governments, which managed international economic relations, regulated business and aggregate demand and, above all, tightly controlled financial markets (see Crotty, 2005). And it was generally believed that finance had been brought under control through government regulation and capital mobility controls because of its responsibility in causing the financial crisis of 1929 and the subsequent Great Depression. Yet, unfortunately, after the breakdown of the post-war institutional framework of financial regulation, finance came to the fore again!

The real problem with the breakdown of the post-war institutional framework, however, was that, just like the other main features of the *Golden Age*, it had been designed on the basis of the protectionist world background that had arisen in the years of the Great Depression. Thus, the way out of the stagnation that was produced within this institutional framework in the 1970s was sought in a new wave of expansion of free trade and capital mobility, in the hope that a larger free world market and wider investment opportunities would improve the profit opportunities of big business.

This new trend in international politics is what is usually called "neoliberal globalisation", which is, in turn, seen by most post-Keynesian economists as a shift to a new model of capitalism. This interpretation of the recent evolution of capitalism as a structural change in its *accumulation regime* and related *mode of regulation* is closely linked to the theoretical paradigms proposed by the *Regulation approach* and the *Social Structures of Accumulation approach*, which we will examine more closely in the next chapter.

However, for many people, the *Golden Age* seemed to make the *American dream* come true.[1] And the general idea of most post-Keynesian economists is that a global prosperity – as experienced during this period – structurally needs strong regulation by governments, but it has been undermined by the deregulation taken further by neoliberalism, seen as the ideological expression of the reasserted power of finance.

Thus, sometimes, in this literature, finance and financiers are seen as the resurgent dark side of capitalism, and monetarism and neoliberalism are seen as their ideological instruments to advance their short-sighted private interests against a more general interest. However, it is a typical old tendency of American liberal ideology to distinguish between good, competitive and democratic capitalism and rogue capitalism, led by *robber barons* and tending towards monopoly and political control of civil society, as well as seeing the state as a potential counterbalance to the economic power of monopoly capital (see Hofstadter, 1955). But unfortunately, in fact, industrial and economic regulatory laws are usually driven precisely by the interests and objectives of big business lobbies (see Kolko, 1963; O'Connor, 1973/2009).

Moreover, all golden ages are typically myths. And the end of the *Golden Age*, as many post-Keynesian theorists admit, was the consequence of its inherent contradictions (see Crotty, 2005).

Furthermore, have changes in the financial sector been driving forces or reflections of recent transformations of capitalism in the rich countries? In the following pages of this book, we will try to show that they were not odd, incidental occurrences but rather the consequence of more basic tendencies in the historical course of capitalism's evolution.

Financial investment vs real investment

However, a considerable number of post-Keynesian economists focus on a more specific meaning of financialisation, defining it as a progressive shift from real capital investment to financial investment. This shift is particularly significant for them because their theories, as well as Marxian theory, traditionally emphasise the role of physical capital accumulation as the main driving force behind economic growth and the increasing prosperity of nations. And, in fact, there is empirical evidence that, in the last two decades of the 20th century, the major OECD economies were characterised by an increase in investment in financial assets and a simultaneous slowdown in the accumulation of physical assets.

In fact, if we use the Stock Market Capitalisation to GDP ratio[2] as a proxy for the significance of financial investment, we can see that there was an exponential growth of this index in the 1980s and the 1990s, rising from 20% to just under 120% in the OECD countries (see Figure 1.1). The values of this ratio in these countries are consistently higher than those showed by the world economy as a whole – even though the latter, of course, are closely influenced by the first.

As might be expected, given that they are characterised by market-oriented financial systems, the United States and the United Kingdom, of all the OECD countries, show the highest values of this ratio, reaching a value – respectively – close to 160% and above 170% in the late 1990s (see Figure 1.2). After an initial drop in this index in 2001, following the burst of the *dot.com bubble*, and a drastic fall during the financial crisis of 2007–2008, the value of the ratio has resumed sustained growth, recently exceeding, at least in the United States, the levels recorded at the end of the 1990s.

However – albeit with lower values – we can also detect similar trends in countries traditionally characterised by bank-oriented financial systems, such as Japan and France, and indeed, albeit to an even lesser extent, in Germany, which has a financial system historically characterised by a close relationship between banks and firms, known as the *hausbank system* (see Figure 1.2).

In the same years, a downward trend in gross capital formation as a percentage of GDP is also evident in all the OECD countries and especially in the United Kingdom, which is characterised by a pronounced process of financialisation of its economy (see Figure 1.3).

Many post-Keynesian economists have therefore taken the view that there must be a structural link between the increase in investment in financial assets and the slowdown in the accumulation of physical assets, because financial investment, from the point of view of a single country, seems to replace investment in capital goods (see Crotty, 2002, 2005; Stockhammer, 2004a, 2004b, 2005; Krippner, 2005; Pariboni and Tridico, 2019; Pariboni et al., 2020). In many OECD economies, moreover, over the past 30 years, profit rates have been increasing, while physical investments have tended to slow down. In this respect too, therefore, it seems that increasing shares of profits went into financial channels rather than productive investment.

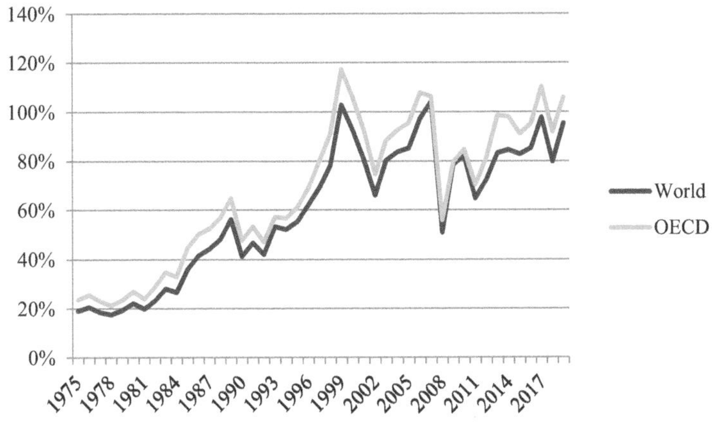

Figure 1.1 Stock Market Capitalisation to GDP ratio (1975–2020).
Source: World Bank national accounts data, and OECD National Accounts data files.

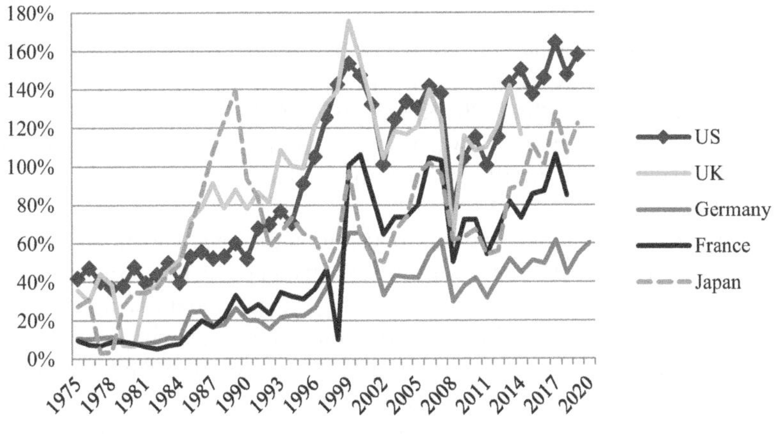

Figure 1.2 Stock Market Capitalisation to GDP ratio in main OECD countries (1975–2020).
Source: World Bank national accounts data, and OECD National Accounts data files.

However, from a theoretical viewpoint, financial investment is no more than a transfer of liquidity from some economic agents to others, not a final use of national income. Thus, at the aggregate global level, financial investment cannot substitute investment in capital goods (see Tobin, 1997; Stockhammer, 2004a). Consequently, to truly understand the change in the composition between financial and real investment in each country, we should rather explain the behaviour of the main OECD economies in the context of globalisation and international capital movements.

This strand of analysis, however, is often based on a firm-centred view of financialisation, although it can also have important macroeconomic

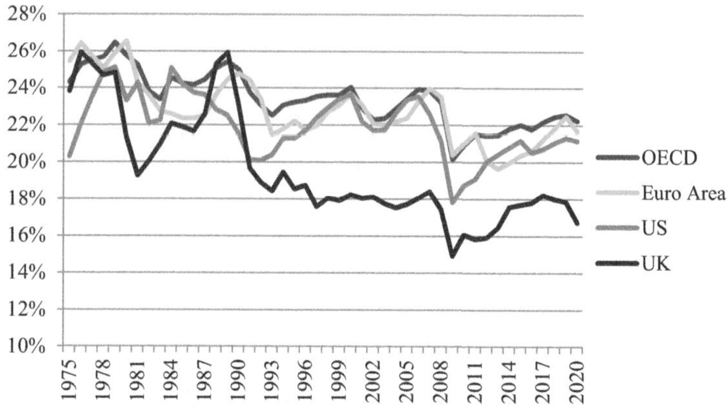

Figure 1.3 Gross capital formation as a percentage of GDP (1975–2020).
Source: World Bank national accounts data, and OECD National Accounts data files.

implications (see van Treeck, 2009). It starts from the evidence that many NFCs seem to have decided to move away from the real sector and towards financial operations to increase their profits (see Boltanski and Chiapello, 2005; Crotty, 2005; Epstein, 2005; Krippner, 2005).

In fact, from the 1980s onwards, in the United States, the total assets of NFCs have exponentially grown more than non-financial assets (see Figure 1.4).

Crotty (2005) explains this trend focusing on the negative effects that were produced by neoliberal policies and the expansion of financial markets in the structure, performance and behaviour of large NFCs, identifying a veritable vicious circle. In fact, according to him, these companies, which are the main actors in capital investment, technological change and productivity growth, are usually characterised by "illiquid" assets due to their strong specialisation in markets with few competitors. For this reason, they are exposed to considerable losses if prices fall to marginal costs due to the entry of new competitors. Thus, they can be highly profitable only if run under oligopolistic conditions – characterised by what Schumpeter called "corespective competition" – and adequate economic growth.

Unfortunately, over time, increasing competition from new firms in the emerging countries, together with the slowdown in global aggregate demand caused by neoliberal policies, drastically reduced their profits. In order to survive in this new environment, many NFCs in OEDC countries were forced to undertake massive restructuring investments that, at a time of declining profits, forced them to increase their debt (see Crotty, 1993). However, because of the growing power of finance, they were compelled to replace committed and "patient" financiers with impatient financial markets that, through manager incentives and threats of hostile takeovers, entailed for

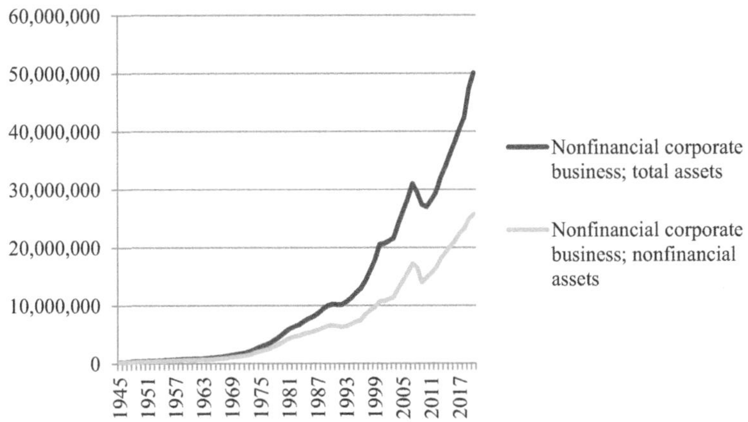

Figure 1.4 Total assets and non-financial assets in the US NFCs (1945–2020).
Source: Federal Reserve Board – Financial Accounts data.

them the necessity to pay increasing shares of their profits to investors and financial agents and to shorten their planning horizons to reduce uncertainty (see Crotty, 2003, 2005). All this developed new business behaviours that, in turn, further weakened the already weak demand (see Crotty, 2000, 2005).

Moreover, shareholders tend to see NFCs as "portfolios" of liquid assets that their managers should continually be modifying to maximise the stock price at every point in time. As a result, they have tended to radically change the structure of management rewards from one that linked managers' salaries to the long-term success of the company to one that links them to short-term movements in the share price. However, in doing so, they have drastically shortened the planning horizons of the NFCs they own (see Crotty, 2003).

Lazonick and O'Sullivan (1996), in turn, pointed out that the most important feature of successful large NFCs has long been their long-term improvement in process and product innovation. This kind of strategy, however, needs *organisational integration* – i.e. a strong attachment to the long-term objectives of the company by all its main stakeholders – and *financial commitment* – which is particularly necessary because innovation typically is an uncertain and expensive long-term project. Thus, only investors with a long-term commitment to the enterprise, such as those prevailing in the *Golden Age*, can provide adequate financial resources to support innovation processes (see Crotty, 2003).

Ultimately, according to this literature, many NFCs have responded to the fall in their profits and the rise in their financing costs by increasing their investments in financial assets to capture their high returns. In addition, for the same purpose, they have created or acquired financial subsidiaries, or expanded the financial subsidiaries they already controlled. This process is what has been called "financialisation of NFCs" (see Crotty, 2005; van Treeck, 2009), which is in fact the main focus of our book.

However, according to most post-Keynesian scholars, even this change in corporate behaviour was ultimately linked to changes in the capital markets and the growing power of market finance, as well as the economic policies that underpinned them (see Aglietta and Reberioux, 2005). In fact, increased capital market liquidity has profoundly affected listed companies by expanding risk transfer possibilities. Above all, however, transformations in the financial sphere have profoundly changed *corporate governance* – i.e. the procedures and practices that determine the exercise of power within listed companies. Thus, a common company-level explanation for financialisation-induced changes in NFC behaviour – which would lead companies to prefer financial returns to physical investments – is found by many post-Keynesian economists in the increasing *pursuit of shareholder value* as the main corporate objective, in turn, induced by the so-called "shareholder revolution" (see Stockhammer, 2004a, 2004b).

The shareholder revolution

The rise of joint-stock companies in capitalist economies has, as we know, progressively made control of the production process theoretically independent of the right of appropriation of the surplus by the owners of the capital. In listed companies, moreover, the dispersion of shareholders can enhance the discretion of managers and their independence from the interests of the equity owners. In fact, the most capable and sought-after managers may not undergo a real selection process and, once in office, are usually unwatched and not accountable. Thus, since the appearance of the book *The Modern Corporation and Private Property*, published by Berle and Means in 1932, the separation of ownership and control and the substantial managerial discretionary powers have constituted a path-breaking issue in the debate on corporate decision-making, generating an extensive literature on corporate governance and the connected forms of corporate finance (see Tirole, 2006).

The corporate governance way of functioning ultimately depends on whether equity is held by "insiders" (managers or entrepreneurs) or "outsiders", but also on the shareholding concentration and the nature and dimension of the claimholders. Thus, from this viewpoint, who holds the claims definitely matters.

An *agency conflict* can arise whenever managers have different objectives from their shareholders. And severe agency problems can impair corporate performance in both public companies, such as those operating in Anglo-Saxon countries, and companies with a controlling shareholder, such as those prevailing in European countries. In fact, there are many ways in which managers may not act in the shareholders' best interests, although mainstream economists bring them all under the aggregate label "moral hazard" (Tirole, 2006, p. 16).

One of these ways, in particular, is defined by Tirole "extravagant investments". However, insiders can operate on the basis of criteria other than those of the fund providers, not necessarily against their long-run interests, but on the basis of strategic considerations that are not easy for the mass of outsiders to understand. Some extravagant investments may, therefore, sometimes be simply strategic moves over a horizon longer than that of the financial investors, who are often victims of the short-sighted view of the discount rate.

In any case, if firms are viewed as mere instruments operating in the interest of the equity owners, given the *agency problem*, the organisation structure of firms needs to be structured to provide proper incentives for managers to act in the shareholders' interest. From this point of view, the internal control by means of the board of directors usually appears to have hardly any effect at all and the main external mechanism of corporate governance in Anglo-Saxon countries is usually considered to be the *market for corporate control*, ultimately implemented through threats of hostile takeovers. However, in other countries, this external mechanism seems rare or completely non-existent and in bank-oriented financial systems, the same role is mainly performed by monitoring banks and other financial institutions as well as close relationships between firms and banks (see Allen and Gale, 2000).

Thus, corporate governance is closely connected to corporate finance and can be defined as "the ways in which the suppliers of finance to corporations assure themselves of getting a return on their investment" (Shleifer and Vishny, 1997; see, also, Becht et al., 2002). Therefore, its main problem seems to be how corporations' insiders can attract external financial funds, committing themselves to paying back funds with an adequate rate of return to external investors. Consequently, although they can also affect firm behaviour in product and labour markets, corporate governance mechanisms are closely connected to the nature of flows of external capital to firms and are closely correlated with the expansion of articulated financial systems, while they are practically non-existent in the less developed countries (see Shleifer and Vishny, 1997).

However, in the real world, contrary to popular belief, most corporate finance comes from internally generated funds in all the financial systems, whether market-oriented or bank-oriented. Thus, corporate financing depends mainly on retained earnings (see Allen and Gale, 2000). Of course, in order to bring forward the implementation of strategic investments or to withstand competitive pressure, companies may use outsider lenders. But even in this case, as lenders wish to limit their risks, the funds a company can obtain from banks or financial markets ultimately depend on its retained earnings.

All this is perfectly in line with the post-Keynesian theory of the firm, which is founded on Kalecki's principle of increasing risk, closely linked, in turn, to the Keynesian notion of fundamental uncertainty (see Lavoie, 2006). According to this principle, in fact, companies are expected to limit the proportion of borrowed funds in order to reduce the possibility of putting themselves in an illiquid or default situation. Consequently, it is profits that allow companies to ensure a healthy financial position and improve their access to bank credit and other types of debt.

In the usual description of external financing of enterprises, moreover, accountants and economists distinguish between debt and equity. However, on a closer look, debt and equity are only the two extremes of a long claim series on corporate income held by a number of different claimholders (see Tirole, 2006). Common stockholders, of course, have voting rights in shareholders' meeting, by means of which they can exercise direct control over the board of directors. Other claimholders can, however, vote with their feet in financial markets, if the latter are sufficiently liquid. From this viewpoint, therefore, it would seem that who holds the claims among the outsiders does not matter at all.

However, market control over the allocation of corporate resources seems to be a relatively recent phenomenon because, for most of the 20th century, salaried managers apparently exercised this kind of control in relative autonomy (see O'Sullivan, 2000). In fact, in the first three post-war decades, the role of shareholders in corporations was severely limited by heavily restrictive financial regulation and capital flow control, which were the political reactions to the financial and real crisis of the 1930s. And this lack of control was quietly accepted by the small savers – such as American households – who had long been feeding the market of industrial securities, demanding only the protection provided by the limited liability enjoyed by public shareholders and the liquidity of the shares they owned.

Moreover, in the 1950s and 1960s, giant corporations usually aimed at financial independence through retained earnings (see Baran and Sweezy, 1966). They were able to borrow from the financial institutions and markets, but were not normally forced to act in accordance, and could avoid subjection to control by the financial corporations and outside shareholders.

Thus, for a long time, public stockholders could exercise little, if any, control over the allocation of corporate profits. And in giant corporations, the managers seemed to be a self-perpetuating group that identified itself with the corporation and its fate. The board of directors and the chief executive officers were "organization men" and control rested securely in their hands. Their major objectives seemed to be the corporation market share and its strategic positions in the market. And, according to most post-Keynesian economists, this alleged way of running businesses encouraged large NFCs to increase their scale of production as the market expanded, continuously increasing their physical investments.

However, according to most post-Keynesian authors, it is a situation that has been changing since the late 1970s, through the progressive erosion of financial regulation by means of the invention of new financial instruments – such as junk bonds and other high-risk and high-return securities – which favoured *leveraged buy outs* (LBOs). Through these financial operations, in fact, stockholders of a public company may be bought out by new groups of investors, which usually include a specialised *buyout firm* supported by old managers, banks and public debt holders (see Shleifer and Vishny, 1997). In this way, the buyout firm could typically buy enough equity to control a public company.

Moreover, up to 1982, the *Securities and Exchange Commission* (SEC) could counteract massive stock repurchases as illegal attempts by the companies to manipulate stock prices. Since the end of 1982, instead, during the onset of the neoliberal phase with deregulation, the SEC has partially liberalised stock repurchases – provided that they be less than 25% of the average daily trading volume over the previous four weeks and the buybacks be carried out at neither the beginning nor the end of the trading day (see Lazonick, 2013).

Thus, according to many post-Keynesian economists, owing to this financial deregulation, the financial markets have progressively exerted increasing pressure on NFCs, by means of hostile takeovers first, and then with the so-called "shareholder revolution", largely characterised by a growing presence of institutional investors within their shareholding (see Lowenstein, 2004; Orhangazi, 2008). The exercise of ownership interests is, in fact, enhanced insofar as a large number of small individuals are replaced by few powerful financial institutions. And *French Regulation Approach* followers had already been pointing up new corporate governance problems since the 1970s, since, as they saw it, the "pursuit of shareholder value" appeared closely associated with an increasing *short-termism* of NFCs (see Aglietta, 2000; Boyer, 2000; Froud et al., 2000; Grahl and Teague, 2000; Jürgens et al., 2000; Morin, 2000; Williams, 2000; Aglietta and Breton, 2001).

In fact, there is a great deal of empirical evidence thrown up by sociological studies that in the 1980s and 1990s, many US companies were reorganised by selling unrelated product lines, engaging in mergers with other companies in similar industries and drastically reducing their workforce (see Davis and Stout, 1992; Davis et al., 1994; Appelbaum and Berg, 1996; Zuckerman, 2000; Fligstein, 2001). And all these actions were ultimately driven by the objective of increasing stock prices to signal to the financial markets that the companies were focused on maximising profits (see Useem, 1993; Zuckerman, 2000; Fligstein and Shin, 2007). Moreover, Lazonick and O'Sullivan (2000) have effectively demonstrated a connection between the pursuit of *shareholder value* and *corporate downsizing* during the neoliberal phase of capitalist development.

Thus, according to these analyses, NFCs have ended up being managed solely on the basis of the principles of *maximising shareholder value* (see Fligstein and Shin, 2007). Their managers have to pay more attention to stepping up the returns on the assets of the company – in order to drive up the value of shareholders' equity – and less attention to other stakeholders, such as employees (see van Treeck, 2015; Blecker, 2016; Palley, 2016; Hein, 2017). Thus the ascendancy of the "maximising shareholder value" principle as the main objective of management totally transformed the previous modes of corporate governance (see Froud et al., 2000, 2006; Lazonick and O'Sullivan, 2000; Williams, 2000).

However, in doing so, the managers end up running their companies as financial portfolios. In fact, if they resisted the principles of financial analysis, they would find their stock price decreasing and their companies subject to hostile takeovers, with the risk of losing their jobs (see Fligstein and Shin, 2007).

It is precisely this prevalence of shareholder interests over those of other stakeholders – fostered by the transformations that have taken place in the financial markets – that has been labelled the "shareholder revolution". This phenomenon is considered one of the main features of financialisation and the current neoliberal era, which is held to be producing radical changes in corporate behaviour in the name of *pursuing* and *creating shareholder value* (see Stockhammer, 2006; Onaran et al., 2011; van der Zwan, 2014).

According to many post-Keynesian authors, this revolution was a direct consequence of financial liberalisation and the emergence of very liquid stock markets in the 1980s and 1990s – for they fostered an increase in the shareholders' ability to influence public company managers by means of the creation of a more efficient *market for corporate control*. The managements of large corporations are, in fact, seen as committed to producing ever greater shareholder value because of the expanded possibilities for financial investors to use the capital market to estimate and compare the performance of their corporations and to discipline them with the threat of hostile takeovers. In this new setting, the managers of large corporations could easily be replaced by shareholders if corporate performance proved inadequate in creating value for them (see Stockhammer, 2006).

Thus, the threat of growing control by large financial intermediaries in public companies becomes an incentive for managers to change their investment behaviours, increasingly orienting them towards short-term profit investment and discouraging "extravagant" or long-term strategic investments. However, this change is also supported by an incentive system for managers that closely connects their salaries to the company stock prices – encouraging financial operations like share repurchasing by means of retained earnings, which are consequently diverted from company investment to new capital goods and technologies. And according to Froud et al. (2000), shareholder value became "the business cliché and social mantra" of the 1990s also on the wave of the ideological consultancy campaigns of the 1980s, summarised in the books by Alfred Rappaport (1986) and Bennett Stewart (1991).

In any case, starting from the 1980s, there has been an evident and significant shift in the US corporate behaviour. Strategic managers of US public corporations, incentivised by ample personal rewards, have explicitly accepted that the prime, if not only, responsibility of the corporation is to "create value for shareholders" or "maximizing shareholder wealth" (see O'Sullivan, 2000).

In the end, according to many post-Keynesian economists, the market for corporate control, and with it the market-oriented managerial compensation schemes, have fostered corporate policies of "downsizing and distributing" – characterised by the managers' sole objective of maximising and distributing dividends to shareholders by squeezing production, cutting workers' wages and downsizing firms to maintain high stock prices (see Lazonick and O'Sullivan, 2000; Hein and Truger, 2013; Lazonick, 2014; van Treeck, 2015; Blecker, 2016; Palley, 2016; Hein, 2017). And all these corporate policies, of course, contrast radically with the policies of "retaining and investing" that characterised the *Golden Age*.

In other words, the increase in shareholder power ended up by reducing productive investment through the imposition of short-term strategies and the draining of internal company resources available for real investment purposes (see van Treeck, 2009; Onaran et al., 2011; Stockhammer, 2013a, 2013b; Tomaskovic-Devey et al., 2015; Barradas, 2017; Tori and Onaran, 2017, 2018a, 2018b). The managers' pursuit of *shareholder value* leads to higher dividend pay-out ratios and share buybacks – which both imply a lower retention ratio and reduce internal means of finance for real investment – while the managers' preference for growth – and hence willingness to invest in capital stock – is weakened by remuneration schemes based on short-term profitability and financial market results (see Hein, 2013).

Thus, according to the post-Keynesian literature, changes in corporate governance mechanisms, produced by the evolution and expansion of financial markets – i.e. financialisation – have ultimately affected the performance of firms in the product and labour markets as well as the financial markets. And the end result cannot but influence the growth regime of the entire economic system.

The role of mutual and pension funds

Many post-Keynesian economists, moreover, consider the "shareholder revolution" largely as a direct consequence of the growing presence of institutional investors in the shareholding of NFCs (see Lowenstein, 2004; Orhangazi, 2008).

In fact, from 1950 to 1990, the share of US corporate equity under the control of institutional investors grew from 8% to 60% (see Porter, 1992). However, the growing presence of institutional investors in NFC shareholding structures decidedly started only in the 1970s, when institutional investors, often by means of LBOs, began to step up their holdings in large industrial conglomerates and gradually became dominant shareholders in many large US companies (see Crotty, 2002). Yet, successively, corporate ownership in the United States has been progressively re-concentrated by a small number of investment funds that own hundreds of companies simultaneously, creating networks of corporate ownership that are significantly concentrated by global standards (see Davis, 2008).

Eventually, by 2019, the world's top 500 asset managers were collectively running a truly impressive mass of corporate assets, amounting around \$104.4 trillion. And the more "activist" of the institutional investors, such as private equity and hedge funds, influenced the corporate governance of the companies in which they invested by exercising their voting rights to significantly restructure them, in order to increase their equity price (see van der Zwan, 2014; Walker, 2016).

Minsky was one of the first to point out that institutional investors – he called them "money managers" – were becoming the main actors in the US economy. He consequently thought that since the 1980s, the US economy – having passed through the phases of "commercial capitalism", "financial capitalism" and "managerial capitalism" – had entered a real new phase of development which he called "money manager capitalism" (see Minsky, 1990, 1993; Whalen, 1997, 2001). And, according to him, money managers, by forcing maximisation of the value of their assets in each short period, put pressure on the corporate managers to raise share prices – radically changing their previous attitude of focusing on corporate growth.

However, most institutional investors are, as we know, financial intermediaries who pool the savings of many small savers to buy securities and other real and financial assets. Their expansion has therefore often been viewed as involving positive effects on economic growth. In fact, they can theoretically stimulate savings opportunities – by better allocating and monitoring the use of funds – and can thus contribute to faster growth by promoting more investment (see Gemzik-Salwach and Opolski, 2017).

They include most traditional financial intermediaries, such as commercial banks, credit unions and insurance companies, although in recent decades they have seen an increasing role played by pension and mutual funds, as well as sovereign wealth and hedge funds. Operating companies, which invest excess money capital in financial assets, may be included under the term, too.

The institutional investors' behaviour is theoretically more sophisticated than that of the retail investors, because the former are entities handled by professional investment managers who are deemed able – on the basis of sound financial principles and avoiding herd effects – to improve the risk-return ratio on behalf of their clients, who are usually small private savers and workers building their pensions. Theoretically, the only direct interest of these institutions is commissions and investment management fees. From this point of view, therefore, they are only companies that make a profit by producing and selling particular services in the financial field.

However, while previous models of share ownership by *holding companies* and *cross-shareholdings* had long severely limited the market for corporate control, the rise of institutional investors made the potential threat of takeovers more pressing, increasing market pressure on corporate management to increase returns and market values of the shares they held (see Lazonick and O'Sullivan, 2000). And the empirical literature on institutional investors highlights the fact that equity markets dominated by them tend to undervalue firms with good prospects of gains in the long term but low current profitability, discouraging long-term investment in R&D as opposed to the distribution of dividends (see Davis and Steil, 2001; Orhangazi, 2008).

Institutional investors often have no direct knowledge of the companies whose shares they put in their portfolios. Their influence on corporate behaviour, therefore, results mainly from their ability to move large funds in very liquid financial markets and their consequent mass action effects on shares pricing. Yet, in any case, they manage their portfolios subject to strict performance criteria embedded in the formal procedures of their corporate governance arrangements, guided by common opinions and evaluations based on the principles of financial analysis, which – theoretically – ultimately determine the public valuation of companies in stock markets (see Aglietta, 2000).

In this setting, the emergence of mutual and pension funds as entities that held increasing shares of stock and were increasing their ownership at the expense of cross-shareholdings among non-financial firms was identified as a relevant trend for business behaviour as from the 1990s.

Mutual and pension funds, although innovative in the services provided, have often been set up by very traditional financial intermediaries, such as banks and insurance companies, especially in Europe (see Levine, 2003). However, they allocate capital among industries and firms in a decidedly market-based way, imposing profitability standards on companies and seeking short-term profit. Creating shareholder value is, in fact, the institutional mission of these funds, which are often viewed as guardians of the small investors whose interests they represent and whose rights they protect. And they have long been seen by many mainstream economists and politicians as the "watchdogs" protecting small savers from the arbitrariness of corporate managers and their "extravagant investments".

Since the mid-1980s, over half of America's households have participated in the stock market by buying mutual funds. The new system of widespread ownership, therefore, is much more of a representative democracy than a direct one, as it is the financial intermediaries who have come to own more than three-quarters of the stock of large corporations in the United States (see Davis, 2008). Thus, since the early 1990s, the growth of institutional investors' ownership has attracted the attention of analysts for its implications for corporate control, as activism on the part of a handful of public pension funds seemed to be the harbinger of genuine corporate governance reform (see Davis and Thompson, 1994; Useem, 1996). However, at the time many legal experts were already pointing out that a series of legal restrictions made it extremely difficult for financial institutions to accumulate sufficient control to effectively steer companies.

In any case, since the mid-1990s, a few mutual funds have become the leading large-scale corporate owners in the United States due to a shift in America's pension financing. They have discretion over buying, selling and voting corporate equities, giving some of them the potential to exert influence over large networks of American corporations. And, from a formal viewpoint, today's concentration of corporate ownership in a few hands is similar to that of finance capitalism described by Brandeis and Hilferding more than a century ago, when productive activities were under the control of a few big investment banks (see Davis, 2008).

Thus, mutual and pension funds, as well as insurance companies, investment banks and private equity funds, have certainly become the main owners of shares in many NFCs and are interested above all in their share prices. According to their institutional mission, in fact, all the managers of institutional investors have interests in the performance of the corporations whose equity they own insofar as it is reflected in the equity price. Furthermore, the higher frequency of trading, allowed by financial markets liquidity, reduces the average span of time for which an equity is usually held, and this ultimately places the emphasis on short-term share-price performance rather than on longer-term growth prospects (see Aglietta and Reberioux, 2005; Sawyer, 2017). Indeed, institutional investors' portfolios subject to continuous change, and capital gains connected to the changes in stock market valuation become more significant for the rates of return of their financial products than interest rate.

However, institutional investors have not so far been behaving like the big investment banks of the early 20th century and have not usually derived their controlling power from majority holdings or even strong minority interests. In the United States, large funds long avoided active participation in corporate management, in stark contrast to ownership networks in other countries (see Davis, 2008). In particular, mutual funds and private pension funds, despite owning a very large proportion of the stock in the US companies, have not been actively participating in shareholder meetings for a long time, unlike public pension funds, which have often taken positions on corporate governance issues and opposed corporate mismanagement (see Davis and Kim, 2007).

Thus, mutual and private pension funds have exerted their power over management mainly with exit strategies, making it difficult for companies to obtain new financing. Moreover, their arrival triggered competition between companies for global savings, which forced them to seek short-term capital gains to avoid the risk of being displaced by competitors (see Parenteau, 2005). This led Davis to label this system of ownership without direct control as "new financial capitalism", involving a historically unique combination of concentration and liquidity (Davis, 2008).

Thus, shareholder activism, potentially coming from large institutional shareholders in the United States, contrary to popular belief and in accordance with empirical evidence, has actually had little effect on corporate performance. Once again, the threat of hostile takeovers has probably been their most effective stimulus for changes in corporate strategy by managers (see Black, 1998).

However, since the financial crisis of 2007–2008, *index mutual funds* and *exchange traded funds* (ETFs) – often all subsumed under the common label of "passive index funds" because they share the key feature of replicating existing equity indices in their portfolios – have seen a dramatic expansion of their role. This was the result of an increasing number of passive investors who shifted their assets from expensive actively managed mutual funds to passive funds that actually minimised expense ratios. Yet in the United States, this sector is strongly dominated by the three largest US asset managers (BlackRock, Vanguard and State Street), which in 2015 collectively owned around 18% of the shares of the large companies included in the S&P 500 index and were the major shareholders in 88% of these companies (see Fichtner et al., 2017). Thus, the rise of passive investment strategies by small savers is actually leading to an unprecedented concentration of corporate ownership.

Thus, according to Fichtner et al. (2017), the rise of the *Big Three* may be able to generate a fundamental transformation of the "new financial capitalism" because of their position of "structural prominence" in the market for corporate control. Moreover, when analysing the proxy voting strategies of the *Big Three* in co-owned companies, these authors found clear evidence of coordination, on the one hand, and management support, on the other. They also highlighted that the managers of the companies the *Big Three* have permanently invested in could also be easily influenced through private engagements, ending up by internalising some of the objectives of the managers of passive index funds.

Thus, according to these authors, the *Big Three* may be able to exercise forms of direct control over the companies held in their portfolios. Moreover, since passive index funds, unlike active mutual funds, simply replicate existing equity indices in their portfolios and then tend to hold the purchased securities until the composition of the index changes, the *Big Three* could, in principle, act as "patient" investors, reversing the markets' traditional attitude towards short-termism (see Braun, 2015).

In summary, however, even if mutual funds and pension funds have led to a concentration of ownership of public companies, they do not seem to have exercised, to date, any significant form of direct and conscious pressure on management choices. Their rise may have influenced the behaviour and performance of the companies they invest in only through their market strategies, facilitated by the deregulation and liquidity of financial markets.

From this point of view, the actual effects produced by these funds may only be the dynamic consequence of the patterns of their evolution over time. A possible perverse effect has, in fact, been attributed to the process of expansion of pension funds, which, because of the huge injection of funds from their members' contributions to buy securities, was considered the main cause of "capital market inflation" – i.e. a rapid and exceptional rise in securities prices – in the period from the mid-1970s to the late 1990s (see Toporowski, 2000).

Since as long ago as the 1970s, in fact, funded pension schemes have been extolled as an optimal way to relieve taxpayers of the burden of paying for old age pensions, while at the same time channelling workers' savings into financing long-term capital investment. Thus, the US and the UK governments have from the outset favoured their introduction as a way to compensate for their lack of direct commitment to supporting their ageing populations, while many continental European governments have only later identified them as a means of reducing their previous high-spending commitments under the new fiscal austerity programmes imposed by the European Monetary Union (see Toporowski, 2000).

Moreover, funded pension schemes have also been accused of making the economy less efficient and weakening the financial system, because of the irregular flow of savings they can inject into the capital markets – especially at the beginning of their lives, when the flow of contributions increases but the subscribers have yet to retire or can only retire with a very small annuity. Furthermore, their expansion over time is limited by the fact that the inflow of contributions is generally restricted by the size of the well-paid workforce and the growing prevalence of precarious employment.

Nevertheless, funded pension schemes were often conceived by the UK and the US governments as a way to provide companies with a source of long-term funding in the capital market, so as to reverse the historical trend of declining investment in fixed capital. Thus, employers and employees have been systematically encouraged, through various tax benefits, to move away from income-related state pensions and into funded occupational pension schemes.

However, the idea that cheap, long-term finance would improve productive investment has proved illusory. In fact, when securities prices rise due to a sudden increase in demand, security yields fall. Thus, securities become cheaper and more attractive ways of raising finance for large companies, as compared with bank borrowing. And, in fact, so it was during the expansion phases of pension funds. Yet, this cheaper way of financing did not give rise to a boom in company investment, but was, rather, utilised to repay the previous bank debt. Governments in the United States and the United Kingdom, in turn, rapidly followed the company example, increasing issues of bonds and bills.

According to Toporowski (2000), this process primarily had devastating consequences for the banking systems of the United Kingdom and the United States, because loans to large companies and government bonds are usually the least risky part of bank assets. The change in corporate and government financing strategies, therefore, forced banks to acquire riskier assets – such as loans to less financially secure borrowers and financial derivatives – which turned out to be the main causes of the subsequent banking and financial crises.

Thus, the capital market inflation in the late 1980s and the 1990s – produced by the large inflow of liquid funds through pension funds – only drove large corporations to replace their short-term loans from banks by issuing short-term corporate bonds, while banks were forced to replace their loans to large corporations with corporate bonds in their balance sheets. And, according to Toporowski (2000), not only was this cheaper financing unable to increase the amount of productive investment, but paradoxically it ended up by reducing it.

In fact, companies facing increasing demand for their shares – due to the immaturity of funded pension schemes – were able to reduce their interest burden by issuing shares and using the proceeds to repay bank loans. And this improved their accounting profitability as their interest costs were reduced – all other economic conditions being equal. As the demand for shares continued to increase, companies found it convenient to take over other indebted companies and use their share issue to repay their bank loans. The companies taken over, by reducing their interest costs, were, in turn, able to prove more profitable without any substantial change, but only on the basis of accounting effects. However, the improved profitability of the acquired companies also improved the profitability of the shareholders of the parent company. And this kind of strategy, of course, was a first step in the direction of moving from manufacturing to financial activities – i.e. towards the financialisation of NFCs.

Thus, according to Toporowski, financial manoeuvres induced by capital market inflation – and, in turn, fuelled by the immaturity of pension schemes – ended up by competing with real capital investment by companies. This, in turn, further depressed aggregate demand, reduced profit expectations in the real sector and prompted many companies to entrust their money to commodity traders or to buy derivatives – in order to offset the possible losses associated with issuing securities to finance new investment in fixed capital in the context of a stagnant goods market. In fact, assets in financial markets are more liquid than fixed capital and therefore less risky as long as there is no prospect of excessive volatility or financial collapse.

Thus, even when analysing the role played by pension and mutual funds, post-Keynesian authors point to the possibility that financial investments can absorb large amounts of additional money capital, to the detriment of real capital accumulation. These financial strategies are, of course, supposed to be encouraged by the brokers and bankers who organise financial markets and profit from brokerage services. And this reiterates the centrality of the growing power of finance in determining regulations and policies.

However, taking over indebted companies to replace their bank debt with their own equity financing is only an appropriate business strategy if there are no suitable profit alternatives. This means that the expected return on new productive investment is less than the sum of the current profit of the firm taken over and the difference between bank interest and the profit distributed on equity. Indeed, the acquiring company could alternatively still raise cheaper funds and invest them in new productive activities earning at least the normal rate of profit. If they do not do so and prefer to acquire existing companies, it is because they fear oversupply in the target markets, which would lead to the risk of losses or at least lower profits than those of the acquired companies. What follows, however, is only a typical process of restructuring productive sectors through centralisation of capital, aimed also at acquiring economies of scale and scope – a process that, in a world of listed companies, is obviously achieved through financial manoeuvres.

Thus, this kind of strategy implies expectations of diminishing returns on new investments and current bank interest rates that are too high – in addition to the inflationary conditions in the financial markets that are blamed on pension funds. And, from the point of view of the post-Keynesian economists themselves, the low profitability of new investments and the current high interest rates in those years were due to the lack of support for aggregate demand by governments and central banks, on the one hand, and to the power of financial intermediaries, on the other. However, at this point, the role played by pension funds is reduced to stimulating an intermediate vicious circle and cannot be seen as the initial driver of stagnation.

The false myth of managerial capitalism

Thus, while they have the merit of focusing on the financialisation of NFCs and its effects on capital accumulation in the developed countries, many post-Keynesian authors usually end up by making the big NFCs appear as victims of the increasing power of the financial markets and the agents and institutions involved within them – in short, as victims of the increasing power of "finance". In other words, the "shareholder revolution" – fostered by the market for corporate control in the context of deregulated and liquid financial markets – is seen by them as an external imposition on NFCs of the tyranny of the pursuit of shareholder value, which, in turn, obliges them to reduce real long-term investment and squeeze the interests of other stakeholders, such as workers.

However, *pursuing shareholder value* is just another way of saying maximising expected profit over time – i.e. maximising *net present value* or *equity* of the firm – which, in accordance with mainstream economics, has long been held the main objective of firms as organisers of production processes in capitalist economies.

The post-Keynesian belief that before the "shareholder revolution" NFCs pursued objectives other than profit maximisation is closely connected to their theory of the firm. This theory, in fact, usually focuses on large firms operating in oligopolistic markets characterised by imperfect competition and strategic decisions, whereby each firm knows that its own decisions have consequences for other firms – including firms that might eventually enter the market – which will, in turn, react (see Lavoie, 2006, 2014; Hein, 2013). In this theoretical context, according to Kalecki, if supply is sufficiently elastic – i.e. firms operate below the point of practical capacity and prime costs per unit of output are stable – prices in the short run are not determined by impersonal "market forces", but can be set by firms through application of the *mark-up rule*, depending on their degree of monopoly (see Kalecki, 1971). Thus, according to this theoretical framework, profit maximisation by companies seems to be either a pure tautology or a non-sense!

Most post-Keynesians, moreover, have long emphasised the separation of owners and managers as one of the main characteristics of large corporations, where the managers theoretically pursue the long-term survival of the firm as their main objective (see Lavoie, 2014). In fact, in order to maintain their oligopolistic position over time, companies need to gain control of their economic environment by preventing new rival firms from entering the industry, developing R&D and exercising control over suppliers, lenders and government legislation. Yet, all these forms of control involve some social and political power held by the firm, which depends on the place it occupies in the social hierarchy and is closely related to its size. And, according to post-Keynesians, it is precisely the objective of maximising the size of the companies that fostered capital accumulation and growth during the three decades of the *Golden Age* (see Tabb, 2010).

This alleged way adopted by the managers running companies is believed by many post-Keynesian economists to characterise what has been called "managerial capitalism", in which the primary objective of top management is supposed to be "the long-term reproduction, growth, and safety of the firm itself, and, through these, its own status and security" (Crotty, 1990, p. 533). In this context, the shareholders' interests are not an objective but rather a constraint for the management.

Managerial capitalism is thus seen by post-Keynesians as a "specific historical construct" that ensured the spectacular results of the *Golden Age* (see Lavoie, 2014). Unfortunately, this virtuous construct was eventually challenged by the financial markets bursting onto the scene from the 1980s onwards and the subsequent financial euphoria of the 1990s – often seen as sudden anomalies in history and structural breaks with the previous mode of functioning of the capitalist economy (see Hein et al., 2015).

Indeed, many seminal empirical studies have shown that managers of large companies may have multiple objectives and not only maximising profit. Since 1939, in fact, when some empirical evidence on the behaviour of firms in the real world emerged – first from the influential work of Hall and Hitch (1939) in the United Kingdom, then from similar research in the United States (see Gordon, 1945, 1948; Lester, 1946; Machlup, 1946; Oliver, 1947) – many theoretical contributions have been produced dealing with the weaknesses of the traditional theory of profit maximisation and questioning the traditional neoclassical theory of the firm and its assumptions.

Hall and Hitch were among the first authors to analyse the actual behaviour of 38 mainly manufacturing companies in the United Kingdom and showed that they aimed not so much at short-term profit maximisation as at long-term profit maximisation by pricing according to the *average cost principle* – i.e. companies set a price to cover average variable cost, average fixed cost and a "normal" profit margin. And this "full cost theory" has, in fact, some points in common with Kalecki's *mark-up rule* – although there is no reference to the influence of other firms' prices stressed by Kalecki (1971).

Gordon, in turn, emphasised that firms are generally guided by "semi-pecuniary" considerations, which are spurred by the pressures of their institutional environment. According to him, all real businessmen who – in contrast to the abstract atomistic entrepreneur of neoclassical theory – are aware of the identity of their own competitors are continually engaged in strategic manoeuvres to safeguard the existence of their firms or to strengthen their position in the market. These manoeuvres may, of course, have effects on profit, but they cannot be accurately assessed. Consequently, when determining business strategies, businessmen usually apply rules of thumb, shortcuts of various kinds and also policy considerations, such as maintaining the company's traditional market share or squeezing labour costs as much as possible – which have a certain influence on the profits earned in the long run. And, incidentally, it is also worth noting that labour cost squeezing is clearly a microeconomic behaviour consistent with the inverse macroeconomic relationship between the rate of profit and wages shown by the profit-wage curve derived from Sraffa's approach or the Marxian theory of surplus value, which accounts for the uniform normal level of the rate of profit at the macroeconomic level.

Of course, it is not easy to treat these empirical strategies with the conventional analytical apparatus of theory, even though they are too important to be ignored as exceptions. Gordon therefore proposed to express the relation between profit maximisation and these semi-pecuniary considerations by treating the latter as subordinate objectives, given the ultimate objective of maximum profit.

From Gordon's point of view, of course, it does not matter whether the businessmen are owner-entrepreneurs or managers, because the semi-pecuniary considerations are the result of the complexity of the business environment and not of the business organisation.

In the 1950s and 1960s, however, some empirical evidence was found that profits were higher in owner-controlled firms than in firms where there was separation of ownership and control (see Lanzillotti, 1958; Kamerschen, 1968; Monsen et al., 1968). This evidence supported the view that managers may have some discretion in pursuing goals other than profit maximisation in the context of agency conflict, prompting many managerial theories of the firm. And all these theories postulate that the separation of ownership and control allows managers some discretion in selecting objectives that maximise their own utility function, such as salaries, prestige, market share, job security and so on.

Managerial theories of the firm, in fact, constituted academic recognition of the fact that a growing trend towards managerial control over the allocation of corporate resources had been taking place since the early decades of the 20th century. And it is no coincidence that the issue of corporate governance, based on the potential conflict between shareholders and managers, has been at the centre of the scene from the Great Depression onwards, because it was in the context of the regulatory interventions of the New Deal that the debate began about which institutions could provide the best conditions for making corporate investment decisions and distributing profits in large corporations.

However, despite all these debates, managers have certainly been exercising considerable control over the allocation of corporate resources for a long time (O'Sullivan, 2000). The so-called "managerial capitalism", which seemed to be increasingly characterising North America, Western Europe and Japan, was presented as a system in which production was concentrated in the hands of large joint-stock companies in which entrepreneurship was taken on by a "transcendent" management, different in type from the traditional subordinate kind (see Marris, 1964).

In these companies, managers can theoretically exercise considerable power without necessarily holding equity, sharing profits or bearing risks, either. Only the legal entity of the company is, in fact, at risk. And it is the company, in its capacity as a legal person that is also the real owner of capital goods.

By law, of course, managers have certain duties towards shareholders, but the extent of these duties is not well defined. If managers refuse to maximise profits because, for example, they also take into consideration the competing social interests, they cannot be legally penalised (Marris, 1964).

Managerial theories of the firm have largely supported the post-Keynesian view, allowing the inference that growth can be slower under the maximisation of "shareholder value" than under the maximisation of managers' utility functions (see Hein, 2013). These theories can, however, only arrive at these conclusions insofar as they see companies as "coalitions" of different stakeholders – i.e. managers, workers, shareholders, suppliers, customers, tax-collectors and so on – who have conflicting objectives that must be harmonised for companies to survive (see Marris, 1964). Conflicts, in turn, can be solved only by top management, which is the most important component of the "coalition" because of its privileged access to information and power in decision-making – which includes corporate goals-setting, basic decisions on investment and expansion, but also promotions and appointments of subordinate management staff.

However, many empirical tests of the predictions of management theories have proved inconclusive or based on inadequate data to truly distinguish between owner-controlled and manager-controlled firms (see Nyman and Silbertson, 1978; Francis, 1980a, 1980b). Moreover, the *Oxford Growth of Firms Project*, conducted in 1980 by interviewing 200 senior executives and directors in a number of large firms in the United Kingdom and West Germany, came up with evidence in sharp contrast to the hypothesis that top management pursues growth more than profitability. The two most important stated objectives were in fact "maximising total profit growth" and "maximising the rate of return on capital" (see Francis, 1980b).

Furthermore, some evidence of cross-country differences in managers' objectives was provided by a survey of the stated attitudes of top managers in several countries (see Institute of Fiscal and Monetary Policy, 1996). With all due caution, considering the possible desire of managers to apply a virtuous veneer to their behaviour, respondents who answered that the only real goal of a company is to make a profit came to only 8% in Japan, 16% in France, 24% in Germany, 33% in the United Kingdom and 40% in the United States. This could demonstrate the relevance of national corporate governance rules in determining the actual objectives of management.

Nevertheless, it is hard to interpret these answers accurately because of the extreme theoretical abstraction of the idea of "maximising profit" as an objective. Even according to neoclassical theory, in fact, *net present value* of the firm or similar concepts is the most explicit objective of entrepreneurs and managers in practice. And growth, market share, as well as other aspects of the company can all be taken as proxies of the notion of net present value, insofar as they affect future profitability (see Allen and Gale, 2000).

However, even the leading theorists of the managerial enterprise have always recognised that the market price of shares – which, according to the fundamental theorem of asset pricing, should theoretically exactly reflect the company's net present value – have always influenced the managerial utility function, because of the prestige associated with their healthy levels and the takeover risk associated with their low values, but also because share prices influence corporate financing, not only in terms of new share issues but also reputation and interest rates in the bond market and in relations with banks (see Marris, 1964).

In summary, as long as the economists' debate on the actual degree of managerial discretion has proved, since the late 1930s, there has been no final consensus.

Most economists have continued to argue that managers do not have unlimited discretion and can only pursue other objectives if these are "subsidiary" or subordinate to profit maximisation. In fact, due to competition, which operates like natural selection, only profit-maximisers survive in the long run, as they can accumulate financial assets that allow them to grow and innovate faster than non-profit-maximisers, who then see their share gradually decline and are eventually eliminated from the market (see Alchian, 1950; Penrose, 1952; Winter, 1964).

Profit maximisation may, of course, not be identified with the solution of the basic *economising problem* assumed by neoclassical theory in its most simplified and idealised abstract representation of firm behaviour, and can be empirically approximated by means of the rules of thumb and other shortcuts described by Gordon. However, managerial discretion is limited because a *comparatively adequate level* of profit is necessary for a dividend policy to be acceptable to shareholders, but also to undertake the necessary investments to maintain or expand the company's market share, and to maintain a sound financial position and a good reputation with the banks. If this *comparatively normal level* of profit is not met, top managers run the risk of exposing themselves to hostile takeovers or other forms of reaction by the owners of capital and losing their job.

Moreover, as is recognised by many post-Keynesian authors, it is profits that – either directly as retained earnings or by allowing firms to borrow from both financial markets and banks – ultimately allow firms to finance their capital expenditures and R&D necessary to achieve any dimensional growth objectives (see Lavoie, 2006).

Furthermore, as we have seen, most analyses on the effects of the "shareholder revolution" have focused on public companies, where there is no controlling group of shareholders and which may therefore be easily exposed to hostile takeovers by institutional investors. Nevertheless, similar changes in corporate behaviour can also be observed in other types of large NFCs.

To account for this evidence, some analysts have argued that the spread over other companies of the objective of maximising shareholder value is partly the result of the pressure exerted by public enterprises undergoing reorganisation on the rest of their industries (see Han, 1994; Greve, 1996; Fligstein and Shin, 2007). However, some so-called "shareholder value maximisation tactics", such as mergers and layoffs, are also of frequent occurrence as attempts to boost profits in industries where they are low. Thus, these "tactics" are perfectly consistent with the objective of obtaining at least a normal level of profit, also in companies that are not victims of the "shareholder revolution".

But above all, the post-Keynesian approach – as well as all the theories that have assumed the existence of a *Fordist accumulation regime*, which we will consider in more detail in the next chapter – was mainly influenced by Burnham's belief that the so-called "managerial revolution" was producing a radical and structural change in the way contemporary capitalism worked (see Burnham, 1941).

According to Burnham, in fact, the rise of joint-stock enterprises had fostered a "struggle for power" by the social group of the managers, who, after a transition period, had achieved social dominance, becoming the new effective *ruling class* in society by exercising the absolute control over the means of production and receiving preferential treatment in the distribution of social product. Thus, since 1914, the world societies had been going through a change analogous to that from feudalism to capitalism – this time moving on from capitalism to what Burnham called the "managerial society".

Burnham's vision was not, of course, limited to private joint-stock companies but extended to the broader technocratic socio-political regimes that were emerging in the 1930s all over the world, such as Leninism-Stalinism in Soviet Union, Fascism-Nazism in many European countries and even "New Dealism" in the United States. In these new social and political contexts, the managers – or rather the bureaucrats – exercised their control over the means of production through their control – guaranteed by appropriate political institutions – of the state, which, in turn, controlled the instruments of production. The state, understood in the broadest sense as the totality of all the socio-institutional systems, was in fact the true "property" of the managers, placing them into the position of ruling class (see Burnham, 1941). The "managerial revolution", therefore, took decision-making power away from the capitalists and reduced them to a position of impotence.

In the early post-war years, many influential post-Keynesian economists, including Minsky, agreed with this view, at least on a purely corporate level, believing that "managerial capitalism" was, at the time, characterised by considerable independence of business executives from bankers and stockholders (see Whalen, 2002).

And according to this view, financialisation is now seen as a crucial new shift from *managerial capitalism* – understood as the "integrated unit dedicated to long-term growth" that characterised the *Golden Age* (Tabb 2010, p. 153) – to *finance-dominated capitalism*, which is the hallmark of the new neoliberal era. And the alleged nature of this shift is closely connected to the analytical paradigms of the *French Regulation School* and the *Social Structures of Accumulation Approach*, which we will analyse in depth in the next chapter.

In any case, this view raises the fundamental issue of understanding the social nature of managers.

Who managers really are and how they run corporations

According to Burnham, managers have been brought to the fore by the growth of large-scale industry and large corporations and are usually engineers and technicians whose specific function is the "direction and coordination" of industrial production processes – a function that, contrary to the early days of liberal capitalism, is no longer performed by the owners of capital (see Burnham, 1941). Managers, therefore, are *de facto* controllers of the means of production because most production processes in modern industry are actually highly complex in technical organisation and call for technical coordination of a large number of separate tasks.

However, are managers a *new ruling class* or just a *new personnel* for the old ruling class?

Of course, for every particular ruling class, we must specify the social relations by virtue of which it occupies its dominant position (see Sweezy, 1942). A group of individuals can, in fact, only be defined as a *ruling class* on the basis of the position it takes in the structure of economic relations in society. And, historically, the ruling classes have mostly been constituted by the people who individually or in association owned the means of production, because ownership generally implies effective control. It is precisely from the ownership of capital that capitalism derives its designation.

However, capitalists are concerned not with means of production as such, but with capital – i.e. means of production reduced to a "qualitatively homogeneous and quantitatively measurable fund of value" (Sweezy, 1942). Their position in society depends on the quantity of capital value they control. Consequently, the capitalists' main concern turns out to lie in the expansion of capital value because, while their social status is determined by the quantity of capital value they control, the forces of competition and technological change continuously work against this value. The objective of expanding capital value, therefore, must be constantly pursued, on pain of elimination from the capitalist class (see Sweezy, 1942).

Nevertheless, this also applies to those who enter into the "management" of capital, on pain of their elimination from the staff of the enterprise or the elimination of the enterprise itself from the market. And, from the point of view of corporate finance, profits are the main instrument to increase capital. Managers, like capitalists in Marx's view, are not free agents but ultimately just "functionaries of capital" (Sweezy, 1942). Insofar as all the forms of control needed by oligopolistic firms imply their social and political power, if this is linked to their "size", then the size that really matters is not their market share – which can only count in the process of determining prices – but rather the size of capital value controlled.

Moreover, if they are not simultaneously shareholders in their company, managers may well be the best paid workers in the capitalist system, but, at every intermediate level of the corporate hierarchy, their objectives are entirely tied to those of their superiors; and those who eventually form the top management, serving as directors or officers, are almost always large-block shareholders or their representatives (see Holderness, 2003; Davis, 2008). In fact, as Marris himself recognised, in the United Kingdom, since the late 1930s, it has been possible for directors in public companies to be removed by a simple majority (Marris, 1964). If this were not the case – as indeed could theoretically be the case in public companies – the owners of the capital could eventually vote with their feet, generating the market for corporate control. Furthermore, provided that a large number of shareholders in public companies were passive and the financial markets illiquid, the dominant-block shareholders could gain control of the company by owning very few shares. Thus in both the United States and the United Kingdom, where public companies are more widespread, it is only the majority of small shareholders who have been deprived of the power of control associated with their ownership rights.

In fact, Burnham himself grouped the main stakeholders of corporations – according to their relations with the means of production – into four different categories: managers, finance-executives, finance-capitalists and stockholders.

He strictly identified managers as individuals who had charge of the actual technical process of production – i.e. operating executives, production managers, plant superintendents and their associates. Thus, he considered managers to be only the people directly involved in the technical production of use-values, who, in the corporate hierarchy, are in reality totally subordinate in terms of the objectives they have to achieve – as was amply pointed out by Veblen (1904, 1921).

Finance-executives, however, had the functions of "guiding the company toward a profit" (Burnham, 1941), dealing with sales, negotiating the prices paid for raw materials and labour, organising the terms of financing the company and so on. All these functions are now usually seen as an integral part of management. But Burnham chose to emphasise only the function of organising the production of use-values in the identification of real managers and, consequently, considered the pursuit of profit to be a goal of personnel other than managers. And once this arbitrary distinction was made, he acknowledged the possibility that finance-executives could often themselves be stockholders in their company, having substantial ownership interests in it.

Burnham also recognised that "finance-capitalists" were often the directors of the companies themselves or that it was the bankers and big financiers who actually appointed the directors. The finance-capitalists' function was neither control of the technical process of production nor pursuit of profit in a particular company, because through holding companies, boards of directors, banks and various legal devices, they were in fact interested in the financial aspects of many companies and in many market operations at the same time. They could, for example, merge several companies to boost sale of shares or bonds to the public, without considering the effects of the merger on the technical process of production or on the profits of each company. Just as they might wish, for tax or speculative reasons, to lower the profit of one company by raising the prices charged by the supplier companies they also owned.

The finance-capitalists were, of course, also stockholders who, although not usually owning a majority of the shares, did own a substantial block of them, and had at their disposal liquid funds and other resources with which they could get enough "proxies" on the shares from the small shareholders to vote as if they had a majority. Thus, they had ultimate control over the assets of the company.

In summary, the finance-capitalists described by Burnham in the era of *the managerial revolution* already had all the characteristics of the institutional investors of today's *shareholder revolution*. One revolution may have followed another, but the only change is that today other types of institutional investors have replaced the banks.

Hence, from a historical point of view, only small shareholders have actually lost control over the means of production owned by the companies they theoretically own, while large shareholders have actually expanded the extent of control attached to their shares.

Moreover, as was highlighted by Baran and Sweezy (1966), top managers are usually recruited from the middle and upper ranks of the capitalist class itself. They are often rich men in their own right, regardless of the large incomes and ample privileges they get for their managerial performance. Thus, even if there were a theoretical separation between "ownership" and "control", they are no strangers to ownership as a whole and, if they are not among the biggest owners, they work as the guardians of all ownership on a large scale. They are the "leading echelon of the property-owning class" (Baran and Sweezy, 1966).

Like other fractions of the ownership class, of course, they may have interests distinct from those of other owners. However, the most likely conflict of interest is with small shareholders rather than with the big shareholders they usually represent, as in the case of dividend policy. Indeed, top managers in the past were often oriented towards generating the most internal company funds possible by lowering as much as possible the dividend pay-out rate that shareholders should wish to maximise. However, on this front, top managers, who were often themselves large shareholders, proved to be the main allies of the largest shareholders, who, like all very wealthy people, are used to saving a large part of their income and may find it agreeable that a large part of the profits be invested directly in corporations in which they already own large shares – provided the corporation is still adequately profitable, of course.

In summary, as some Marxist economists have pointed out (see Baran and Sweezy, 1966; Mandel, 1990), managerial capitalism – seen as a new form of capitalism oriented to growth rather than profit – has long been another myth with no foundation. The myth has often served to promote the idea of a "soulful corporation" (see Kaysen, 1957), in which corporate management may subordinate the pursuit of shareholder value to a variety of more socially worthy objectives and to looking after the interests of other stakeholders. And it is this apology of managerial corporations that has probably prompted some post-Keynesian economists to draw a sharp contrast between the "innocent" NFCs and the greedy financial markets.

However, the belief that large or giant corporations, run by professional managers, could afford not to pursue the maximum viable profit by largely freeing themselves from competition and constraints of demand that arise from the business cycle and technological innovation – i.e. by guaranteeing a specific demand for their products (see Galbraith, 1967/2007) – was an illusion born of a hasty extrapolation from the exceptional conditions that prevailed during the long boom following the end of the Second World War (see Mandel, 1990).

In capitalist economies, decisions crucial for society, such as investment decisions, are made neither by society as a whole nor by "associated producers", but by independent firms – be they small producers or large, multi-national corporations – which are the essential economic institutions of capitalism. The juridical form does not matter. The social functioning of private property of capital – i.e. fragmented social labour – does not depend on the kind of agents who take the independent firms' decisions, be they individual capital owners, representatives of stockholders or managers. The decision-makers' behaviour is, in fact, socially and historically determined by the same set of impersonal forces that characterise competition – be it free or monopolistic.

NFCs as main actors of their own financialisation

In conclusion, if the alleged compulsion to growth maximisation by managerial corporations is recognised to be a mere function of the traditional pursuit of profit – as growth is in fact capital accumulation that can result only from surplus value production and realisation (see Mandel, 1990) – large NFCs may play a far less passive role as agents of their own financialisation than assumed by some post-Keynesian economists.

Financial control of productive activities has traditionally been seen by top managers as a particular organisation controlling model (see Fligstein, 1990). Thus, what may appear to be the "pursuit of shareholder value" may simply be the effect of the traditional maximisation of the self-valorisation of the capital of the main owners – especially in companies with a controlling interest, which use mass shareholders and their financial intermediaries as mere holders of less secured claims. From this viewpoint, however, the alleged "shareholder revolution" may in the end play a minor role.

The dynamics of large industrial corporations have historically largely influenced "the wealth of nations" – i.e. their "national income", to put it in modern economic terms – during the past century and a half (see Chandler et al., 1997). Such enterprises, in fact, are key microeconomic agents that employ productive assets, human resources and technological knowledge on a vast scale. Their importance has risen over time. In 1900, only 113 companies were listed on the New York Stock Exchange, while today they number 2,800. In the United States, the share of all manufacturing firms covered by corporations rose from 49% in 1947 to 78% in 2017. And today, in the United States, around 95% of all the value added in the manufacturing sector is produced by corporations that account for more than 94% of all new capital expenditures (see U.S. Census Bureau).

As we know, the rise of large corporations was the direct consequence of the new needs connected to managing the new technologies of the "Second Industrial Revolution". During the first industrial revolution, in fact, all the enterprises were small and managed by their owners and – up until the mid-19th century – their activities became increasingly specialised, handling a single product or service in the different spheres of production, distribution, transportation, finance and other services – in full accordance with Adam Smith's vision of the relationships between specialisation and the extent of the market (see Chandler and Straus, 1978). The modern multi-unit and multi-functional enterprise appeared only as from the mid-19th century, when new technologies of production and transportation permitted an unprecedented expansion of markets. In this new economic scenario, the evolution of the enterprises in a number of economic sectors moved in the direction of combination and integration of the activities of several productive and distributive units. Yet, this required new forms of organisation to mobilise the necessary capital and employ the large number of workers and managers needed – and indeed to coordinate the large flow of goods through the processes of production and distribution and monitor the different functional activities involved. And the liquid funds needed to finance most of the new production processes could be efficiently raised only through the limited liability of corporate form of organisation and raising money by selling shares of stock.

Starting from the 20th century, these multi-functional enterprises began to diversify their production activities in an attempt to further enlarge their market, moving into new sectors and other countries. In this way, big modern enterprises became multi-industry and multi-national, and these new expansion strategies also changed the structure of many industries and national economies as a whole. Giant corporations have become the hallmark of modern times, dominating production, distribution, transport, finance and services and playing an important role in all the industrial economies (see Chandler and Straus, 1978). Given their size, they are inevitably bureaucratic in organisation. Their control requires a hierarchy of offices – each with its own functions and responsibilities – and therefore the implementation of a very complex managerial structure.

However, very early on financial control proved to be an effective corporate control model for multi-industry and multi-national organisations, leading to the creation of *holding companies* – which are financial institutions in their own right, managing a portfolio of stocks to control the companies in which they hold a share of the equity capital. It is only the struggle for corporate control which distinguishes them from other financial institutions. Nevertheless, NFCs – whether controlled by holding companies or not – remain the only place where money capital can actually be spent to purchase the factors of production that combine to produce tradable goods and services for the exclusive purpose of making a surplus value – which only then, if ever, can be redistributed by financial institutions in the form of interest, dividends, capital gains or even the winnings of gambling.

Since the 1970s, after the collapse of the Bretton Woods international order, the big NFCs were faced with a massive new effort to rapidly enhance their competitiveness on a global scale. The attempt to overcome the constraints of national markets required new financial funds at a time when self-financing was severely limited by low profit rates. This incited recourse to the financial markets, increasing the demand for loanable funds and *money capital* and raising interest rates and dividends. And the intense restructuring process called for given the need to raise profitability levels also led to the waves of mergers and layoffs, as well as the decisions to squeeze production, cut workers' wages and downsize companies that have so often been blamed on the effects of the "shareholder revolution".

In this context, according to some economists, the emergence of the "shareholder value conception of control" was in fact the solution attempted to cope with the economic crisis of the 1970s (see Fligstein and Shin, 2007). It was the falling rates of profit that prompted the US business and financial lobbies from breaking away from the government-run system of regulation they had hitherto, on the whole, accepted. The structural crisis of the 1970s spurred the large concentrations of private capital – until then acting only in non-financial sectors of the economy – to resume financial strategies and reorganise themselves on a global scale (see Useem, 1984; van der Pijl, 1984; Helleneir, 1994; Duménil and Lévy, 2005).

Indeed, the very difference between long-termism and short-termism may be no more than a reflection of the difference in competitive conditions resulting from the transition from regulated and relatively controlled oligopolistic national markets to a free global market in which even large concentrations of private capital have to compete with each other on a no-holds-barred basis. In reality, the choice between short-term and long-term profit maximisation depends on the actual competitive conditions faced by firms. Short-termism is typical of competitive capitalism, while long-termism was long allowed by monopoly capitalism – which, however, is only able to effectively limit competition in the market for its products within the boundaries of protected national markets (see Mandel, 1990).

We thus agree with the idea that the financialisation of NFCs is a new phenomenon that can generate dramatic changes in the daily life and social welfare of developed countries because of its impact on investment decisions and employment (see van der Zwan, 2014). However, it can be correctly explained only in the context of the new international relationships that characterise globalisation.

Indeed, we believe that the financialisation of NFCs is not an accidental distortion of previous capitalist tendencies – as sometimes appears in the post-Keynesian literature – but an organic development within the developed countries oriented towards a better reorganisation of capitalist power relations on a global scale. And the very rise to prominence of financial markets and their main actors and products – rather than as aberrations hampering the normal functioning of the "real" economy – must be seen as a set of institutional innovations promoting new types of capitalist rationality within the new global "capital circuit", where NFCs remain the main actors. Financialisation and globalisation are, in other words, just two sides of the same coin.

In order to better understand the new developments in world capitalism and their initial turning point, however, we must first delve into the exceptional features of the so-called *Golden Age* and the reasons for its implosion.

Notes

1 See, as an emblematic case of this identification, Lazonick's description of what a prosperous economy should look like and how this was embodied by the US economy during the *Golden Age* (Lazonick, 2013).

2 The ratio compares the value of all stocks at an aggregate level to the value of the country's total output.

References

Aglietta, M. (2000). "Shareholder Value and Corporate Governance: Some Tricky Questions". *Economy and Society*, 29 (1): 146–59.

Aglietta, M. and Breton, R. (2001). "Financial Systems, Corporate Control and Capital Accumulation". *Economy and Society*, 30 (4): 433–66.

Aglietta, M. and Reberioux, A. (2005). *Corporate Governance Adrift: A Critique Of Shareholder Value*. Cheltenham and Northampton, MA: Edward Elgar.

Alchian, A. (1950). "Uncertainty, Evolution, and Economic Theory". *Journal of Political Economy*, 58 (3): 211–221.
Allen, F. and Gale D. (2000). *Comparing Financial Systems*. Cambridge, MA and London: The MIT Press.
Appelbaum, E. and Berg, P. (1996). "Financial Market Constraints and Business Strategy in the U.S.". In: Michael, J. and Smith, J. (eds.), *Creating Industrial Capacity: Towards Full Employment*. New York: Oxford University Press, pp. 192–221.
Arestis, P. (2016). "Financial Liberalization, the Finance-Growth Nexus, Financial Crises and Policy Implications". In: Arestis, P. and Sawyer, M. (eds.), *Financial Liberalisation. Past, Present and Future*. Cham: Palgrave Macmillan, pp. 1–42.
Arestis, P., and Sawyer, M. (2005). "Financial Liberalization and the Finance-Growth Nexus: What Have We Learned?". In: P. Arestis and M. Sawyer (eds.), *Financial Liberalization: Beyond Orthodox Concerns*. Houndmills and Basingstoke: Palgrave Macmillan, pp. 1–42.
Arestis, P. and Sawyer, M. (eds.) (2018). *Inequality. International Papers in Political Economy*. Cham: Palgrave Macmillan.
Baran, P. and Sweezy, P. M. (1966). *Monopoly Capital. An Essay on the American Economic and Social Order*. New York: Monthly Review Press.
Barradas, R. (2017). "Financialisation and Real Investment in the European Union: Beneficial or Prejudicial Effects?". *Review of Political Economy*, 29 (3): 376–413.
Becht, M., Bolton, P. and Roell, A. (2002). "Corporate Governance and Control". In: Constantinides, G., Harris, M. and Stulz, R. (eds.), *Handbook of the Economics of Finance, Volume 1 A*. Amsterdam: North-Holland, pp. 3–109.
Berle, A. Jr. and Means, G. (1932). *The Modern Corporation and Private Property*. Chicago, IL: Commerce Clearing House.
Bernanke, B. S. (2015). *Why Are Interest Rates So Low?*. Available at: http://www.brookings.edu/blogs/ben-bernanke/posts/2015/03/30-why-interest-rates-so-low
Black, B. (1998). "Shareholder Activism and Corporate Governance in the United States". In Newman, P. (ed.), *The New Palgrave Dictionary of Economics and the Law*. New York: Stockton Press, pp. 459–65.
Blecker, R. A. (2016). "The US Economy Since the Crisis: Slow Recovery and Secular Stagnation". *European Journal of Economics and Economic Policies: Intervention*, 13 (2): 203–14.
Boltanski, L. and Chiapello, E. (2005). *The New Spirit of Capitalism*. London and New York: Verso.
Boyer, R. (2000). "Is a Finance-Led Growth Regime a Viable Alternative to Fordism? A Preliminary Analysis". *Economy and Society*, 29 (1): 111–45.
Braun, B. (2015). "From Performativity to Political Economy: Index Investing, ETFs and Asset Manager Capitalism". *New Political Economy*, 21 (3): 257–73.
Burnham, J. (1941). *The Managerial Revolution. What is Happening in the World Now*. New York: John Day Co.
Cecchetti, S. G. and Kharroubi, E. (2012). "Reassessing the Impact of Finance on Growth". *BIS Working Papers*, 381.
Cecchetti, S. G. and Kharroubi, E. (2015). "Why Does Financial Sector Growth Crowds Out Real Economic Growth". *BIS Working Papers*, 490.
Chandler, A. D. and Straus, G. (1978). "The United States: Evolution of Enterprise". In: Mathias, P. and Postan, M. M. (eds.), *Economic History of Europe. Volume VII. The Industrial Economies. Capital, Labour, and Enterprise Part 2. The United States, Japan, And Russia*. Cambridge: Cambridge University Press, pp. 70–133.

Chandler, A. D., Amatori F. and Hikino T. (eds.) (1997). *Big Business and the Wealth of Nations*. Cambridge: Cambridge University Press.

Crotty, J. R. (1990). "Owner–Manager Conflict and Financial Theories of Investment Instability: A Critical Assessment of Keynes, Tobin, and Minsky". *Journal of Post Keynesian Economics*, 12 (4): 519–42.

Crotty, J. R. (1993). "Rethinking Marxian Investment Theory: Keynes Minsky Instability, Competitive Regime Shifts and Coerced Investment". *Review of Radical Political Economics*, 25 (1): 1–26.

Crotty, J. (2000). "Structural Contradictions of the Global Neoliberal Regime". *Review of Radical Political Economics*, 32 (3): 361–68.

Crotty, J. (2002). "The Effects of Increased Product Market Competition and Changes in Financial Markets on the Performance of Nonfinancial Corporations in the Neoliberal Era". *PERI, University of Massachusetts, Amherst, Working Paper Series*, 44.

Crotty, J. (2003). "The Neoliberal Paradox: The Impact of Destructive Product Market Competition and Impatient Finance on Nonfinancial Corporations in the Neoliberal Era". *Review of Radical Political Economics*, 35 (3): 271–79.

Crotty, J. (2005). "The Neoliberal Paradox: The Impact of Destructive Product Market Competition and 'Modern' Financial Markets on Nonfinancial Corporation Performance in the Neoliberal Era". In: Epstein, G. A. (ed.), *Financialization and the World Economy*. Cheltenham and Northampton, MA: Edward Elgar Publishing Ltd, pp. 77–110.

Davis, G. F. (2008). "A New Finance Capitalism? Mutual Funds and Ownership Re-Concentration in the United States". *European Management Review*, 5: 11–21.

Davis, G. F., Diekmann, K. A. and Tinsley, C. (1994). "The Decline and Fall of the Conglomerate Firm in the 1980s: The Deinstitutionalization of an Organizational Form". *American Sociological Review*, 59: 547–70.

Davis, G. F. and Kim, E. H. (2007). "Business Ties and Proxy Voting by Mutual Funds". *Journal of Financial Economics*, 85: 552–70.

Davis, E. P. and Steil, B. (2001). *Institutional Investors*. Cambridge, MA: The MIT Press.

Davis, G. F. and Stout, S. (1992). "Organization Theory and the Market for Corporate Control, 1980–1990". *Administrative Science Quarterly*, 37: 605–33.

Davis, G. F. and Thompson, T. A. (1994). "A Social Movement Perspective on Corporate Control". *Administrative Science Quarterly*, 39: 141–73.

Duménil, G. and Lévy D. (2004). "The Economics of US Imperialism at the Turn of the 21st Century". *Review of International Political Economy*, 11 (4): 657–76.

Duménil, G. and Lévy D. (2005). "The Neoliberal (Counter-)Revolution". In: Saad-Filho, A. and Johnston, D. (eds.), *Neoliberalism. A Critical Reader*. London: Pluto Press, pp. 9–19.

Epstein, G. A. (2005). "Introduction: Financialization and the World Economy". In: Epstein G.A. (ed.), *Financialization and the World Economy*. Cheltenham and Northampton, MA: Edward Elgar Publishing Ltd, pp. 3–16.

Epstein, G. and Jayadev, A. (2005). "The Rise of Rentier Incomes in OECD Countries: Financialization, Central Bank Policy, and Labor Solidarity". In: Epstein, G. A. (ed.), *Financialization and the World Economy*. Cheltenham and Northampton, MA: Edward Elgar Publishing Ltd, pp. 46–74.

Epstein, G. and Power, D. (2003) "Rentier Incomes and Financial Crises: An Empirical Examination of Trends and Cycles in Some OECD Countries". *Canadian Journal of Development Studies / Revue canadienne d'*études du développement, 24 (2): 229–48.

Fama, E. F. and Miller, M. H. (1972). *The Theory of Finance.* New York: Holt, Rinehart, & Winston.

Ferreiro, J. and Gómez C. (2016). "Financialization and the Financial Balance Sheets of Economic Sectors in the Eurozone". In: Arestis, P. and Sawyer, M. (eds.), *Financial Liberalisation. Past, Present and Future.* Cham: Palgrave Macmillan, pp. 87–131.

Fichtner, J., Heemskerk, E. M. and Garcia-Bernardo J. (2017). "Hidden Power of the Big Three. Passive Index Funds, Re-Concentration of Corporate Ownership, and New Financial Risk". *Business and Politics*, 19 (2): 298–326.

Fligstein N. (1990). *The Transformation of Corporate Control.* Cambridge, MA: Harvard University Press.

Fligstein, N. (2001). *The Architecture of Markets: An Economic Sociology of Twenty-First-Century Capitalist Societies.* Princeton, NJ: Princeton University Press.

Fligstein, N. and Shin, T. (2007). "Shareholder Value and the Transformation of the U.S. Economy, 1984–2000". *Sociological Forum*, 22 (4): 399–424.

Francis, A. (1980a). "Families, Firms and Finance Capital: The Development of UK Industrial Firms with Particular Reference to Their Ownership and Control". *Sociology*, 14 (1): 1–27.

Francis, A. (1980b). "Company Objectives, Managerial Motivations and the Behaviour of Large Firms: An Empirical Test of the Theory of 'Managerial' Capitalism". *Cambridge Journal of Economics*, 4 (4): 349–61.

Froud, J., Haslam, C., Johal, S. and Williams, K. (2000). "Shareholder Value and Financialization: Consultancy Promises and Management Moves". *Economy & Society*, 29 (1): 80–110.

Froud, J., Johal, S., Leaver, A. and Williams, K. (2006). *Financialization and Strategy. Narrative and numbers.* London and New York: Routledge.

Galbraith, J. K. (1967/2007). *The New Industrial State.* Princeton, NJ: Princeton University Press.

Gemzik-Salwach, A. and Opolski, K. (2017). "Introduction". In: Gemzik-Salwach, A. and Opolski, K. (eds.), *Financialization and the Economy.* London and New York: Routledge, pp. 1–5.

Gordon, R. A. (1945). *Business Leadership in the Large Corporation*, Washington, DC: The Brookings Institution.

Gordon, R. A. (1948). "Short-Period Price Determination in Theory and Practice", *American Economic Review*, 38 (3): 265–88.

Grahl, J. and Teague, P. (2000). "The Régulation School, the Employment Relation and Financialization". *Economy and Society*, 29 (1): 160–78.

Greve, H. R. (1996). "Patterns of Competition: The Diffusion of a Market Position in Radio Broadcasting". *Administrative Science Quarterly*, 41 (1): 29–60.

Hall, R. L. and Hitch, C. J. (1939). "Price Theory and Business Behaviour". *Oxford Economic Papers*, 2: 12–45.

Han, S. K. (1994). "Mimetic Isomorphism and Its Effects on the Audit Service Market". *Social Forces*, 73 (2): 637–64.

Hein, E. (2013). "The Crisis of Finance-Dominated Capitalism in the Euro Area, Deficiencies in the Economic Policy Architecture, and Deflationary Stagnation Policies". *Journal of Post Keynesian Economics*, 36 (2): 325–54.

Hein, E. (2017). "Financialisation and Tendencies Towards Stagnation: The Role of Macroeconomic Regime Changes in the Course of and after the Financial and Economic Crisis". *Institute for International Political Economy, Working Paper*, 90.

Hein, E, Dodig N. and Budyldina N, (2015). "The Transition Towards Finance-Dominated Capitalism: French Regulation School, Social Structures of

Accumulation and Post-Keynesian Approaches Compared". In: Hein, E., Detzer, D. and Dodig N. (eds.), *The Demise of Finance-Dominated Capitalism. Explaining the Financial and Economic Crises.* Cheltenham, UK: Eldward Elgar, pp. 7–53.

Hein, E. and Truger, A. (2013). "Finance-Dominated Capitalism in Crisis – the Case for a Global Keynesian New Deal". *Journal of Post Keynesian Economics*, 35 (2): 187–213.

Hein, E. and van Treeck, T. (2010). "'Financialisation' in Post-Keynesian Models of Distribution and Growth: A Systematic Review". In: Setterfield, M. (ed.), *Handbook of Alternative Theories of Economic Growth.* Cheltenham: Edward Elgar, pp. 277–92.

Helleneir, E. (1994). *States and the Reemergence of Global Finance: From Bretton Woods to the 1990s.* New York: Cornell University Press.

Hofstadter, R. (1955). *The Age of Reform.* New York: Vintage Books.

Holderness, C. G. (2003). "A Survey of Blockholders and Corporate Control". *Federal Reserve Board of New York Economic Policy Review*, 9 (1): 51–64.

Institute of Fiscal and Monetary Policy (1996). *Socio-Economic Systems of Japan, the United States the United Kingdom, Germany and France.* Tokyo: Ministry of Finance.

Jürgens, J., Naumann, K. and Rupp, J. (2000). "Shareholder Value in an Adverse Environment: The German Case". *Economy & Society*, 29 (1): 54–79.

Kalecki, M. (1971). *Selected Essays on the Dynamics of the Capitalist Economy. 1933–1970.* Cambridge: Cambridge University Press.

Kaysen, C. (1957). "The Social Significance of the Modern Corporation". *The American Economic Review*, 47 (2): 311–9.

Kamerschen, D. R. (1968). "The Influence of Ownership and Control on Profit Rates". *American Economic Review*, 58 (3): 432–47.

King, R. G. and Levine, R. (1993a). "Finance and Growth: Schumpeter Might Be Right". *Quarterly Journal of Economics*, 8: 717–37.

King, R. G. and Levine, R. (1993b), "Finance, Entrepreneurship, and Growth: Theory and Evidence", *Journal of Monetary Economics*, 32 (3): 513–42.

Kolko, G. (1963). *The Triumph of Conservatism. A Reinterpretation of American History, 1900–1916.* New York: Free Press.

Krippner, G. R. (2005). "The Financialization of the American Economy". *Socio-Economic Review*, 3: 173–208.

Lanzillotti, F. (1958). "Pricing Objectives in Large Companies". *American Economic Review*, 48 (5): 921–41.

Lavoie, M. (2006). *Introduction to Post-Keynesian Economics.* Basingstoke: Palgrave Macmillan.

Lavoie, M. (2014). *Post-Keynesian Economics: New Foundations.* Cheltenham: Edward Elgar Publishing Ltd.

Lazonick, W. (2013), "The Financialization of the U.S. Corporation: What Has Been Lost, and How It Can Be Regained", *Seattle University Law Review*, 36: 857–909.

Lazonick, W. (2014). "Profits Without Prosperity". *Harvard Business Review*, 92 (9): 46–55.

Lazonick, W. and O'Sullivan, M. (1996). "Organization, Finance and International Competition". *Industrial and Corporate Change*, 5 (1): 1–49.

Lazonick, W. and O'Sullivan, M. (2000). "Maximizing Shareholder Value: A New Ideology for Corporate Governance". *Economy and Society*, 29 (1): 13–35.

Lester, R. A. (1946). "Shortcomings of Marginal Analysis for Wage-Employment Problems". *American Economic Review*, 36 (1): 63–82.

Levine, R. (2003). "More on Finance and Growth: More Finance, More Growth?". *Federal Reserve Bank of St. Louis Review*, 85 (4): 31–46.

Lowenstein R. (2004). *Origins of the Crash: The Great Bubble and Its Undoing*. London: Penguin Books.

Machlup, F. (1946). "Marginal Analysis and Empirical Research". *American Economic Review*, 36 (4): 519–54.

Mandel, E. (1990). "Introduction by Ernest Mandel". In: Marx, K., *Capital. Volume I*. London: Penguin Books, pp. 11–86.

Marris, R. (1964). *The Economic Theory of 'Managerial' Capitalism*. London: Palgrave Macmillan.

McKinnon, R. I. (1973). *Money and Capital in Economic Development*. Washington, DC: Brookings Institution.

McKinnon, R. I. (1988). "Financial Liberalization in Retrospect: Interest Rate Policies in LDCs". In: Ranis, G. and Schultz, T. P. (eds.), *The State of Development Economics. Progress and perspectives*. Oxford: Basil Blackwell, pp. 386–410.

McKinnon, R. I. (1989). "Financial Liberalization and Economic Development: A Reassessment of Interest-rate Policies in Asia and Latin America". *Oxford Review of Economic Policy*, 5 (4): 29–54.

McKinnon, R. I. (1991). *The Order of Economic Liberalization: Financial Control in the Transition to a Market Economy*. Baltimore, MD: John Hopkins University Press.

Miller, M. H. (1998). "Financial Markets and Economic Growth". *Journal of Applied Corporate Finance*, 11 (1): 8–14.

Minsky, H. P. (1982). *Can "It" Happen Again: Essays on Instability and Finance*. Armonk, NY: M.E. Sharpe.

Minsky, H. P. (1990). "Schumpeter: Finance and Evolution". In: Heertje, A. and Perlman, M. (eds.), *Evolving Technology and Market Structure: Studies in Schumpeterian Economics*. Ann Arbor: The University of Michigan Press, pp. 51–74.

Minsky, H. P. (1993). "Finance and Stability: The Limits of Capitalism". *The Levy Economics Institute, Working Paper*, 93.

Monsen, R. J., Chiu, J. S. and Cooley, D. E. (1968). "The Effects of Separation of Ownership and Control on the Performance of the Large Firm". *Quarterly Journal of Economics*, 82 (3): 435–51.

Morin, F. (2000). "A Transformation in the French Model of Shareholding and Management". *Economy and Society*, 29 (1): 36–53.

Nyman, S. and Silberston, A. (1978). "The Ownership and Control of Industry". *Oxford Economic Papers*, New Series, 30 (1): 74–101.

O'Connor, J. (1973/2009). *The Fiscal Crisis of the State*. New Brunswick and London: Transaction Publishers.

O'Sullivan M. (2000). *Contests for Corporate Control. Corporate Governance and Economic Performance in the United States and Germany*. Oxford: Oxford University Press.

Oliver, H. M. (1947). "Marginal Theory and Business Behaviour", *American Economic Review*, 37 (3): 375–83.

Onaran, Ö, Stockhammer, E. and Grafl, L. (2011). "Financialisation, Income Distribution and Aggregate Demand in the USA". *Cambridge Journal of Economics*, 35 (4): 637–61.

Orhangazi, Ö (2008). "Financialisation and Capital Accumulation in the Non-Financial Corporate Sector: A Theoretical and Empirical Investigation on the US Economy: 1973–2003". *Cambridge Journal of Economics*, 32 (6): 863–86.

Pagano, M. (1993). "Financial Markets and Growth: An Overview". *European Economic Review*, 37 (2–3): 613–22.

Palley, T. I. (2007). "Financialization: What It Is and Why It Matters". *The Levy Economics Institute Working Paper*, 525.

Palley, T. I. (2012). *From Financial Crisis to Stagnation: The Destruction of Shared Prosperity and the Role of Economics*. Cambridge: Cambridge University Press.

Palley, T. I. (2013). *Financialization: The Economics of Finance Capital Domination*. Basingstoke: Palgrave Macmillan.

Palley, T. I. (2016). "Inequality, the Financial Crisis and Stagnation: Competing Stories and Why They Matter". *Real World Economics Review*, 74: 1–18.

Parenteau, R. W. (2005). "The Late 1990' US Bubble: Financialization in the Extreme". In: Epstein, G. A. (ed.), *Financialization and the World Economy*. Cheltenham and Northampton, MA: Edward Elgar Publishing Ltd, pp. 111–48.

Pariboni, R., Paternesi Meloni, W. and Tridico, P. (2020), "When *Melius Abundare* Is No Longer True: Excessive Financialization and Inequality as Drivers of Stagnation", *Review of Political Economy*, 32 (2): 216–42.

Pariboni, R. and Tridico, P. (2019). "Labour Share Decline, Financialisation and Structural Change". *Cambridge Journal of Economics*, 43: 1073–102.

Penrose, E. (1952). "Biological Analogies in the Theory of the Firm", *American Economic Review*, 42 (5): 804–19.

Phillips, K. (2002). *Wealth and Democracy. A Political History of the American Rich*. New York: Broadway Books.

Porter, M. E. (1992). "Capital Disadvantage: America's Failing Capital Investment System". *Harvard Business Review*, 70: 65–82.

Power, D., Epstein, G. and Abrena, M. (2003) "Trends in Rentier Incomes in OECD Countries: Estimates, Data, and Methods". PERI, University of Massachusetts, Amherst, *Working Paper Series*, 58a.

Rappaport, A. (1986). *Creating Shareholder Value*. New York: The Free Press.

Sawyer, M. (2014). "What Is Financialization?". *International Journal of Political Economy*, 42 (4): 5–18.

Sawyer, M. (2017). "Financialization and Economic and Social Performance". In: Gemzik-Salwach, A. and Opolski, K. (eds.), *Financialization and the Economy*. London and New York: Routledge, pp. 9–25.

Sawyer, M. (2018). "Financialisation, Financial Crisis and Inequality". In: Arestis, P. and Sawyer, M. (eds.), *Inequality. Trends, Causes, Consequences, Relevant Policies*. Cham: Palgrave Macmillan, pp. 43–87.

Shaw, E. S. (1973). *Financial Deepening in Economic Development*. New York: Oxford University Press.

Shleifer, A. and Vishny, R. W. (1997). "A Survey of Corporate Governance". *The Journal of Finance*, 52 (2): 737–83.Stewart, B. (1991). *The Quest for Value*. New York: HarperCollins.

Stockhammer, E. (2004a). "Financialisation and the Slowdown of Accumulation". *Cambridge Journal of Economics*, 28 (5): 719–41.

Stockhammer, E. (2004b). *The Rise of Unemployment in Europe. A Keynesian Approach*. Cheltenham, and Northampton, MA: Edward Elgar.

Stockhammer, E. (2005). "Shareholder Value-Orientation and the Investment-Profit Puzzle". *Journal of Post-Keynesian Economics*, 28 (2): 193–216.

Stockhammer, E. (2006). "Shareholder Value Orientation and the Investment-Profit Puzzle". *Journal of Post Keynesian Economics*, 28 (2): 193–215.

Stockhammer, E. (2013a). "Rising Inequality as a Cause of the Present Crisis". *Cambridge Journal of Economics*, 39 (3): 935–58.

Stockhammer, E. (2013b). "Financialization, Income Distribution and the Crisis". In: Fadda, S. and Tridico, P. (eds.), *Financial Crisis, Labour Markets and Institutions*. London: Routledge, pp. 98–119.

Summers, L. (2014a). "U.S. Economic Prospects: Secular Stagnation, Hysteresis, and the Zero Lower Bound". *Business Economics*, 49(2): 65–73.

Summers, L. (2014b). "Reflections on the 'New Secular Stagnation Hypothesis'". In: Teulings, C., Baldwin, R. (eds.), *Secular Stagnation: Facts, Causes and Cures*. London: CEPR Press, pp. 27–38.

Sweezy, P. M. (1942). "The Illusion of the 'Managerial Revolution'". *Science & Society*, 6 (1): 1–23.

Tabb, W.K. (2010). "Financialization in the Contemporary Social Structure of Accumulation". In: McDonough, T., Reich M. and Kotz D.M. (eds.), *Contemporary Capitalism and Its Crises: Social Structure of Accumulation Theory for the 21st Century*. Cambridge: Cambridge University Press, pp. 145–67.

Tirole, J. (2006). *The Theory of Corporate Finance*. Princeton, NJ: Princeton University Press.

Tobin, J. (1997). "Comment". In: Pollin, R. (ed.), *The Macroeconomics of Savings, Finance and Investment*. Ann Arbor: University of Michigan Press, pp. 299–304.

Tomaskovic-Devey, D., Lin, K. H. and Meyers N. (2015). "Did Financialization Reduce Economic Growth?". *Socio-Economic Review*, 13 (3): 525–48.

Toporowski, J. (2000). *The End of Finance. The Theory of Capital Market Inflation, Financial Derivatives and Pension Fund Capitalism*. London and New York: Routledge.

Tori, D. and Onaran, Ö. (2017). "Financialisation and Physical Investment: A Global Race to the Bottom in Accumulation?". *PKSG. Post Keynesian Economics Study Group, Working Paper*, 1707.

Tori, D. and Onaran, Ö. (2018a). "The Effects of Financialization on Investment: Evidence from Firm-Level Data for the UK". *Cambridge Journal of Economics*, 42, 1393–416.

Tori, D. and Onaran, Ö. (2018b). "Financialization, Financial Development and Investment. Evidence from European Non-Financial Corporations". *Socio-Economic Review*, 0: 1–43.

Tridico, P. (2017). *Inequality in Financial Capitalism*. London and New York: Routledge.

Tridico, P. and Pariboni R. (2018). "Inequality, Financialization, and Economic Decline". *Journal of Post Keynesian Economics*, 41 (2): 236–59.

Useem, M. (1984). *The Inner Circle: Large Corporations and the Rise of Business Political Activity in the U.S. and U.K.* London: Oxford University Press.

Useem, M. (1993). *Executive Defense: Shareholder Power and Corporate Reorganization*. Cambridge, MA: Harvard University Press.

Useem, M. (1996). *Investor Capitalism: How Money Managers Are Changing the Face of Corporate America*. New York: Basic Books.

van der Pijl, K. (1984). *The Making of an Atlantic Ruling Class*. London and New York: Verso.

van der Zwan, N. (2014). "Making Sense of Financialization". *Socio-Economic Review*, 12: 99–129.

van Treeck, T. (2009): "The Political Economy Debate on 'Financialization' – A Macroeconomic Perspective". *Review of International Political Economy*, 16 (5): 907–44.

van Treeck, T. (2015). "Inequality, the Crisis, and Stagnation". *European Journal of Economics and Economic Policies: Intervention*, 12 (2): 158–69.

Veblen, T. (1904). *The Theory of Business Enterprise*. New York: Charles Scribner's Sons.

Veblen, T. (1921). *The Engineers and the Price System*. New York: B. W. Huebsch.

Walker, O. (2016). *Barbarians in the Boardroom. Activist Investors and the Battle for Control of the World's Most Powerful Companies*. London: Pearson Education Limited.

Whalen, C. J. (1997). "Money Manager Capitalism and the End of Shared Prosperity". *Journal of Economic Issues*, 31 (2): 517–25.

Whalen, C. J. (2001). "Integrating Schumpeter and Keynes: Hyman Minsky's Theory of Capitalist Development". *Journal of Economic Issues*, 35 (4): 805–23.

Whalen, C. J. (2002). "Money Manager Capitalism: Still Here, but Not Quite as Expected". *Journal of Economic Issues*, 36 (2): 401–6.

Williams, K. (2000). "From Shareholder Value to Present-Day Capitalism". *Economy and Society*, 29 (1): 1–12.

Winter, S. (1964). *Economic "Natural Selection" and the Theory of the Firm*. New Haven, CT: Yale Economic Essays.

Zuckerman, E. (2000). "Focusing the Corporate Product: Securities Analysts and De-Diversification", *Administrative Science Quarterly*, 45: 591–619.

2 The French Regulation School and the Social Structures of Accumulation Approach

Accumulation regimes and stages of capitalism development

As we mentioned several times in the previous chapter, the idea that financialisation is a structural change in the recent evolution of capitalism is closely linked to the theoretical paradigms proposed by the so-called *French Regulation School* and the *Social Structures of Accumulation Approach* (SSAA). According to many post-Keynesian authors, in fact, both these approaches provide some fundamental interpretations not only of the dynamics of financialisation, but also of the beginning of its structural crisis, which some see as coinciding with the financial crisis of 2007–2008 (see Hein et al., 2015).

Each of these two approaches deals with the interaction between social institutions – considered in a very broad sense – and the way the capitalist economy works, trying to explain the dynamics of the institutional structure development and the related phases of economic development. Both these currents of economic analysis share the insight that the historical developments of capitalism are embedded in social institutions and there is a close interdependence between these institutions and different *accumulation regimes* or different *stages of development*. Both approaches also share the idea that some insights can be gained into the dynamics of these regimes or stages, and focus in particular on *structural breaks* or *regime changes* in the long-run development of modern capitalism, which, according to most post-Keynesian authors, can also help explain the emergence and consolidation of financialisation (see Hein et al., 2015).

In fact, the two approaches, while using different terminologies and showing some mutual differences – as well as many internal facets – have some common theoretical roots and tend to converge in many final interpretations of capitalist development (see Kotz, 1990).

The so-called *French Regulation School* is in fact a broad research programme of radical political economy which has also reached out well beyond economics, winning a major role in many historical and sociological explanations of capitalist societies. However, despite its name, it does not prove a truly homogeneous school of thought, as some of its leading ideas have changed

DOI: 10.4324/9781003223221-3

substantially over time (see De Vroey, 1984). Thus, following Jessop (1997), we prefer to define it more generally as the *Regulation Approach* (RA).

This approach was originally influenced by *French structural Marxism*, which borrowed the concept of *regulation* from systems theory and structuralism to apply it to the ways the configurations of social relations characterising different historical stages of social production – called, following Marx, "modes of production" – work out in the context of the historical development of "socioeconomic formations". The RA, therefore, has deep-rooted relations with Marx and various types of Marxist theories. Indeed, it is not by chance that its early formulations highlighted the crucial role played by the class struggle in the genesis, dynamics and crisis of the various periods of capital accumulation and the policies that accompanied and sustained them. However, the main Marxist components were progressively diluted over time with other institutionalist and post-Keynesian approaches (see Jessop, 1997; McDonough, 2010). And more recent analyses have gradually come to focus more on issues of structural cohesion than on problems of social conflict (see Jessop, 2006).

RA's formal distancing from Marxism was probably linked more to the political than the scientific crisis of the latter in the early 1980s (see Nadel, 2002). However, the RA shook off its explicit tie with Marxism, although its research programme conserved many links with the Marxian vision.

The SSAA, in turn, was from the outset jointly inspired both by American neo-Marxists and by long-wave theorists – such as Kondratief and Schumpeter – and developed some of Minsky's long-run visions (see Kotz, 1994; Lippit, 2010; Hein et al., 2015). However, unlike many orthodox Marxist theories which focused on the possibility of the collapse of capitalism, the SSAA has always been strictly concerned with the ability of capitalism to regenerate itself after each period of crisis.

Thus, the RA and the SSAA both share some Marxist views regarding the nature and preconditions of capital accumulation and emphasise the historical and social nature of capitalist economies, highlighting the variability of capitalism across time and space.

They also assume that society as a whole, including economic activities, is characterised by social relations that are inherently contradictory, given the conflicting objectives and interests of the different social groups, and that these structural contradictions sooner or later generate structural crises. But they share with Marx above all the idea that capitalism, while showing an enormous productive potential, is a contradictory system that does not contain any self-regulating mechanisms able to set it in the direction of the perpetual accumulation of capital it needs to survive in the long run (see Aglietta, 1979/2015).

In the Marxian paradigm, in fact, the capitalist mode of production is founded on the accumulation of capital, which continuously transforms a surplus value into additional capital. It is this process that periodically expands and accelerates economic growth, but in an unsustainable way, because of the contradictions between the development of productive forces and the needs of distribution of social product between labour and capital. And it is precisely these growing contradictions that create the conditions for new phases of crisis, which constantly characterise the expanded reproduction of the capitalist system.

Thus, according to Marx as well as the RA and the SSAA, capital accumulation is essentially an expression of the labour-capital relation, by which the share of surplus value in the social product is determined. Marx, moreover, saw the tendency of the rate of profit – i.e. the market form of distribution of the surplus value among capitalists – to decline as an inevitable underlying consequence of the capitalist mode of production. However, even according to Marx, this tendency to decline can be continuously counteracted by forces that, in the RA and SSAA perspectives, are, respectively, summarised as *modes of regulation* and *social structures of accumulation* (SSA).

Consequently, according to both the RA and the SSAA, although the capitalist mode of production makes accumulation an imperative, there is no simple and invariable relation between it and forms of accumulation. The main objective of both these approaches, therefore, is to analyse the social and economic patterns that enable a stable accumulation over time – defined as "accumulation regimes" by the RA and "stages of development" by the SSAA.

In the SSAA, however, a "stage of development" is simply an empirical concept, corresponding to a historical long wave in capital accumulation, which tends to last for several decades (see Lippit, 2010). In the RA, instead, an "accumulation regime" is, rather, a macroeconomic concept, corresponding to a specific form of organisation of production and distribution of value and surplus value that is able to coordinate, over a long period, changes in the conditions of production – such as the volume of capital invested in the different productive branches – with transformations in the conditions of final consumption (see Lipietz, 1988; Jessop, 1997). Thus, an accumulation regime is defined by a set of complementary patterns of production and consumption that is capable of self-reproducing over a long period and is consequently characterised by its own *reproductive requirements*. And the regular patterns which define it have often been formalised by the regulationists with macroeconomic models of "steady growth", inspired by Kalecki and other Cambridge economists and based on Kaldor's celebrated "stylized facts" (see Kaldor, 1957).

According to both the RA and the SSAA, these regular patterns of accumulation do not, of course, exclude crises and typically take shape between two structural crises. According to the early versions of these approaches, in fact, capitalism can experience transitory periods of stable growth only through two kinds of stable arrangements – an appropriate balance between wages and profits and a society-wide acceptance of a set of regulations, procedures and cultural expectations that give rise to appropriate policies (see Aglietta, 1979/2015; Lipietz, 1987). If even one of these two arrangements becomes unstable, then a radical restructuring has to take place before economic growth can resume and social conflict disappear (see Cohen and Kennedy, 2013). Economic and financial crises, therefore, periodically highlight breakdowns in the regular reproduction process of social relations and promote new forms of social relations.

Most SSAA authors and regulationists share the Keynesian idea that "without a stable and favorable external environment, capitalist investment in production will not proceed" (Gordon et al., 1994). On the basis of the experience of the Great Depression, in fact, Keynes made a decisive contribution in the direction of a definitive dismantling of the business cycle paradigm previously prevailing in economics, arguing that the phenomenon of the business cycle was no longer a characteristic feature of capitalist development because the economic system tends rather towards equilibria with unemployment that cannot change endogenously (see Hillinger, 1987). And most SSAA authors share Keynes' view that the internal mechanisms of business cycles, under the conditions of modern monopoly capital, are no longer autonomously able to restore the conditions for rapid accumulation (see Gordon et al., 1983).

This assumption implies that prolonged stability in the enlarged reproduction of capital in any accumulation regime or stage of development can be achieved only when it is "institutionalized" in a set of practices, norms and conventions that form a *mode of regulation* – according to the RA – or an *SSA* – according to the SSAA – where social structures are all those human relations which have a stable existence over relatively long periods of time. Essentially, therefore, study of social and economic changes consists in study of changes in social structures. And, given the Keynesian assumption of a tendency towards equilibria with unemployment, any upswing phase of capitalist development can only be the result of a new adequate SSA or mode of regulation, without which there could only be stagnation.

All this also implies that both accumulation regimes and stages of development are transformed over time and also vary in space. They can be characterised by different *industrial paradigms* – which, according to the RA, summarise at the microeconomic level the main features of the technical and social division of labour, such as mass production – as well as different intensity of technical change, volume and composition of demand and workers' lifestyles.

According to the RA, furthermore, when an industrial paradigm, a regime of accumulation and a mode of regulation are sufficiently consistent to ensure for a certain period of time the conditions for a long wave of capitalist expansion, their combination defines a *development model* (see Jessop, 1997; Boyer, 2000, 2005, 2010, 2013). Thus, we can say that the main purpose of both approaches is to explain the rise and subsequent structural crisis of such development models. In doing so, both approaches consider a wide range of institutional factors and social forces directly and indirectly involved in capital accumulation. Aware of the anarchic role of market forces, in fact, they stress the significant complementary functions of other social mechanisms in capitalist reproduction which try to regularise and normalise capital accumulation against the volatility and uncertainty produced by these forces.

Thus, according to both the RA and the SSAA, the chances of a long-term accumulation period can only depend on social and economic regularities at the micro, meso and macro levels concerning the forms of organisation of production and competition – both domestically and internationally – the time horizon of the decision-makers involved in capital accumulation, an adequate distribution of the social product between wages and profits and, above all, an adequate size and composition of aggregate demand able to absorb an increasing production capacity, guaranteed by an active intervention of the state (see Boyer, 1986; Gordon et al., 1987; Lippit, 2010).

In this theoretical context, therefore, *Fordism* – i.e. the concept the RA is perhaps best known for – is precisely a development model, based on conditions, both economic and extra-economic, conducive to mass production and consumption and generalised application of scientific methods in the organisation of production processes, which is believed by regulationists to have characterised the *Golden Age* (see Amable, 2002). In fact, the RA arose precisely to explain the sudden structural crisis in the mid-1970s – characterised by an unexpected combination of stagnation and inflation – in this exceptional expansionary phase (see Jessop, 1997). Thus, the concept of the *Fordist accumulation regime* was coined precisely to describe the prolonged period of stable growth after the Second World War in the major industrialised countries, based on an unprecedented "compromise" between capital and labour (see Boyer, 2010).

Similarly, the SSAA emphasises the "accord" between capital and labour – characterised by strong trade unions and wages rising in tandem with labour productivity – as a key feature of the period between the end of the Second World War and the "great stagflation" of the 1970s.

Once again, therefore, in explaining the exceptional upswing of the *Golden Age*, the two approaches place emphasis on the oligopolistic competition conditions and the connected *wage relations*, on the one hand, and the role of the state in supporting aggregate demand on the other. For both approaches, the alleged typical features of managerial capitalism – which we highlighted in the previous chapter – coupled with the welfare state provided by governments were the fundamental conditions for the long upswing that characterised the Fordist accumulation regime.

Modes of regulation and social structures of accumulation

Thus, according to both the RA and the SSAA, empirical regular patterns of accumulation can only be supported by adequate institutional forms and arrangements, which, in turn, are transformed over time. The main objective of both the approaches is, therefore, to analyse the interconnections between these institutional forms and the regularities of capitalist development, as well as the crisis tendencies of modern capitalism and the possible sources of crisis resolution. To this end, they focus on the changing combinations of economic and extra-economic institutions and practices which help to temporarily secure a certain stability in the accumulation process despite the fundamental contradictions and conflicts generated by the dynamic of capitalist societies itself.

In the RA, institutional forms create a logical passage from micro- to macroeconomics, socially determining the behaviour of economic agents, which are not homogeneous rational market subjects interacting in a series of complete markets, as in mainstream approaches, but are social individuals, socially and historically determined, as in the Marxian approach. A hierarchy among the different institutional forms is generated by the *mode of regulation* that characterises a country in every period under consideration.

In the SSAA, in turn, the set of institutions existing in a particular time and place, and encouraging capital accumulation, is referred to as a "social structure of accumulation" (see Kotz, 1994).

Thus, in essence, both modes of regulation and SSAs are "emergent"[1] sets of institutions, norms, organisational forms, practices and individual and collective behaviour patterns historically determined that accompany an accumulation regime and provide the conditions for its long-run social reproduction (see Jessop, 1997; Boyer and Saillard, 2002; McDonough, 2010). Both modes of regulation and SSAs provide consistency to a set of decentralised decisions, without any need for the agents to be aware of the principles governing the overall dynamics of the system (see Boyer and Saillard, 2002). In other words, they are a social "invisible hand", alternative to the market relations assumed by mainstream economics.

However, the social relations that characterise modes of regulation and SSAs must be susceptible of being reproduced over time – that is, the totality of their agents must be reproduced in their material existence and put in a position to accept or impose the establishment of the same relations. Every stable social relationship, therefore, must be embodied in individuals in the form of acquired habits and routines.

The capacity of a dominant class to impose social practices that benefit it over a long span of time is called *hegemony* – as, for example, in the case of the "American model" in Western advanced economies in the 1950s and 1960s. However, dissatisfaction experienced by some social groups as a consequence of the contradictory characteristics of some social relations can periodically create the demand for new norms and relations. Consequently, different social groups can enter into conflict, but, despite the struggle among their agents, social relations can still be temporarily reproduced, until crisis sets in. The way this happens, in turn, is closely connected to the problem of regulation itself. And social procedures and authority structures for conflict resolution, providing for the modification of norms, constitute an integral part of the forms of regulation (see Lipietz, 1988).

The major form among these in the modern era is, of course, the state, which defines the legitimacy and durability of social relations – instituting, for instance, the market and money, and codifying the *wage relation*. The state has hegemony armed with coercion, and society as an abstraction is in practice shaped by politico-juridical systems. Thus, the social relations between the members of every organisation are closely influenced by the laws, political frameworks and customs of the larger social entities within which they operate.

However, other forms of regulation may only be codified by conventions and habits – through which agents enter into stable relations – even with no legal status (see Lipietz, 1988). In fact, the original French word "régulation" indicates social regularisation, rather than legal or state regulation, and, according to Jessop, it might be better translated as *regularisation* or *normalisation* (see Jessop, 1997). Thus, the regulationists look more to various forms of "governance" used to regularise economic activities than to legal arrangements. The expression "mode of regulation" in the RA is therefore simply an abbreviation for "social mode of economic regulation", which can be set in antithesis with a pure "economic mode of economic regulation", guaranteed by market relations alone, which is typical of mainstream economic approaches (see Jessop, 1997).

However, according to the regulationists, state forms and legal arrangements also matter and are an integral part of any mode of regulation. In their early definitions, in fact, modes of regulation as well as SSAs are usually characterised by four main institutional forms: the *wage relation* – i.e. structural features of labour markets, ways of wage bargaining, levels of individual and social wages, workers' lifestyles and so on; the *enterprise forms* – i.e. firms' internal organisation, sources of profits, forms of competition, ties among different enterprises, links to the banking system and so on; and the *monetary standard* and the *social and economic functions of the state*, which, in turn, contribute to determining the monetary regime, forms of competition and the wage relations (see Jessop, 1997; Guttmann, 2015).

The *wage relation*, in the early formulations of both approaches, was seen as a fundamental component of any mode of regulation or SSA and synthesised the set of relationships between types of work organisation, forms of wage bargaining and the ways in which the workforce reproduces itself. Of all institutional forms, in fact, the RA and the SSAA originally paid particular attention to this relationship because it was assumed to dominate all other social institutions, determining as it does the form of appropriation of surplus in the capitalist mode of production.

Money itself is another important institutional form, as general equivalent that connects all economic units. Many monetary regimes, moreover, function as possible ways to offset shortfalls and oversupply in the economic systems. These particular institutional forms can obviously involve major intergovernmental relations within extensive international areas of circulation and exchange, like the Bretton Woods agreements in the Fordist accumulation regime or, now, the Euro and its centralised regulation in the Eurozone.

From the outset, the regulationists also shared with Minsky a particular interest in financial settings and, above all, they shared the idea that modern economies are dominated by the choice between productive and financial investments, determined by the difference between the interest rate and the rate of profit. This implies, for example, that, as the euphoria of an economic boom spreads, companies tend to choose increasingly risky investment plans, so that the slightest shock makes clear the latent imbalance between financial returns and the returns on productive investments, sparking off a crisis. The latter can then become cumulative if the credit crunch, in turn, reduces the overall demand rather than financial speculation.

Another key factor of both modes of regulation and SSAs is the *international regime* within which they work, and which shapes the relations between a single nation-state and the international "Concert of Nations". Indeed, if a single state can exert political sovereignty over a defined territory, relations between it and the rest of the world are rarely pure market relationships, while they typically arise from political choices and the diplomatic balance of power, as well as being influenced by currency exchange management and openness to foreign capital movements. Thus, the international regime obviously interacts with the country's other institutional forms and arrangements.

All significant social relations, therefore, imply regularity in some social practices, characterised by a certain permanence over time. And regulation of a social relation is precisely the way in which this relation can be reproduced despite its conflictual nature. Any mode of regulation or SSA must, however, inevitably go through a cyclical chain of cause-and-effect relationships in four stages: relation-reproduction-contradiction-crisis (see Lipietz, 1988). Given the contradictory nature of capitalist societies, in fact, while social relations create the conditions to reproduce capital accumulation over time, their interaction progressively generates new contradictions that eventually provoke a structural crisis. Finally, structural crises enhance the generation of new social relations that create the conditions for a new cycle of capital accumulation.

Most contradictions emerge over time in every mode of regulation and SSA due to class conflicts, competition between companies, economic wars between governments and the struggle between different political groups (see Brenner and Glick, 1991). These contradictions, in turn, act on the accumulation regime and eventually lead to a structural crisis. Thus, crises are to be seen essentially as discontinuities in the reproduction of social relations resulting from the accumulation of divergences and contradictions between the different levels of the institutional forms of the current mode of regulation.

Consequently, the transition from one development model to another is discontinuous and "creatively destructive" (Jessop, 1997, p. 292). Naturally, the new development model that can emerge from structural crises is not usually predictable (see Brenner and Glick, 1991). Yet, above all, because social institutions are complex historical outcomes, after the collapse of a previous mode of regulation or SSA, the emergence of new social institutions that can guarantee a new accumulation regime usually takes a long time, generally involving a transition period characterised by economic stagnation.

In Fordism, according to the regulationists, the fundamental institutional arrangements lay in the new role played by the state, credit money, an original wage relation, an oligopolistic form of competition and strict governmental control of international trade and capital movements (see Boyer and Saillard, 2002). From the point of view of state forms, the Fordist mode of regulation was characterised by the "Keynesian welfare state" (Jessop, 1997), whose main feature was to ensure full employment in the context of relatively closed economies, and to influence income distribution through the regulation of collective bargaining and thus support economic growth by ensuring adequate levels of effective domestic demand. In fact, according to both the RA and the SSAA, collective mass consumption was the real crux of the Fordist development model (see Hein et al., 2015).

In this theoretical context, therefore, Keynesian economic policies appear to be a part of the mode of regulation that served for the Fordist accumulation regime to exit from the long stagnation produced by the Great Depression in the 1930s and ensure a long-term accumulation in the first three post-war decades. However, according to the regulationists, the Keynesian policies served only to counter unemployment determined by a lack of effective demand in a situation of excess of productivity compared to real wages (see Boyer, 1986).

Unfortunately, the Fordist mode of regulation worked well only between 1948 and the early 1970s. In fact, the regulationists see the crisis of the 1970s as the exhaustion of the Fordist accumulation regime, which reached its limits because of the accumulation of new internal contradictions, especially in terms of income distribution between wages and profits (see Boyer, 1986). The conflict in income distribution was long mitigated – at least in a part of the economic system – by monopolistic extra profits, obtained by restricting competition in internal markets, but especially with a continuous increase in productivity, obtained by intensifying the mechanisation of production processes. But the latter way also produced a growing stock of fixed capital, which contributed to reducing the normal rate of profit in the non-financial sectors.

Finally, the crisis of this accumulation regime coincided with the crisis of its specific Keynesian mode of regulation, which, in turn, lost its effectiveness and accumulated a growing mass of new internal contradictions (see Lordon, 2002). In particular, full employment policies saw real wages rising, contributing to shrinking the share of profit in the national income and so reducing the prospects of profitability in new investment. In this way, the 1970s and the early 1980s were characterised by the crisis of the monopolistic and state-managed mode of regulation that opened the way out of the 1929 crisis.

The way out of decreasing profitability was sought in the expansion of free trade and capital mobility, on the one hand – in the hope that a larger free world market and a wider range of investment opportunities would improve profit opportunities – and, on the other hand, squeezing real wages through inflation as well as production delocalisation in emerging countries. However, the escalation of the new conflict between capital and labour undermined the wage relation, which constituted the pivot of the Fordist mode of regulation as a whole, leading to its final crisis.

Subsequent to the crisis of the post-war accumulation regime, according to most regulationists, a new *post-Fordist mode of regulation* gradually took shape as from the mid-1980s. It was characterised by internationalisation of competition, liberalisation of capital movements and consequent intensification of monetary constraints and sharp transformations in the wage relation: in short, by the neoliberal mode of regulation still dominant, which, according to most post-Keynesian economists, essentially boosted financialisation.

Finance-dominated capitalism

Of course, both the RA and the SSAA have provided their own interpretations of financialisation, seeing it as a phase of transition from the Fordist development model to – respectively – a "finance-led growth regime" or a "global neoliberal SSA". And both approaches have also come up with views on the consequences of the new regime for long-run economic and social development and presages of its possible final structural crisis (see Lippit, 2010; Guttman, 2015).

The main merit of these contributions on financialisation is that, in contrast to many post-Keynesian approaches – where, as we saw in the previous chapter, the institutional changes of neoliberalism are often considered as exogenous shocks, based on changing power relations between financial capital and the main actors of the real production – they address institutional changes as the result of the internal dialectic and final structural crisis of the previous development model or SSA (see Hein et al., 2015). In these theoretical approaches, also these institutional changes are seen as the result of the very laws of motion of capitalism.

Thus, the structural crisis of the Fordist development model – according to the RA – or the "regulated capitalist SSA" – according to SSAA – has in fact been seen by many interpreters of these approaches as a consequence of the collapse of the profitability enjoyed in the previous regime.

To account for the empirical decrease of profitability from the mid-1960s to the late 1970s, many regulationists originally looked to Marx's law of the tendency of the general rate of profit to fall (see Aglietta, 1979/2015; Boyer, 1987). Thus, they attributed the fall in the rate of profit to the inability of labour productivity growth to increase the growth of surplus value at a rate sufficient to counteract the growing organic composition of capital (see Brenner and Glick, 1991).

The subscribers to SSAA, however, explicitly refer to the Marxian theory of the cyclical *profit squeeze* – according to which, under the conditions of full employment reached at the end of each expansionary phase, the bargaining power of the workers is able to temporarily squeeze the rate of surplus value and, consequently, the rate of profit (see Kotz, 2013).

For both approaches, however, first the collapse of profitability had negative impacts on real investment and growth, and then it went on to undermine the very foundations of the "compromise" or "accord" between capital and labour. Thus, the trade unions' wage demands in excess of productivity gains, allowed by full employment conditions, were first counterbalanced by rising inflation rates and subsequently by redundancy discipline. Yet, these capitalists' reactions, undermining the foundations of the previous compromise between capital and labour, determined the structural crisis of the "Fordist–Keynesian regime of accumulation" itself (see Arrighi, 1994/2010).

As we have seen, from the theoretical point of view of both approaches, a structural crisis undoubtedly opens a transitional phase, which should eventually lead to the emergence of new social relations that should create the conditions for a new regime of accumulation.

Thus, according to many regulationists, the collapse of the Fordist development model prompted various attempts to establish new accumulation regimes. Of these, on the basis of the empirical evidence of the 1990s, Boyer listed "competition-led" and "service-led" regimes in many OECD countries, the "knowledge-based economy" in the United States, "Toyotism" in Japan and "export-led growth" in East Asia (see Boyer, 2000).

However, none of these alleged regimes has shown temporal duration and spatial spread comparable to those of Fordism. Therefore, for a long time, there has been no agreement as to precisely how to characterise the new *post-Fordist regime* (see Stockhammer, 2008).

Finally, what seems to have emerged as the best candidate over the last two decades is what the RA called the "finance-led growth regime" and the SSAA labelled the "neo-liberal global SSA", both believed to have characterised the United States and the United Kingdom from the 1980s onwards and gradually expanded to the rest of the world as the last long-wave accumulation regime in a chronological order (see Lippit, 2010; Guttman, 2015; Hein et al., 2015).

In this new accumulation regime or SSA, the hierarchy among institutional forms had dramatically changed, with financial relations taking over the centre of the scene previously occupied by the wage relation (see Boyer and Saillard, 2002). In this new context, in fact, the dominant capital-labour relation is a "discord" rather than an "accord", based on flexibility, higher cost of job loss, downward pressure on wages and increasing individualism of workers displacing solidarity and the propensity to unionism (see Tabb, 2010).

The global neoliberal SSA, in particular, is characterised both by all the main features usually utilised to describe globalisation – such as developments in *information and communication technology* (ICT), decreasing transportation and communication costs, increasing international free trade, reorganisation of production on a global scale, complex production networks and global chains, free movements of capital and so forth – and all those usually utilised to define financialisation and neoliberalism (see Tabb, 2010). Within this social structure, globalisation plays the role of a new industrial paradigm, comprising the reorganisation of production due to dramatic innovation, reduction of costs in transportation and communication, the development of *ICTs* and international free movements of capital. Neoliberalism, however, is seen as a major subset of emergent social relations, constituted by attitudes, practices and policies globally consistent and mutually reinforcing, which has, from the functional point of view, taken the place of the previous Keynesian mode of regulation (see Tabb, 2010). While financialisation is seen as the creation process of the new set of pivotal relations – which have been replacing the former wage relation – linking globalisation and neoliberalism as key components of the new SSA (see Tabb, 2010). From this point of view, therefore, the growth of the financial sector and its functions is nothing but the emergent mechanism for lubricating adjustment to the new developments of the emerging industrial paradigm.

Of course, other major changes are taken into account in defining the new SSA – most regarding the spatial configuration of capital accumulation processes. Internationally, in fact, the new dominant core-periphery relationship is that between the newly industrialised emerging economies and the former manufacturing core, which is undergoing significant de-industrialisation and transformation into a pure financial centre (see Arrighi, 1994/2010).

In this theoretical context, however, some authors have ended up by identifying the very concept of financialisation with "finance-dominated capitalism" – i.e. a new stage of development of modern capitalism as opposed to the previous "manager-dominated capitalism" – whose SSA is characterised by deregulation of the financial sector, shareholder dominance at the firm level, the rise of shadow banking, the financialisation of everyday life and macro-policies dominated by financial interests (see Jessop, 2002; Hein, 2012, 2013, 2015, 2016; 2017; Hein et al., 2015; Tridico, 2017).

On the income distribution side, finance-dominated capitalism is characterised by an increase in the share of gross profits, dividends and interest, on the one hand, and a corresponding fall in the share of labour income – associated with a growing inequality between workers' wages and top managers' salaries – on the other.

On the corporate side, instead, it is characterised by increasing shareholder power over managers and workers – with shareholders able to align management with their own interests through short-term performance-related remuneration schemes – and an increasing rate of return on equity and debt instruments held by "rentiers".

On the consumption side, finally, finance-dominated capitalism is characterised by boosting wealth-based and debt-financed consumption – through stock market and house price booms that increase the notional wealth against which households could borrow. This has long been offsetting the depressing demand effects of neoliberal policies, the shareholder revolution and falling real wages (see Hein, 2015; Hein et al., 2016). In doing so, however, finance-dominated capitalism has generated new contradictions over time – such as growing debt-income ratios of private households that can only be sustained by speculative bubbles.

But above all, the rise of finance-dominated capitalism is believed to be a new system of "profits without investment" in many advanced countries, with the share of financial and foreign profits in total corporate profits exceeding 50% in the United States (see Arrighi, 1994/2010; van Treeck, 2009a, 2009b; Krippner, 2011; Hein 2012; Hein and Mundt, 2012; van Treeck and Sturn, 2012; Hein et al., 2015; Krippner et al., 2017).

This new growth regime in which the profitability of stock market assets has taken on a decisive central role is also defined by some regulationists as "finance-led capitalism" (see Aglietta and Reberioux, 2005). And this theme, of course, is widely linked with the process of financialisation of NFCs that is the main focus of this book.

However, all the inconsistencies and new contradictions of finance-dominated or finance-led capitalism are seen by many as the general causes of all the global financial and economic crises of the last few decades and, above all, as the major harbingers of the financial crisis of 2007–2008, seen by many authors as the final systemic crisis of this new accumulation regime (see Lippit, 2010; Tabb, 2010; Guttman, 2015; Hein et al., 2015). According to the latter reading, therefore, we now probably find ourselves in a new phase of transition between the already failed finance-dominated capitalism and a future and as yet unknown stage of development that will have to rise from the ashes of the previous one.

However, there has been no general agreement among regulationists and SSAA interpreters on the reproductive conditions of this alleged finance-led accumulation regime.

Of course, by definition, an accumulation regime of this type is only theoretically possible if the diffusion of financial norms and practices leads to stable growth over a long period.

Boyer, on the basis of empirical evidence limited to the 1980s and 1990s, developed a formal macroeconomic model to study the short-term stability of this kind of regime (Boyer, 2010). According to him, stable growth can be possible if the norm of increasing profitability imposed by shareholders on corporations and management has a positive effect on real investment and, thus, on aggregate demand. But this can only come about if the financial markets support the investment behaviour induced by higher profitability, and provided that the wealth effects on consumption, in turn, generate sufficient additional aggregate demand to compensate for under-consumption due to falling wages. And this requires that most current household incomes be made up of a mix of wages and financial income or debts against assets.

However, according to Boyer himself, the development of financial markets can itself also provoke increasing structural instability. Thus, there is probably a threshold beyond which financialisation can even destabilise the economy as a whole. And only appropriate regulation by the central banks, designed to prevent financial bubbles and market volatility, can stabilise the system over time.

Does a new accumulation regime really exist?

In summary, both the RA and the SSAA have from the outset had the ambition of explaining *Kondratiev cycles* – i.e. the long economic cycles, with an average duration of 50 or 60 years that have characterised historical capitalist development – by identifying above all the social institutions and modes of regulation that guaranteed the long phases of upswing, on the one hand, and the internal contradictions that determined the final structural crises on the other (see Arrighi, 1994/2010; Jessop, 1997; Wolfson, 2003). And in both these approaches, systemic crises play the role of structural breaks and adjustments that transform the existing regime on the different institutional fronts of wage relations, as well as forms of competition, state intervention and the monetary and banking environment, and, indeed, international relations.

In this theoretical context, furthermore, finance-led capitalism has been seen as the last regime of long-wave accumulation that emerged in the early 1980s and lasted at least until the financial crisis of 2007–2008, if not beyond (see Lippit, 2010; Guttman, 2015; Hein et al., 2015).

However, according to the earlier definitions of both modes of regulation and SSAs, the only new institutional structures that can aspire to play these roles have to lead to both stability and strong economic growth (see Wolfson and Kotz, 2010). Furthermore, according to the earlier formulations of the SSAA, a stage of development, enhanced by an adequate SSA, has to be an entire cycle of growth and decline, each lasting approximately 25 years (see Wolfson, 2003). Thus, in the early versions of both approaches, a long period of stable growth was the essential and qualifying element to identify a regime of accumulation or the upswing phase of a stage of development.

Unfortunately, however, this does not really seem to be the case with neoliberalism and financialisation (see Wolfson, 2003).

In the final decades of the 20th century, in fact, the global economy was slowing down and characterised by greater volatility (see Tabb, 2010). The GDP growth rates in the main industrialised countries in the neoliberal era remained significantly lower than those recorded during the Fordist regime (see Wolfson, 2003; Kotz and McDonough, 2010; Wolfson and Kotz, 2010). Moreover, in this period, the United States and other advanced economies entered into a new phase of cyclical behaviour. The cycles in the United States averaged about six years in length and showed highly variable GDP growth rates in the first cycle, which covered the period 1981–1987 (see Dymski, 2009). In the following two cycles – covering the period 1988–1999 – the US GDP growth rates showed relatively less variability, but the second cycle ended with the burst of the *dot.com financial bubble* and the serious threat of the first major financial crisis in the country after the crisis of 1929.

Subsequent monetary policies and further financial deregulation helped to halt the fall in asset prices and reinforce a new phase of growth in speculative financial incomes – which fuelled the real estate price bubble and the associated subprime mortgages boom – but they simply shifted the outbreak of the crisis to 2007.

Thus, neoliberalism and financialisation can certainly be considered new institutional structures. And an upswing phase might even not necessarily be characterised by high growth rates to be recognised as such (see Tabb, 2010). However, neoliberalism and financialisation have been recognised as major sources of uncertainty and instability – as well as of increasing risk of financial turmoil and crises – too often to be easily reconciled with the canonical idea of mode of regulation or SSA.

Consequently, we share the view that it is very difficult to consider neoliberalism and financialisation as components of an SSA if – according to its original meaning – this is defined as a social structure that guarantees stable and regular capital accumulation and economic growth in all the countries that are characterised by it. This difficulty is even greater if the stable growth is identified with the post-Keynesian concept of "steady growth", as many regulationists have often done.

But above all, if we understand capital accumulation as the growth of the stock of capital goods and productive capacity of a single country, how can a social structure that promotes "profits without investment" be defined as a "social structure of accumulation"?

Similar questions have even been raised by some notable representatives of the SSAA. And many analysts initially viewed neoliberalism and financialisation simply as ways of going back to the original nature of capitalism – after an exceptional historical parenthesis – rather than as functional components of a new SSA (see Tabb, 2010).

Other SSAA interpreters, on the basis of the inconsistencies between its original definition and current uses, have instead proposed a revision of the very concept of SSA (see Wolfson, 2003). Kotz himself, who is one of the founding fathers of the SSAA, agreed with Wolfson's proposal and concluded that the long-term development of capitalism can probably be better understood through the concept of a succession of "institutional structures" (ISs) – each of which may or may not promote rapid capital accumulation and growth – rather than exclusively through that of SSA (see Kotz, 2003). Kotz also pointed out that the only case of rapid and sustained economic growth in the neoliberal era occurred in China, where, although economic activities were partly liberalised, the neoliberal model was never definitively adopted, resulting in an unprecedented combination of state ownership and central planning with the free market and the pursuit of private profit (see Kotz and McDonough, 2010).

However, Kotz eventually found it acceptable to define the "neoliberal institutional structure" as an SSA no longer on the basis of its effect on the rate of economic growth, but insofar as it "promotes profit-making and serves as a framework for the process of capital accumulation" (Kotz and McDonough, 2010).

From this viewpoint, however, the new social structures of the neoliberal era can be qualified as structures of accumulation only if we consider capital accumulation not as the growth of the stock of capital goods – in accordance with post-Keynesian approaches – but rather – in accordance with Marx – as the process of self-valorisation of capital value. Only in this way can the capital value of a country grow independently of the stock of capital goods operating within it, insofar as it is able to finance real investment and growth in other countries – i.e. insofar as it is able to appropriate surplus value produced in them.

This different perspective, moreover, is also more consistent with the idea that financialisation amounts simply to a change in the accumulation of the personal wealth of the rich in the advanced countries (see Krippner, 2011). From this viewpoint, however, financialisation becomes no more or less than globalisation seen from the perspective of the rich countries.

Furthermore, in our view, the evidence that the wage relation in the Fordist development model has been replaced by financial relations in finance-led capitalism opens up only two possibilities on the theoretical ground. Either the wage relation in an accumulation regime is not as essential an element as was assumed in the early formulations of the RA and the SSAA, or the financial relations – with their inherent aspects of long-term unsustainability – cannot truly characterise an accumulation regime or SSA, according to their own early definitions.

In the first case, the substitution of the wage relation with financial relations can only mean that a mode of regulation or an SSA needs a social relation that guarantees adequate support for consumption demand – not specifically an accord between capital and labour. Yet, the need is then to explain why the wage relation rose to be the pivot of the Fordist mode of regulation, although – by its very nature – it limited the profit share in national income.

In the second case, financialisation can only characterise a transition period between two successive modes of regulation or SSAs. And transition periods can, of course, show nothing but stagnation – in accordance with the early versions of the RA and the SSAA – or instability and turbulence – in accordance with the anarchic nature of unregulated capitalism itself.

Moreover, having observed the coexistence of economic growth and full employment coupled with wage growth from the late 1940s to the early 1970s, the question arises, what is the mutual causal relation? Was it the growth of mass consumption, fuelled by wage growth, that influenced economic growth, or was it the upswing phase that allowed the conflict between wages and profits to be mitigated, as long as the latter grew within the limits of productivity gains? Of course, in any upswing phase, virtuous circles can be generated. But what was the real main driver?

For most economists influenced by the Keynesian belief in a general tendency of the economic system towards equilibria with unemployment, the only possible answer is the obvious one: Keynesian policies! However, it is also empirically evident that in the 1970s, Keynesian policies without the support of any others showed their limits in sustaining growth processes and ended up by producing stagflation.

Thus, on the one hand, we believe that the exceptional upswing phase after the Second World War has not yet been adequately explained and that its genesis was probably due mainly to the great upheavals of the war itself – such as the immense mass destruction of infrastructure and capital goods and the subsequent need for reconstruction. Above all, however, major factors were acceleration in the process of technological innovation, linked to the needs of war, and the dramatic rupture of the previous world order, with the implosion of the great European colonial empires and "Pax Americana" bursting onto the scene (see Gordon et al., 1987). On the other hand, we believe that, when discussing the role played by policies, we need to clarify better why governments do what they do. Industrial and economic policies are not exogenous variables controlled by paternalistic politicians who follow the general interests of society as a whole – as is sometimes assumed by theoretical economists – but are usually oriented by the interests and objectives of the large economic lobbies themselves.

Finally, the truly extraordinary upswing phase after the Second World War, characterised by financial tranquillity and no serious threat of financial crises, in reality covered less than 20 years – from 1946 to 1965. And even during this period there were significant cumulative changes in the US financial structure that eventually led to increasing market turbulence as from the mid-1960s and progressively undermined the dollar-based international monetary system created with the Bretton Woods Agreement (see Minsky, 1982/2016). Indeed, as early as 1966, financial turmoil began to appear again, prompting massive interventions by the central banks to avert a crisis that nevertheless eventually broke out in the mid-1970s (see Minsky, 1982/2016; Crotty, 2005). Thus, the process of financialisation was actually a karst current that ran through all the years of the *Golden Age*, only to resurface with impetus when the regulatory superstructure collapsed.

However, the main problems with most of the concepts formulated by the RA and the SSAA are, as we see them, purely epistemological. In fact, they are essentially *empirical* or *a posteriori* concepts. They are certainly very useful to classify, periodise and compare the historical forms of development of capitalist society. And, in fact, *Fordism* and *post-Fordism*, as historical stages in the development of capitalism, have acquired a reputation even in research fields outside economics, such as sociology and history (see Jessop, 1997). However, they are not *theoretical concepts* that can help to formulate a general theory or to understand the laws of motion of economic systems and predict their future developments.

At first glance, in fact, the distinction between an accumulation regime and its corresponding mode of regulation may be reminiscent of the Marxian distinction between base and superstructure. However, according to Marx, the base has a dynamic of its own, which can obviously be favoured or hindered by the superstructure, but in any case shows an autonomous tendency of development determined by the historical development of the productive forces. On the contrary, an accumulation regime, although characterised by the structural elements of its industrial paradigm, is actually the result of its own specific mode of regulation. By definition, in fact, an accumulation regime can only exist if there is an appropriate mode of regulation. Thus, the connection between an accumulation regime and a mode of regulation or an SSA becomes a pure tautology.

Indeed, as we have seen, both the RA and the SSAA are founded on the assumption that any upswing phase of capitalist development needs an adequate SSA or mode of regulation, without which there could only be stagnation. And it is precisely this Keynesian-derived assumption – by definition without demonstration – that makes the relation between capital accumulation and modes of regulation or SSAs a pure tautology. In fact, if it is only adequate social institutions of accumulation that allow capital accumulation, then any empirical capital accumulation implies the existence of such institutions. At this point, however, every social institution empirically characterising a phase of capital accumulation can legitimately be supposed to be part of its mode of regulation or SSA. Unfortunately, however, this circular logical process does not help us any further in understanding the dynamics of capitalism.

Therefore, in our opinion, the categories formulated by both the RA and the SSAA, despite having provided extensive and suggestive scenarios representing the social complexity of the forms of development of capitalism, remain *classificatory concepts*, which only help to systematise, periodise and compare historical phenomena *ex post*. In doing so, they certainly provide useful pointers to identify the internal contradictions of the different stages of development, and these are surely the dialectical elements that set in motion the subsequent transformations. But they do not help to discover the actual laws of movement of social structures, as was the original intention of their authors.

From this point of view, therefore, we believe that, within the context of heterodox interpretations, many Marxian categories remain more powerful as tools to explain the dynamics of capitalism and identify its lines of future development, as we will try to show in the following chapters.

In fact, we agree with Arrighi – who greatly appreciated the concepts developed by the RA and used them extensively to describe the historical development of capitalism in its transition from the Fordist to the post-Fordist phase – that the key formula to understand financialisation at both the national and international levels remains Marx's general formula of capital circuit: *M–C–M′* (see Arrighi, 1994/2010).

This formula, as we know, shows how a capital self-valorisation circuit must generally pass through three different metamorphoses. Capital, which must enter into every process of self-valorisation – i.e. investment – in the form of *money capital* (*M*), must usually be transformed into *commodity capital*

(C), which must then be transformed into new money capital (M'), greater than the initial capital. At the end of this self-valorisation process, M' – which is of exactly the same nature as M – can potentially enter into a new process of self-valorisation and start a new cycle.

In this self-valorisation process, money capital is therefore synonymous with "liquidity, flexibility, freedom of choice" (Arrighi, 1994/2010). Commodity capital, instead, is capital immobilised in a particular production or exchange process in view of some profit, which will depend on market conditions – i.e. competition and demand. It therefore amounts to concreteness, rigidity and a narrowing down or closing of options. Ultimately, M' means new expanded liquidity, flexibility and freedom of choice (see Arrighi, 1994/2010).

According to Arrighi, therefore, Marx's formula shows that all capitalists – be they individuals or collective agents of capital, such as companies – do not invest money capital in particular production or exchange processes – with the consequent loss of flexibility and freedom of choice – as an end in itself. They accept the loss of flexibility and the associated risk only insofar as it appears a necessary means of ensuring greater flexibility and freedom of choice in the future – i.e. as a necessary means to increase capital value.

Thus, if there is no expectation that the undifferentiated capital value will increase, or if this expectation remains systematically unfulfilled, money capital by its very nature tends to more flexible forms of investment. In short, capital agents "prefer" liquidity (see Arrighi, 1994/2010). The liquidity preference can lead to hoarding – which is the main reason for lack of aggregate demand – or, under peculiar environmental conditions, periodic excitement in trying to increase the value of capital without going through real production – i.e. looking for "profits without real investment" or "money breeding money".

Moreover, according to Braudel – the famous historian who, together with Wallerstein, is one of the main references for Arrighi's theses on the current evolution of the world-economy – "financial expansions" are typically symptoms of maturity in particular capitalist phases of development. The withdrawal of capital value from commerce or industry, and its transformation into banking and financial capital, is in fact a recurrent world-systemic tendency, as is well attested by the historical experience of the Genoese, Dutch and British capitalist oligarchies over the last centuries (see Marx, 1867/1990, p. 920; Braudel, 1977).

To explain capitalist development in its transition from Fordism to post-Fordism, Arrighi introduces the notion of the "systemic cycle of accumulation". This notion is closely connected with both Braudel's notion of capitalism as the "nonspecialized" top layer in the hierarchy of the world-economy and Marx's general formula of capital (M-C-M') – interpreted as depicting a recurrent pattern of historical capitalism.

In fact, according to Braudel, the capitalist top layer in the world system is characterised by the flexibility to switch its investments continually from businesses with diminishing returns to those with growing returns (see Braudel, 1983). The historical consequence of this intrinsic tendency is the alternation of phases of material capital accumulation (*M-C* phases) with phases of financial expansion (*C-M′* phases). In *M-C* phases, the increasing investment of money capital favours the production of an increasing mass of commodities and accumulation of capital goods. In the *C-M′* phases, however, an increasing mass of money capital is freed from its commodity form and the accumulation of capital value seeks to proceed exclusively through financial transactions – as in the periodic phases of financial excitement described by Marx with the abbreviated formula *M-M′*. A complete systemic cycle of accumulation ultimately consists of the conjunction of these two types of phases.

Thus, following Arrighi and paraphrasing Braudel's observations on merchant capital in the modern age (see Braudel, 1977), we can say that money capital does not generally tend to specialise because no one branch of the commerce and industry available to it is sufficiently developed to absorb all its ability to expand. Thus, the best form of capital in general is money capital, which changes its fields of investment so frequently because high profits are constantly shifting from one sector to another.

As Braudel pointed out, "capitalism is essentially conjunctural" (Braudel, 1977), because it accommodates the dictates of changes in the economic situation, and its greatest strength lies in its ability to adapt and change. However, this means that capitalism is, by its very nature, against every "accumulation regime" – in the sense of a regular and stable pattern of development. The only specialisation that sometimes tends to develop in the life of capital is *money trading* – i.e. the use of money capital as *interest bearing capital* – because this is the most general application of it.

From this viewpoint, therefore, contemporary neoliberalism and financialisation are not components of a new accumulation regime, nor a return to the origins, but rather re-emergence of the karst tendencies of capitalism that had been kept at bay or simply concealed over an exceptional span of time – resulting from the catastrophes of the Great Depression and the ensuing Second World War – in which attempts were made to regulate the development of market capitalism in its own interest. Financialisation, in particular, is no more or less than the re-emergence of the permanent aptitude of capitalism for flexibility. And this permanent aptitude – at the end of a systemic cycle of accumulation – is now producing transformation of the former core of the world-economy into a financial centre for the rising new core. In other words, the former advanced economies of the *Golden Age* are progressively becoming the financial centres of the emerging Asia as the new core of the world-economy.

Note

1 Emergent phenomena are typical features of the evolution of complex systems according to complexity theory. They are coherent structures, patterns and

properties that arise during the process of self-organisation of complex systems (see Goldstein, 1999).

References

Aglietta, M. (1979/2015). *A Theory of Capitalist Regulation. The US Experience.* London and New York: Verso.

Aglietta, M. and Reberioux, A. (2005). *Corporate Governance Adrift: A Critique of Shareholder Value.* Cheltenham and Northampton, MA: Edward Elgar.

Amable, B. (2002). "*Régulation* Theory and Technical Change". In: Boyer, R. and Saillard, Y. (eds.), *Régulation Theory. The State of the Art.* London and New York: Routledge, pp. 161–67.

Arrighi, G. (1994/2010). *The Long Twentieth Century. Money, Power, and the Origins of Our Times.* London and New York: Verso.

Boyer, R. (1986). *La théorie de la régulation. Une analyse critique.* Paris: Éditions La Découvert.

Boyer, R. (1987). "Technical Change and the Theory of Regulation". *CEPREMAP Working Papers*, 8707.

Boyer, R. (2000). "Is a Finance-Led Growth Regime a Viable Alternative to Fordism? A Preliminary Analysis". *Economy and Society*, 29 (1): 111–145.

Boyer, R. (2005). "How and Why Capitalisms Differ". *MPIfG Discussion Paper*, 05/4.

Boyer, R. (2010). "The Rise of CEO Pay and the Contemporary Social Structure of Accumulation in the United States". In: McDonough, T., Reich, M. and Kotz, D. M. (eds.), *Contemporary Capitalism and Its Crises: Social Structure of Accumulation Theory for the 21st Century.* New York: Cambridge University Press, pp. 215–38.

Boyer, R. (2013). "The Present Crisis: A Trump for a Renewed Political Economy". *Review of Political Economy*, 25: 1–38.

Boyer, R. and Saillard, Y. (2002), "A Summary of Régulation Theory". In: Boyer, R. and Saillard, Y. (eds.), *Régulation Theory. The State of the Art.* London and New York: Routledge, pp. 36–44.

Braudel, F. (1977). *Afterthoughts on Material Civilization and Capitalism.* Baltimore, MD: Johns Hopkins University Press.

Braudel, F. (1983). *Civilization and Capitalism. 15th-18th Century. Volume II. The Wheels of Commerce.* London: Book Club Associates.

Brenner, R. and Glick, M. (1991). "The Regulation Approach: Theory and History". *New Left Review*, 188: 45–119.

Cohen, R. and Kennedy, P. (2013). *Global Sociology.* Basingstoke and New York: Palgrave Macmillan.

Crotty, J. (2005). "The Neoliberal Paradox: The Impact of Destructive Product Market Competition and 'Modern' Financial Markets on Nonfinancial Corporation Performance in the Neoliberal Era". In: Epstein, G. A. (ed.), *Financialization and the World Economy.* Cheltenham and Northampton, MA: Edward Elgar Publishing Ltd, pp. 77–110.

De Vroey, M. (1984). "A Regulation Approach Interpretation of Contemporary Crisis". *Capital & Class*, 8 (2): 45–66.

Dymski, G. A. (2009). "Does Heterodox Economics Need a Unified Crisis Theory? From Profit-Squeeze to the Global Liquidity Meltdown". In: Goldstein, J. P. and Hillard M. G. (eds.), *Heterodox Macroeconomics. Keynes, Marx and Globalization.* Abingdon: Routledge, pp. 66–84.

Goldstein, J. (1999). "Emergence as a Construct: History and Issues". *Emergence*, 1 (1): 49–72.

Gordon, D., Edwards, R. and Reich, M. (1994). "Long Swings and Stages of Capitalism". In: Kotz, D. M., McDonough, T. and Reich, M. (eds.), *Social Structures of Accumulation: The Political Economy of Growth and Crisis*. New York: Cambridge University Press, pp. 11–28.

Gordon, D., Weisskopf, T. E. and Bowles, S. (1983). "Long Swings and the Nonreproductive Cycle". *The American Economic Review*, 73 (2): 152–157.

Gordon, D., Weisskopf, T. E. and Bowles, S. (1987). "Power, Accumulation and Crisis: The Rise and Demise of the Postwar Social Structure of Accumulation". In: Cherry R. (ed.), *The Imperiled Economy. Book I. Macroeconomics from a Left Perspective*. New York: Union for Radical Political Economics (URPE), pp. 43–57.

Guttman, R. (2015). "The Heterodox Notion of Structural Crisis". *Review of Keynesian Economics*, 3 (2): 194–212.

Hein, E. (2012). *The Macroeconomics of Finance-Dominated Capitalism - and Its Crisis*. Cheltenham and Northampton, MA: Edward Elgar.

Hein, E. (2013). "The Crisis of Finance-Dominated Capitalism in the Euro Area, Deficiencies in the Economic Policy Architecture, and Deflationary Stagnation Policies". *Journal of Post Keynesian Economics*, 36 (2): 325–354.

Hein, E. (2015). "Finance-Dominated Capitalism and Re-distribution of Income: A Kaleckian Perspective". *Cambridge Journal of Economics*, 39 (3): 907–934.

Hein, E. (2016). "Secular Stagnation or Stagnation Policy? Steindl after Summers". *PSL Quarterly Review*, 69 (276): 3–47.

Hein, E. (2017). "Financialisation and Tendencies Towards Stagnation: The Role of Macroeconomic Regime Changes in the Course of and after the Financial and Economic Crisis". *Institute for International Political Economy, Working Paper*, 90.

Hein, E., Detzer D. and Dodig N. (2016). "Financialisation and the Financial and Economic Crises: Theoretical Framework and Empirical Analysis for 15 Countries". In: Hein, E., Detzer, D. and Dodig, N. (eds.), *Financialisation and Financial and Economic Crises. Country Studies*. Cheltenham: Edward Elgar, pp. 1–41.

Hein, E., Dodig, N. and Budyldina, N. (2015). "The Transition Towards Finance-Dominated Capitalism: French Regulation School, Social Structures of Accumulation and Post-Keynesian Approaches Compared". In: Hein, E., Detzer, D. and Dodig, N. (eds.), *The Demise of Finance-Dominated Capitalism. Explaining the Financial and Economic Crises*. Cheltenham: Eldward Elgar, pp. 7–53.

Hein, E. and Mundt, M. (2012). "Financialisation and the Requirements and Potentials for Wage-Led Recovery - A Review Focusing on the G20". *International Labour Organization. Conditions of Work and Employment Series*, pp. 1–67.

Hillinger, C. (1987). "Keynes and Business Cycles". In: Gandolfo, G. and Marzano, F. (eds.), *Keynesian Theory, Planning Models and Quantitative Economics. Essays in Memory of Vittorio Marrama*. Volume I. Milan: Giuffrè Editore, pp. 77–95.

Jessop, B. (1997). "Survey Article: The Regulation Approach". *The Journal of Political Philosophy*, 5 (3): 287–326.

Jessop, B. (2002). *The Future of the Capitalist State*. Cambridge: Polity Press.

Jessop, B. (2006). "Regulation Theories in Retrospect and Prospect". *Economy and Society*, 19 (2): 153–216.

Kaldor, N. (1957). "A Model of Economic Growth". *The Economic Journal*, 67 (268): 591–624.

Kotz, D. M. (1990). "A Comparative Analysis of the Theory of Regulation and the Social Structure of Accumulation Theory". *Science & Society*, 54 (1): 5–28.

Kotz, D. M. (1994). "The Regulation Theory and the Social Structure of Accumulation Approach". In: Kotz, D. M., McDonough, T. and Reich, M. (eds.), *Social Structures of Accumulation: The Political Economy of Growth and Crisis*. New York: Cambridge University Press, pp. 85–97.

Kotz, D. M. (2003). "Neoliberalism and the Social Structure of Accumulation Theory of Long-Run Capital Accumulation". *Review of Radical Political Economics*, 35 (3): 263–270.

Kotz, D. M. (2013). "Social Structures of Accumulation, the Rate of Profit, and Economic Crises". In: Wicks-Lim, J. and Pollin R. (eds.), *Capitalism on Trial. Explorations in the Tradition of Thomas E. Weisskopf.* Cheltenham: Edward Elgar, pp. 335–49.

Kotz, D. M. and McDonough, T. (2010). "Global Neoliberalism and the Contemporary Social Structure of Accumulation". In: McDonough, T., Reich, M. and Kotz, D. M. (eds.), *Contemporary Capitalism and Its Crises: Social Structure of Accumulation Theory for the 21st Century*. New York: Cambridge University Press, pp. 93–120.

Krippner, G. R. (2011). *Capitalizing on Crisis: The Political Origins of the Rise of Finance*. Cambridge, MA and London: Harvard University Press.

Krippner, G., Lemoine, B. and Ravelli, Q. (2017). "An Interview with Greta Krippner". *Revue de la régulation*, 22. https://journals.openedition.org/regulation/12637.

Lipietz, A. (1987). "Rebel Sons: The Regulation School. An Interview Conducted by Jane Jenson". *French Politics and Society*, 5 (4): 17–26.

Lipietz A. (1988). "Accumulation, Crises, and Ways Out". *International Journal of Political Economy*, 18 (2): 10–43.

Lippit, V. D. (2010). "Social Structure of Accumulation Theory". In: McDonough, T., Reich, M. and Kotz, D. M. (eds.), *Contemporary Capitalism and Its Crises: Social Structure of Accumulation Theory for the 21st Century*. New York: Cambridge University Press, pp. 45–71.

Lordon, F. (2002). "*Régulation* Theory and Economic Policy". In: Boyer, R. and Saillard, Y. (eds.), *Régulation Theory. The State of the Art*. London and New York: Routledge, pp. 129–36.

Marx, K. (1867/1990). *Capital. Volume I*. London: Penguin Books.

McDonough, T. (2010). "The State of the Art of Social Structure of Accumulation Theory". In: McDonough, T., Reich, M. and Kotz, D. M. (eds.), *Contemporary Capitalism and Its Crises: Social Structure of Accumulation Theory for the 21st Century*. New York: Cambridge University Press, pp. 23–44.

Minsky, H. (1982/2016). *Can "It" Happen Again? Essays on Instability and Finance*. London and New York: Routledge.

Nadel, H. (2002). "Régulation and Marx". In: Boyer, R. and Saillard, Y. (eds.), *Régulation Theory. The State of the Art*. London and New York: Routledge, pp. 28–35.

Stockhammer, E. (2008). "Some Stylized Facts on the Finance-Dominated Accumulation Regime". *Competition & Change*, 12 (2): 184–202.

Tabb, W. K. (2010). "Financialization in the Contemporary Social Structure of Accumulation". In: McDonough T., Reich, M. and Kotz, D. M. (eds.), *Contemporary Capitalism and its Crises: Social Structure of Accumulation Theory for the 21st Century*. New York: Cambridge University Press, pp. 145–67.

Tridico, P. (2017). *Inequality in Financial Capitalism*. London: Routledge.

van Treeck, T. (2009a). "The Political Economy Debate on 'Financialisation' – A Macroeconomic Perspective". *Review of International Political Economy*, 16 (5): 907–944.

van Treeck, T. (2009b). "A Synthetic Stock-Flow Consistent Macroeconomic Model of 'Financialisation'". *Cambridge Journal of Economics*, 33 (3): 467–493.

van Treeck, T. and Sturn, S. (2012). "Income Inequality as a Cause of the Great Recession? A Survey of Current Debates". *International Labour Organization. Conditions of Work and Employment Series*, 39.

Wolfson, M. H. (2003). "Neoliberalism and the Social Structure of Accumulation". *Review of Radical Political Economics*, 35 (3): 255–262.

Wolfson, M. H. and Kotz, D. M. (2010). "A Reconceptualization of Social Structure of Accumulation Theory". In: McDonough T., Reich, M. and Kotz, D. M. (eds.), *Contemporary Capitalism and Its Crises: Social Structure of Accumulation Theory for the 21st Century*. New York: Cambridge University Press, pp. 72–90.

3 Classical Marxist approaches

Finance capital

As we said in the previous chapter, some economists have seen financialisation as a return to or a re-proposal of old capitalist forms which prevailed over a century ago and were accurately described by famous Marxist authors such as Hilferding, Luxemburg, Bukharin and Lenin.

These Marxist authors tried to explain the deep changes in the capitalist way of working from the late 19th century to the First World War, passing from the competitive conditions of its early stage to what was defined as "monopoly capitalism". By "monopoly", of course, Marxists do not mean a market with a single seller, as is usually the case in mainstream economics. "Monopoly capitalism" is seen as the transition of the capitalist mode of production from the early phase of free competition to one where giant corporations, trusts and cartels dominate the market, under conditions of oligopolistic or monopolistic competition.

Hilferding's contribution came first and focused mainly on a number of financial aspects that are relevant to today's arguments on financialisation. Hilferding, in fact, dealt with what he defined as "finance capital", which is nothing but bank capital – i.e. a specific form of money capital – transformed into industrial capital by investing it directly in industrial activities through the purchase of share capital in joint-stock companies. Thus, according to Hilferding, the rise of finance capital transformed bankers – i.e. financial intermediaries – into the real controllers of industrial activities.

The similarity between this phenomenon and growing control of the NFCs by institutional investors is self-evident. The banks, whose main traditional function is to centralise money capital – gathering together idle funds such as firms' reserves and depreciation funds, on the one hand, and the savings of households on the other – were taking control of production organisations.

However, the rise of finance capital, according to Hilferding, was only the result of the more general process of concentration and centralisation of capital. In other words, it was nothing more than the system of oligopolistic industry controlled by oligopolistic banks (see Davis, 2008).

DOI: 10.4324/9781003223221-4

The process of concentration and centralisation of capital had already been central to Marx's work and was empirical evidence in the major capitalist countries in Hilferding's time (see Sau, 1979; Dutta, 2021). According to Marx, the concentration of capital is nothing more than the accumulation process of an ever increasing mass of capital around an original core through the reinvestment of surplus value. Centralisation, however, is "concentration of capitals already formed, destruction of their individual independence, expropriation of capitalist by capitalist, transformation of many small into few large capitals" (Marx, 1867/1990, p. 777).

Centralisation of capital, therefore, differs from concentration because "it only presupposes a change in the distribution of already available and already functioning capital" (Marx, 1867/1990, p. 777). It results from a mere change in the distribution of already existing components of total capital. By centralisation, "capital grows to a huge mass in a single hand in one place, because it has been lost by many in another place" (Marx, 1867/1990, p. 777).

From Marx's viewpoint, of course, free competition was essentially about the cheapness of goods, which, in turn, depends on the productivity of labour which ultimately depends on the scale of production. Consequently, in free competition "the larger capitals beat the smaller [...] whose capitals partly pass into the hands of their conquerors, and partly vanish completely" (Marx, 1867/1990, p. 777). This means that the capitalist production system, due to competition, requires by its very nature the accumulation and restructuring of capital through seeking economies of scale and/or scope into ever-larger enterprises in order to accrue productivity gains (see Fine, 2014).

In this context, according to Marx, the credit system – which under conditions of free competition plays the role of "assistant of accumulation, drawing into the hands of individual or associated capitalists by invisible threads the money resources" – becomes "a new and terrible weapon in the battle of competition and is finally transformed into an enormous social mechanism for the centralisation of capitals" (Marx, 1867/1990, p. 778).

Centralisation, in turn, accelerates the process of accumulation by favouring the expansion of the scale of productive activities because it is enough to change the quantitative groupings of the existing parts of total capital. The large masses of capital created by centralisation, therefore, can, in turn, grow through accumulation of the surplus value they produce, but, thanks to economies of scale, they can do so more rapidly than smaller activities, accelerating the accumulation and concentration of total capital.

The theoretical extreme limit of this process is only reached when all the individual capitals invested in an industry are merged into a single capital, owned by a single capitalist or a single company. Once again, according to Marx, the creation of joint-stock companies was nothing more than a "smoother process" in this direction, whereas large-scale productive activities, such as the building and running of railways, would have been severely slowed down if one had to wait for individual capital to reach a critical mass to carry them out (see Marx, 1867/1990, p. 779).

Hilferding's analysis, therefore, starts with these views of Marx and his other very fragmentary considerations on the possible crucial role played by the joint-stock company set out in the third volume of Capital – which was published by Engels only after the author's death on the basis of his compilation of notes[1] – and focuses precisely on this rise of the joint-stock company as the new dominant form of organisation of capitalist enterprise.

Hilferding highlights the way owners of large amounts of capital can use the joint-stock form of organisation to gain control of the money capital of many small savers. The joint-stock company can in fact pool the money capital of many small shareholders and allow the centralisation of many capitals into one. Yet, at the same time, it allows the ownership of personal wealth to be concentrated in a few hands – thanks to the opportunities offered by share speculation on the stock markets – and the possibility that the holders of only majority blocks of shares gain control of large masses of capital. The rise of the joint-stock company, eventually, led to an accelerated process of concentration and centralisation of capital in which the largest capitals drove out the smallest, generating a massive concentration of economic power as well as production.

According to Hilferding, moreover, the rise of concentration and centralisation of capital in one sector has inevitable consequences for all the other sectors that interact with it, creating "relations of mutual dependence and dominance" where "it is the amount of capital that principally determines which enterprise shall become dependent upon the other" (Hilferding, 1910/1981, p. 223). Thus, where a relatively more competitive industry deals with a large concentration of capital or cartel, it will fall under its control. Weaker companies will be reduced to the status of mere agents unless they react by forming their own cartel or coalitions. However, this is a further prompt to create new centralisations of capital, spurring the expansion of monopoly capitalism as a fundamental transformation of early competitive capitalism.

According to Hilferding, the main actors in this process in his time were the banks. This focus on the role of the banks was probably influenced by his direct experience of events in Germany and Austria. However, investment bankers have also long been regarded as the overlords of the American corporate system in the last quarter of the 19th century (see Sweezy, 1941). A few years after Hilferding's book was published, Louis Brandeis (1914) described phenomena similar to those in Germany in the United States, where bankers such as J. P. Morgan had taken control of many industries through networks of directors placed on the boards of the companies whose shares they had acquired, resulting in relatively stable interest groups with the banks at the centre. These financial figures did not suffer a dramatic eclipse in the United States until the 1930s, due to the aftermath of the 1929 financial crisis.

In Germany, however, the banks not only held shares in industrial companies themselves, but also acted on behalf of their clients in buying and selling shares, eventually acquiring an extraordinary power of control over all sources of money capital, in a very similar way to today's institutional investors. The tendency towards concentration and centralisation of control was obviously reinforced by the own banks' tendency towards "monopoly", which led them to play a dominant role in the hierarchy of the capitalist system as a whole (see Hilferding, 1910/1981, p. 121, n18; Lenin, 1916/1974, pp. 210–226; Bukharin, 1917/1929, p. 71). The banks, in turn, promoted cartelisation and mergers among their clients to reduce the risk that the companies to which they have lent money would fail, further reinforcing the process of concentration and centralisation of production itself.

Hilferding, therefore, used the term "finance capital" to overcome the Marxian distinction between industrial, commercial and financial capital – which had characterised competitive capitalism. According to him, "finance capital" was not the simple synonym for financial capital, but rather the fusion of the latter with industrial capital. This fusion, in turn, was prompted by a growth in bank deposits on the one hand, and declining opportunities for traditional loans in commerce and industry due to growing industrial monopolies on the other, which increasingly forced banks to invest directly in production and become industrial capitalists. However, this process took more and more of the control of industrial capital away from the pure industrialists who could only dispose of the capital through the banks which were ultimately the real owners (see Hilferding, 1910/1981, p. 225).

Thus, Hilferding's concept of finance capital highlighted how an increasing part of the industrial capital came into the hands of firms via the financial system, but also that a growing part of the production had fallen under the control of the latter.

Finance capital, therefore, is that fraction of total capital in which the functions of financial capital and industrial capital are effectively unified, so that the collection of funds from a variety of sources is carried out by the same entity that effectively controls the productive use of the funds. However, the real structural reason for this unification is the elimination of free competition between individual capitalists by large monopoly groups. This process also involves a change in the relationship of the capitalist class to state power and its regulation forms (see Hilferding, 1910/1981, p. 301).

Thus, in accordance with Hilferding's view, today's large multinational NFCs may be considered to all intents and purposes a part of "finance capital" due to their very nature. Whether or not they are under the control of the banks or other institutional investors, their headquarters perform many of the typical functions of financial capital in collecting money from many sources and channelling capital flows from one subsidiary to another. In other words, it is the very form of the joint-stock organisation, associated with large multinationals and multi-product scopes, that determines the financialisation of NFCs.

However, according to Hilferding, the very financial nature of the share capital increasingly promoted the idea that a growing proportion of industrial capital ceased to "belong to the industrialists who employ it" (Hilferding, 1910/1981, p. 225). In fact, in accordance with the German and American experience, industrial capitalists only obtained the use of money capital through the banks, which, in their eyes, were the representatives of the original owners of capital. However, the banks were induced to sink an increasing part of their funds into industry so that the bankers were themselves increasingly transformed into industrial capitalists. Thus, the progressive transformation of money capital into credit capital eventually resulted, through the establishment of the joint-stock company, in a qualitative inversion of the relationship.

Another peculiar element in Hilferding's analysis is the concept of "promoter's profit". This arises from the possibility of selling shares of a joint-stock company for considerably more than the capital value effectively invested in it because the yield on this capital is higher than the current rate of interest on investments (see Hilferding, 1910/1981, pp. 107–116). The promoter's profit is a further form of extra-profit deriving from monopoly conditions – or rather, it is the present value of expected future monopoly extra-profits – which, in turn, stimulates the centralisation of capital and the growth of giant corporations, cartels and trusts.

Finally, Hilferding also emphasised the role played by the export of capital in the era of monopoly capital, although he only focused on the causes of this export related to the different tariff systems around the world (see Hilferding, 1910/1981, p. 311–336). However, the analysis of capital movements and the role played by nation states in sustaining them help link the analysis of monopoly capital to that of imperialism.

Bukharin's and Lenin's "Imperialism"

The second Marxist contribution that is, in our opinion, interesting as far as an understanding of contemporary process of financialisation is concerned is the analysis of imperialism by Lenin and his collaborator Bukharin.[2]

The term imperialism may be a bit misleading for economists because it would appear to refer to international political and military power relations. However, Bukharin and Lenin actually chose this label to qualify a new phase of development of capitalism. This was because their analysis was closely inspired by Hobson's seminal book *Imperialism: A Study*, published in 1902. In his book, Hobson – who was not a Marxist – had indeed analysed the development of the colonial system as it manifested itself during the last three decades of the 19th century. However, in doing so, he had also paid close attention to the economic interests that promoted this process, focusing in particular on the role played by large concentrations of private capital and capital movements abroad. Hobson, in fact, argued that the "economic root of imperialism" lay in the export of capital in search of new investment opportunities since these were diminishing at home (see Hobson, 1902/2005, pp. 71–93).

Both Bukharin and Lenin, therefore, seized on the fashionable term that was dominating a wide-ranging and heated political debate to point out that the tendencies of the historical development of their time, which had led to the First World War, were the direct consequence of a specific new stage of development of capitalism – which Lenin described as the "highest" one, probably hoping for its imminent end. However, along the lines already outlined by Hilferding and Hobson, Bukharin and Lenin highlighted that the economic foundations of the new stage of capitalism were the "concentration of production and monopolies" (Lenin, 1916/1974, p. 196). Thus "imperialism", according to them, was nothing but "the reproduction of capitalist competition on a larger scale" (Bukharin, 1917/1929, p. 110) or "the monopoly stage of capitalism" (Lenin, 1916/1974, p. 266).

For Bukharin, Lenin and most later Marxists, therefore, imperialism is not a political or ideological phenomenon – limited to colonial expansion, the relationship between the advanced countries and the colonial or semi-colonial areas within their formal or informal empires, and power struggles between states – as is for many historians and political scientists. Instead, it is the expression of "imperative necessities of advanced capitalism" (see Kemp, 1972, p. 17). The Marxist theory of imperialism, indeed, focuses on the features displayed by the capitalist mode of production in its most advanced stage as a result of the functioning of its inherent "laws of motion".

Bukharin's and Lenin's analysis, however, was also a development and extension of some insights into the dominant tendencies in capitalism already seen in Marx and Engels some decades before they manifested themselves so clearly. In fact, although Marx did not explicitly deal with monopoly capital – partly because this was not so developed in his time, but mainly because he provided a model of "pure capitalism" at a relatively high level of abstraction – his analysis of the capitalist mode of production provided many elements for a subsequent expansion of the theoretical reflection in this direction. The parts of Capital which are most relevant to explaining the "monopoly" phase of the capitalism are the reproduction schemes – which deal with the so-called "realisation problem" of the surplus value – the tendency for the rate of profit to fall and, above all, the concentration and centralisation of capital as an inevitable outcome of competition (see Kemp, 1972).

Marxian reproduction schemes, in fact, help understand the permanent problem of private capital which must continuously find new market outlets. This necessity was the starting point of Rosa Luxemburg's theory of imperialist commercial expansion and capital export, based on "under-consumption" (see Luxemburg, 1913/2003, pp. 426–433). Indeed, on the basis of a simplified reading of the "realisation problem" (see Brown, 1972; Kemp, 1972), she believed that, according to Marxian reproduction schemes, in a closed capitalist economy the accumulation of capital ends up finding a definitive upper limit in the fact that consumption, which is closely linked to wages, does not increase in the same way as productive capacity – generated by the growth of investment – does. Although Marx actually thought that this disproportion between investment and consumption can only produce periodic crises, Luxemburg dramatised its consequences, believing that capitalism could only survive in the long run by finding market outlets in non-capitalist areas. This "under-consumptionist" approach found a prominent supporter in Hobson himself and, as we shall see more clearly in the following pages, was successively shared by Kalecky and many American neo-Marxist authors who ended up converging with Keynesian positions in assuming a basic tendency of capitalism towards economic stagnation in the absence of economic intervention by the state.

The tendency for the rate of profit to fall – resulting from technical change that increases the "organic composition of capital" – i.e. the proportion between constant and variable capital – can, in turn, again according to Marx, only be counteracted by other forces such as increased productivity, the expansion of international trade in less developed areas and the use of cheaper finance through the evolution of corporate forms of organisation. All these forces seem to be activated by capitalists in the development stage of monopoly capitalism. In other words, many features of monopoly capitalism appear to be attempts to counteract the tendency for the rate of profit to fall.

However, as we have already seen, it is the relentless process of concentration and centralisation of capital highlighted by Marx that, by its very nature, is closely linked to the structural changes in capitalism that prepare the way for monopoly capitalism.

No "pure capitalism" model, of course, can completely represent actual economic relations in their specific and historically determined context, and this also applies to Marx's analysis. To explain real economic developments, according to historical materialism itself, account has to be taken of the features of superstructure and its interaction with the economic base; this particularly applies to the role played by national states and their relations with each other. The productive forces released by the capitalist mode of production, in fact, cannot be contained within the geographically confined areas of national states. The rise of capitalism and industrialisation has led to the existence of a world market and an international division of labour, with all the new conflicts associated with them. It is precisely through their relationship with the world market that the core and peripheral states of a world economy acquire their status of dominance or dependence.

Thus, Bukharin and Lenin simply pointed out that, on the basis of Marx's theory, monopoly capitalism is a necessary consequence of competitive capitalism due to the processes of concentration and centralisation of private capital. They, nevertheless, starting from Hobson's analysis, linked the formation of large concentrations of capital in advanced countries with the tendencies towards dividing the world into empires and spheres of economic influence – and thus with the international rivalries and tensions that had produced the First World War – connecting the main economic and political tendencies of their time into a single theoretical system.

However, from our viewpoint, the more interesting elements of Bukharin's and Lenin's analysis concern some structural transformations that characterise the rise of monopoly capitalism.

Lenin shared with Hilferding the view that the banks, through the process of banking concentration and centralisation, were transformed from mere intermediaries in the payment system to concentrations of economic power that had control over almost all the money capital of the capitalist class in one or several countries. He also shared with Hilferding the view that capitalist corporations in advanced countries aim to expand their markets – in order to realise surplus value and sustain their profits – by entering the world market and corporations, of course, did so with the aid and support of their governments. However, in this way, economic competition turns into power and military competition between states. Bukharin, in turn, held the "internationalisation" of capital, together with the associated growing conflicts between the interests of the large concentrations of capital, as the very cause of a parallel "nationalisation" of capital – where the latter means a close alliance between the large capitalist corporations and trusts and their home nation states in the new contest for the world market.

The less developed areas of the world, in this context, became economically linked to the advanced countries, making it possible for the latter to acquire cheaper raw materials which – by entering the circulation process as variable capital – helped to counteract the tendency for the rate of profit to fall. Yet, above all, the differences in the levels of profit rates between advanced and peripheral countries, based on different wage levels as well as different tariff systems, enhanced capital exports from the former to the latter.

According to Bukharin and Lenin, therefore, the export of capital is one of the most essential economic features of monopoly capitalism since the latter continuously produces a huge "capital surplus" in the advanced countries, which – due to the very limitations on competition created by the monopoly powers at home – must find new investment opportunities abroad (see Lenin, 1916/1974, p. 241).

However, while Hobson associated capital export essentially with underconsumption (see Kemp, 1972), Bukharin's and Lenin's position was completely different. Bukharin and Lenin, indeed, following Marx, believed that international capital movements are governed by the law of equalisation of rates of profit in the world economy. Thus, they pointed out that the export of capital from advanced countries had become increasingly important in the phase of monopoly capital because of both the tendency of the rate of profit to fall in advanced national markets and the possibility of increasing this rate by penetrating foreign markets with the political and military support and guarantees offered by the home nation states.

Bukharin classified export capital into two main categories: interest-bearing capital and profit-making capital (see Bukharin, 1917/1929, p. 40).

A large part of the first category consisted of state loans, stimulated by the growth of state budgets in colonial or peripheral countries – caused, in turn, by the increasing complexity of their economic systems and the need for new large infrastructures, as well as their growing militarisation. The remainder was credit by the large banks of one country to the banks of another country, with no specific aim.

The second category of capital export was produced by "participation" in the shareholding of foreign companies or by the creation of their own subsidiaries in foreign countries. In less developed countries, indeed, profits are usually higher "for capital is scarce, the price of land is relatively low, wages are low, raw materials are cheap" (Lenin, 1916/1974, p. 241).

Equity participation, in turn, stimulated both financial forms of capital ownership in advanced countries and new forms of financial control over foreign productive activities through the spread of international trusts and holding companies. This formed "international monopolist capitalist associations which share the world among themselves" (Lenin, 1916/1974, p. 266).

Alongside these structural movements of capital, of course, there were also speculative movements which were in any case closely linked to the former.

Capital exports, in turn, produced flows of foreign surplus value back home, in the form of interest or dividends and all these financial flows eventually created an ever closer network of international financial interdependence.

Here, too, we can find close analogies with the events that characterise today's financialisation process. As we have seen in the previous chapters, many crucial phases of today's financialisation were initially associated with the fall of profitability in advanced countries – whether produced by the increasing organic composition of capital or by the squeezing of profit by the rising real wages brought about by full employment. Once again the main solution was found in a new wave of free international capital movements. Bukharin's and Lenin's analysis, therefore, helps to understand why financialisation and "neoliberal globalisation" are two sides of the same coin. In this theoretical context, indeed, their close nexus presents itself as a mutual support and stimulus relation.

In the Marxist theory, however, the expansionism drives of the advanced capitalist economies are closely associated with the rise of large concentrations of both real capital in the industrial sectors and money capital in the hands of the banks and other large financial institutions. Indeed, the confines of the national market become too narrow for the self-valorisation process of huge concentrations of private capital. Continuous capital accumulation combined with a high level of profitability requires larger, growing markets. Growing domestic demand from home governments and expansion abroad have become necessary elements for the self-valorisation of large domestic industrial capitals, while the big banks and other large financial institutions, in turn, need new investment outlets abroad.

However, according to Lenin, monopoly capitalism also produces a tendency to stagnation because monopoly prices and competition discourage technical progress to a certain extent. In Marx's economic theory, in fact, capital accumulation is driven not only by profit, but also by competition, which forces individual capitalists to invest to survive in the market, utilising dynamic economies of scale, increasing returns, technical innovations and progressive mechanisation to defend and expand their market share. The monopolistic limitation of free competition, therefore, weakens the incentive to innovate in order to reduce production costs. The only economy of scale which is, beyond a certain level of concentration and centralisation of capital, actually pursued is that of the capital-value dimension which allows, by means of financial levers, the control of large parts of industrial production in increasingly larger areas of activity.

This view, in our opinion, helps to better understand the nexus between financialisation and a decline in real investment. Indeed, it suggests that financialisation and a decline in real investment in advanced countries may not be in a cause-and-effect relationship – as assumed by many post-Keynesian authors – but may simply be two joint manifestations of the same underlying process: the increasing concentration and centralisation of capital.

Monopoly capital according to the American neo-Marxists

The concept of "monopoly capital" has been partly revised by the American neo-Marxists since the 1960s.

Baran and Sweezy (1966), agreeing with Bukharin and Lenin that in the 20th century the capitalist economic system underwent a profound qualitative change by turning from a competitive into a monopolistic economy, pointed out that Marx's analysis had been partially outdated by the evolution of events because it neglected monopoly conditions – such as administered prices and a tendency towards stagnation. Thus, in their opinion, the "fundamental structural change" of competitive capitalist economy towards monopoly capitalism imposed a change in the laws identified by Marx such as that of the falling rate of profit (see Baran and Sweezy, 1966).

Consequently, they substituted the law of falling profit with the law of rising surplus and the concept of surplus value with that of surplus, since the former "is probably identified in the minds of most people familiar with Marxian economic theory as equal to the sum of profit-interest-rent" (Baran and Sweezy, 1966, p. 10). In their definition, instead, surplus is simply the "difference between what a society produces and costs of producing it" (Baran and Sweezy, 1966, p. 9). Then, this surplus can, in turn, be invested in expanding productive capacity, or consumed in various forms, or wasted in different ways.[3]

Thus, their entire analysis was organised around one central theme: "generation and absorption of the surplus under conditions of monopoly capitalism" (see Baran and Sweezy, 1966, p. 8).

According to Baran and Sweezy, monopoly capitalism tends to generate ever more surplus, both absolutely and as a share of total output, by means of both declining costs, due to innovation policies and consequent increase in productivity, and the market power of the giant corporations, thanks to which they can make the price and so widen profit margins (see Baran and Sweezy, 1966).

Yet, as was highlighted by Mattick's critique, declining costs due to innovation characterised all capitalist development and not only its monopoly phase. Thus, according to Mattick, the new real monopoly strategic means of piling up surplus can be grounded solely on keeping administered prices artificially high (see Mattick, 1978).

However, according to Baran and Sweezy, monopoly capitalism alone fails to provide the demand needed to absorb this growing surplus. It may be consumed – primarily by capitalists but also by a part of the workers[4] – invested, or wasted in "frivolous and often harmful ways" of the "affluent society" and its "vast military establishment"[5] (see Baran and Sweezy, 1966). To the extent that it is consumed by capitalists or wasted in sale efforts and public waste, its share available for investment is reduced.

The greater surplus arises because the production capacity of the economic system grows too rapidly, owing to the imperfect competition conditions in monopoly sectors. As they see it, in capitalist economies there is a permanent tendency for productive capacity to outpace effective consumer demand (see Sweezy and Magdoff, 1972).

Corporate concentration, markedly unequal distribution of personal income and a tax structure more favourable to the corporations and the rich create enormous saving potential that needs, as counterpart, strong and sustained investment performance to prevent the economy from falling into stagnation.

Thus, the limits to capitalist expansion seem to lie in any insufficiency in the modes of surplus utilisation (see Baran and Sweezy, 1966). Under monopoly capitalism, in which the law of rising surplus rules, the usual ways of surplus utilisation, namely capitalists' consumption and investment, are eventually no longer able to absorb all the surplus. Thus, the problem of new forms of surplus utilisation arises.

It is self-evident that American neo-Marxists' theory is essentially a restatement of Luxemburg's "under-consumptionist" approach, updated to the economic conditions of the second post-war period. As we have seen in the previous chapter, their view strictly influenced the successive development of the SSAA, favouring its convergence with the post-Keynesian approaches.

Sweezy, however, was fully aware of the theoretical weaknesses in the theses advocated by Luxemburg whom he called "the queen of the subconsumers" (Sweezy, 1942/1946). In particular, he was aware that Luxemburg, when discussing expanded reproduction, implicitly retained the assumptions of simple reproduction (see Sweezy, 1942/1946, pp. 202–207).

Marx, indeed, constructed a series of numerical examples that illustrate how extended reproduction schemes require quite different proportions of capital goods production and consumption goods production from those required in simple reproduction schemes (see Marx, 1885/1992, pp. 586–595). According to Marx, in order to ensure regular extended reproduction, the composition of the social product must change in favour of the department of capital goods – which drives the accumulation process – and the consumer goods department must see the capital employed grow in such a way as to ensure the growth of variable capital within the capital goods sector. This assumes, of course, the availability of an adequate "industrial reserve army", but shows the theoretical possibility of the absence of a structural deficit in effective demand. Marx, of course, did not presuppose any automatic co-ordination mechanism that would guarantee the proportions between the different departments of social production adequate for a regular development of the accumulation process. In more modern terms, according to Marx, a dynamic equilibrium exists for expanded reproduction, but, under the anarchic conditions of the market, this is by no means stable.

In partial agreement with this Marxian view, Baran and Sweezy held the view that, for monopoly capitalism to be healthy, total income had to rise fast enough to allow the share of surplus which was not consumed to be invested. According to them, however, this is only possible if the surplus that is not consumed rises proportionately less than total income and this can occur only if capitalists' consumption rises as a share of surplus produced, or, alternatively, there is an increase in the share of waste consumption. Alternatively, the investment-seeking part of surplus will rise faster than total income, creating conditions for overaccumulation and crises.

In monopoly capitalism, however, capitalists' consumption is closely connected to the part of surplus consisting of distributed profit. Thus, according to Baran and Sweezy, even if capitalists consumed the entire amount of their dividends, their consumption would not rise as a share of total surplus, because most large companies, even though tending to have a dividend payout rate constant over the long term, do not adjust it immediately in the case of rising profits. So a continuous growth of profit rate is accompanied by an equal decline in the pay-out rate.

The only solution to avoid overaccumulation is a growing absorption of surplus by uses other than consumption and investment. This kind of absorption can be implemented only by conspicuous waste, carried out by the same corporations, in the form of sales efforts and representation expenditures, or the government, in the form of public expenditures made, depending on the circumstances, for social welfare or military and imperialistic purposes.

These sources of effective demand reduce the accumulation rate of the system but stabilise it and allow for "realisation" of surplus.

Magdoff and Sveezy did not think that a theory of the determinants of investment decisions alone could suffice, because the problem is much more complex and includes historical dimensions and the hypothesis that capitalist development takes place in long cycles. They deemed that Keynes had started developing an economic enquiry going in this direction. This conclusion further enhanced convergence between Keynesian and neo-Marxist approaches.

According to Baran and Sweezy, the end of stagnation in the post-war period was largely due to three major causes: a massive role played by government spending and deficits, an exceptional growth in consumer debt and, last but not least, a ballooning of the financial sector, which generated a new class of financial rentiers who increased demand for luxury goods – i.e. capitalists' consumption.

According to them, to clearly understand the new wave of stagnation from the 1970s it needs understand its provisional suspension in the 25 years after the Second World War. In this period, indeed, the incentive to invest was very strong and unusual, producing a growth record that was the best in the entire history of capitalism.

The war had altered the givens of the world economy in several ways: the need for recovery of goods and services diminished greatly during the war; a huge mass of purchasing power accumulated during the war by firms and individuals; a great expansion of international trade, fed by the new US worldwide hegemony, with the dollar operating as the basis of a new international monetary system, most of the pre-war trade and currency blocs dismantled and new conditions for relatively free capital movements; civilian spinoffs from military technology; the building up, mostly in the United States, of a huge peacetime armaments industry.

All these changes raised new long-term optimism in the business world, incentivising a major investment boom in all the major industries.

But all these forces were self-limiting. Investment not only responds to a demand, it also satisfies it, and expanding industrial capacity, in the anarchy regime of capitalist markets, often ends up by creating overcapacity. That obviously is not sufficient to create a general deficit of aggregate effective demand. Theoretically, the excess capacity created in some sectors should correspond to deficits in others. But the excess capacity destroys capital value and the income it can produce and in doing so reduces the actual capital growth rate, which is essential to guarantee long-term full employment equilibrium for the economic system.

The investment boom generated by the incentives of the post-war period eventually undermined the very incentive to invest. Initially, the new tendency to stagnation was countered by debt creation, frantic financial speculation and higher inflation. But ultimately all these palliatives exhausted their capacity to counteract a decreasing propensity to invest and the problem of stagnation was again raising its head, with the addition of a deteriorating financial situation.

Sweezy did not argue that stagnation is a permanent and structural state of mature capitalist economy, as Hansen did in the 1930s. Following Schumpeter's suggestions, he thought that new powerful stimuli to investment could be engendered by new technological revolutions, but that these cannot be forecast and do not act with regularity.

In the normal short business cycles – i.e. Kitchin and Juglar cycles – each of their two basic phases, expansion and contraction, usually contain the "seeds of its opposite". But Sweezy thought this would not happen in long cycles. According to him, in the long post-war expansion the reversal did take place because every investment boom exhausts itself. But the successive stagnation phase could not automatically generate any "forces of reversal". Such forces cannot be generated by the internal logic of the economic system but only by means of greater historical processes, such as major wars or technological revolutions.

According to Magdoff and Sweezy (1987), one of the major forces counteracting the tendency to stagnation in the United States since the 1960s has been the rapid growth in the total outstanding public and private debt. This growth was, in turn, associated with the emergence of a huge and fragile financial superstructure that continuously threatened the stability of the economic system as a whole with its stresses, strains and imbalances.

New financial instruments, providing innovative ways to transfer price risks among investors, and growing competition in financial services, increased financial transactions, stimulating active trading and speculative strategies, which are in fact strictly linked with the outstanding debt explosion. In fact, the growing complexity of new financial superstructure, in turn, increased possibility of settlement failures and price volatility of financial assets. In a *Business Week* editorial of 16 September 1985, reported by Magdoff and Sweezy (1987), it was claimed "Slow growth and today's rampant speculative binge are locked in some kind of symbiotic embrace".

Baran and Sweezy's theses were strongly criticised by some orthodox Marxists, such as Ben Fine, Laurence Harris, David Yaffe and Paul Mattick, for their rejection of Marx's law of the falling rate of profit. This Marxian law had no central place in the previous Marxian political economy, but it was increasingly adopted by "fundamentalist" Marxists in the 1970s as the key concept for developing an economic crisis theory (see Foster, 2014).

In particular, according to Mattick, the falling rate of profit does not depend on competition but on value relations in the expanded capital reproduction. Thus, it is merely another expression for the accumulation of capital along with increasing productivity of labour. Moreover, Mattick asserted that Marx did not use the word "monopoly" in opposition to "competition", as the mainstream theories do. His theory of capital competition is compatible with a theory of monopoly because the latter always remains competitive, and a non-competitive monopoly capitalism would indeed imply the end of all market relations, which are vital for capitalism.

According to Mattick, Marx's theoretical analysis of capitalism disregards competition, which plays a role only in determining production prices, because it rests on the abstract concept of total capital in the aggregate, in which the sum of all production prices equal total value. From this point of view, it is regardless of whether market structure is competitive or monopolistic. Yet, in the descriptive parts of his work, Marx dealt with capital competition and its elimination by way of competition itself, that is the centralisation and concentration process of capital.

Mattick asserted that Marx's analysis was only in terms of value and surplus value because "the relation between wage-labour and capital determines the entire character of the capitalist mode of production" and one of the greatest advantages in Capital lies in "the treatment of surplus-value independently of its particular form of profit, interest, ground rent, etc." (Mattick, 1978).

In this way, according to Mattick, "Marx succeeded where Ricardo had failed, namely, in recognising in the falling rate of profit an immanent law of capital accumulation" (Mattick, 1978).

However, as we shall see in Chapter 5, these theses reinforced neo-Marxists' view that structural changes in the capitalist system at the end of the 20th century turned recurrent business cycles into a chronic tendency towards stagnation – i.e. a sharp slowdown in the real investment process – and prompted "the financialisation of the capital accumulation process" (see Magdoff and Foster, 2014).

Financial oligarchies and rentiers

Marx held that the very formation of joint-stock companies produces

> a new financial aristocracy, a new kind of parasite in the guise of company promoters, speculators and merely nominal directors; an entire system of swindling and cheating with respect to the promotion of companies, issue of shares and share dealings.
>
> (Marx, 1894/1991, p. 569)

Monopoly capitalism, in addition, secures monopoly extra-profits from the simple issuance of bonds and shares, in the form of the promoter's profit identified by Hilferding.

Thus, according to Lenin, based solely on the general conditions of commodity production and private property, the way capitalist monopolies work inevitably favours the rise to power of a financial oligarchy – i.e. the rise to power of finance and financiers that many post-Keynesian authors highlight today.

However, the rise to power of these actors is not the rise to power of a new fraction of the capitalist class against the other ones, but just the transformation of the major capital owners in owners of money capital able to maintain itself in the most liquid, flexible and unspecialised form. It is nothing more than the social manifestation of the rise of "finance capital" as defined by Hilferding of which NFCs are an integral part.

According to Hilferding, moreover, the separation of capital ownership from production management, achieved by the joint-stock system, creates solidarity of all property interests, blurring the differences between land rent, bank interest and industrial extra-profits, since all are eventually based on different forms of monopoly power. Thus, with the establishment of "finance capital", the wealthy classes no longer differentiate, as in the early stages of capitalism, according to their sources of income – whether profit, interest or rent – but they all share a common participation in the distribution of social surplus which is indistinctly presented as the receipt of a financial return on undifferentiated money capital. "Finance capital", indeed, appears on the world stage as the pure form of ownership of any means of production. It is capital according to Marx, in its highest abstraction and quintessence and, above all, it becomes the proper form of capital ownership in the advanced countries that are becoming the financial centre of the entire world economy.

With the "holding system", moreover, few people, representing a relatively small capital, can control enormous capital. This plays a very important role in developing and consolidating what we may define as the "oligarchies of finance capital". In fact, the rise of "finance capital" produces a new power elite, which, according to Mills (1956), is nothing more than the "managerial reorganisation of the propertied classes into the more or less unified stratum of the corporate rich". In this context, the corporate system is nothing but an "apparatus of appropriation" of social surplus (see Mills, 1956, p. 107; Sweezy, 1956).

The rise of capitalist monopolies, moreover, enhances capitalists' interest in strengthening the power of the state, on the one hand, while private capital acquires the economic power to dominate the state on the other.

The capitalist ruling classes have historically established themselves politically through the nation state and, as a result, nation states represent the different interests of their national ruling classes. States define themselves in the economic sphere through their own economic regulations, monetary and tariff systems, and controls on the international movement of production factors. Thus, all the forms of state regulation are generally in the very interests of the capitalist ruling classes. If state regulation changes over time this is because these interests are, in turn, changing. In our view, therefore, also financial deregulation in the 1980s and 1990s was actually the result of the changing interests of the "oligarchies of finance capital" of which the headquarters of the NFCs are an integral part.

Monetarism and neoliberalism, as ideological constructions and policy practices, have certainly helped these oligarchies to reassert their own interests. Neoliberal globalisation, in particular, has allowed a greater appropriation of the surplus created in the sphere of production in emerging countries by the capitalists of the old core of the world economy through financial instruments.

However we disagree with Keynes and post-Keynesians' views on the "role of bad ideas" (Palley, 2012) – i.e. that "the ideas of economists and political philosophers, both when they are right and when they are wrong, are more powerful than is commonly understood" and that "it is ideas, not vested interests, which are dangerous for good or evil" (Keynes, 1936/2013, pp. 383–384).

Indeed, we believe the exact opposite: dominant material interests are prevailing and ideas are simply an attempt to systematise and justify them ex-post. Consequently, from our point of view, if someone does not agree with the course of events, their main objective must be to understand the real economic and social dynamics at work in order to find possible forms of collective action in line with material interests other than the dominant ones.

However, according to Bukharin and Lenin, there is a permanent contradiction between the international unifying tendencies of the new technologies and the constricting influence of the nation state. This is expressed in rivalries and tensions between the major states, alliances and preparation for wars – be they commercial or ultimately military.

At the same time, with the emergence of an international financial system, even countries with a stationary population and stagnant real economy can grow rich by credit and simply lending capital abroad. Thus, today's Western countries may turn into a group of ex-industrial countries whose upper classes draw large incomes, in the form of interest and dividends, from the rest of the world with which they can also support "great tame masses of retainers, no longer engaged in the staple industries of agriculture and manufacture, but kept in the performance of personal or minor industrial services under the control of a new financial aristocracy" (Hobson, 1902/2005). Thus, the advanced Western countries may, as Hobson prophetically predicted, become the place of a "small aristocracy of millionaires, who will have made their money where labour was cheapest, and return to spend it where life is pleasantest" (Hobson, 1902/2005). In these countries life can be so pleasant for the wealthy classes also because within them "no productive work will be possible [...], but such labour as is required for personal service will be procurable at a cheap rate, owing to the reluctance of labour to· keep pace with the migration of capital" (Hobson, 1891/1992).

Therefore, due to the separation of ownership from control implemented by the joint-stock form of production organisation, a more or less extensive part of capital owners can voluntary transform themselves or be forced to transform into pure "financial rentiers". Lenin, for instance, when talking about monopoly capitalism, argued that a large concentration of interest-bearing capital, held in securities in a few countries, enhances the extraordinary growth of a "stratum of rentiers" – i.e. "people who live by 'clipping coupons', who take no part in any enterprise whatever, whose profession is idleness" (Lenin, 1916/1974, p. 277).

However, the term "financial rent" is not usual in economics. In point of fact, in the classical approach, the term *rent* properly denoted the income deriving from the ownership of non-reproducible means of production, such as land and other natural resources. According to Ricardo, for instance, rent was a payment for "the use of the original and indestructible powers of the soil". Thus, in accordance with this approach, it might seem improper to speak of rent referring to income deriving from the ownership of money capital.

However, some precursors of the classical economists had already followed this line. William Petty, for example, in his *Treatise on Taxes and Contributions*, had counterposed interest, as "rent of money", to rent of land and houses. Petty's parallel was then followed by Locke, while North contrasted interest, as "rent of stock", with land rent, and the "stocklords" with the landlords (see Engels, 1878/1987, p. 222).

Neoclassical economic theory, moreover, has successively generalised Ricardo's theory of rent, extending it to all the factors of production (see Quadrio-Curzio, 1998), so that rent has become synonymous with payment for use of a resource, whether it be land, labour, equipment, ideas, or even money (see Alchian, 2008). In other words, rent is viewed as a premium for scarcity, which, in this approach, determines all the prices of goods and services, including the incomes of the primary factors of production. Nevertheless, only land income traditionally retains this name properly, while the rent for labour is usually called "wages", just as the payment for use of money is called "interest" (see Alchian, 2008).

However, in various heterodox economic approaches it is common to use the term *rentier* to refer to someone who only earns interest and dividends on his capital (see Glyn, 2006; Pollin, 2007). This use of the term is also traditionally associated with an ethical judgement that implies a parasitic role of the rentier within society, as he is the one who receives interest and dividends on the capital he has provided, but does not engage in any entrepreneurial activity.

Werner Sombart, the German economist and sociologist who first developed the concepts of *late capitalism* and *creative destruction*, investigating and depicting the main features of the entrepreneur psychology in the ascending phase of the bourgeoisie, explicitly opposed it and the behaviour of haute finance in France and England during the seventeenth and eighteenth centuries, characterised by "wealthy persons, mostly of bourgeois origin, who had enriched themselves as tax farmers or creditors of the nation and who now floated on the surface of the broth as circles of fat, completely removed, however, from the economic life" (Sombart, 1913, p. 46).

According to Sombart, moreover, when Holland declined as trade world centre in the course of the 18th century, Dutch merchants began to live on their "rents", which included land rent as well as interest, and any concern for capitalistic enterprises of any type progressively diminished (see Sombart, 1913, p. 188).

Sombart also quoted Daniel Defoe, the famous 18th-century British novelist, who described the process of the evolution of merchants into coupon-cutters as follows:

> Formerly it had been necessary for him [the merchant.-N.B.] at any rate to be diligent and active in order to acquire his fortune; but now he has nothing else to do than to determine to be indolent and inactive. National rents and land ownership are the only proper investment for his savings.
>
> (Sombart, 1913, p. 201)

However, such behaviour, according to Bukharin (1927), resurfaces whenever a swift accumulation of money capital is associated with the development of various forms of credit, which increase the number of people who have no direct relation whatever to production – i.e. the social group of the "rentiers". The more highly developed the credit system, the greater is the possibility for some people to become "indolent and inactive", delegating the financial management of their assets to others and thus increasing the overall amount of financial services (see Bukharin, 1927). And this trend grows as cross-border capital movements increase.

Thus, from this point of view, we can say that growing financialisation in Western economies, referred to as "the increasing role of financial motives, financial markets, financial actors and financial institutions in the operation of the domestic and international economies" (Epstein, 2005), is nothing but the direct consequence of the increase in the number of rentiers in advanced countries.

This social group is not, of course, a social class in the Marxist sense of the word, but rather a specific group within the ranks of the capitalist class, characterised by certain traits of a specific "social psychology" – which, as we will see in Chapter 5, can in any case generate some relevant effects on aggregate demand and capital accumulation.

This social group looms increasingly large with the expansion of joint-stock corporations and financial intermediaries and the increase in the trade in securities.

According to Bukharin, the subgroup of the capitalist class that exclusively lives on the income from securities predominantly operates in the field of the circulation of financial paper – i.e. the Stock Exchange. However, we can find a number of different nuances within it. There is a stratum, in fact, that is not only independent of production, but also of the circulation process of securities itself. In the past times this was predominantly constituted by the owners of gilt-edged securities, like national bonds and other kinds of secure obligations. Today, however, they can also be largely made up of clients of mutual funds, edge funds and other financial intermediaries that parcel out yield and risk by means of elaborate financial instruments. In the same way, within this stratum there are also people who invest their wealth in real estate too, drawing permanent and secure incomes from this. All these categories avoid the day-to-day disturbances of the Stock Exchange, contrary to shareholders, who are exposed to the ups and downs of speculation, but still depend on the general conditions of credit, summarised by the interest rate.

Thus, in advanced countries some subgroups of the capitalist class and the upper strata of the middle class tend to transform themselves into rentiers who have about the same relation to the great financial intermediaries as they had to the State in the past. In both cases, in fact, they are paid their interest and have nothing else to worry about.

In point of fact, the rise of a group of rentiers in the advanced economies is a truly spontaneous tendency of capitalism. George Ramsey, a Scottish economist widely quoted by Marx (1894/1991, pp. 483–484), argued as early as the first half of the 19th century that:

> as a nation advances in the career of wealth, a class of men springs up and increases more and more, who by the labours of their ancestors find themselves in the possession of funds sufficiently ample to afford a handsome maintenance from the interest alone. Very many also who during youth and middle age were actively engaged in business, retire in their latter days to live quietly on the interest of the sums they have themselves accumulated. This class, as well as the former, has a tendency to increase with the increasing riches of the country, for those who begin with a tolerable stock are likely to make an independence sooner than they who commence with little. Thus it comes to pass, that in old and rich countries, the amount of national capital belonging to those who are unwilling to take the trouble of employing it themselves, bears a larger proportion to the whole productive stock of the society, than in newly settled and poorer districts. [...] As the class of rentiers increases, so also does that of lenders of capital, for they are one and the same.
>
> (Ramsay, 1836, pp. 201–202)

Indeed, Bukharin saw rentiers as people who usually do no work at all and argued that production lay beyond their horizon. Thus, the most characteristic feature of this social group is its removal from the productive economic life. Rentiers participate directly neither in the activities of production nor in trade, and often do not even cut their own coupons. Their main "sphere of activities" is consumption, which is the basis of their entire life, ruled by a peculiar "psychology of pure consumption". Thus, the rentier class is parasitical by its very nature and develops the same psychological features as the decayed nobility and the financial aristocracy at the end of the *ancien régime*, consequently concerned only with their own luxuries.

Bukharin, however, held that it is the capitalist mechanism itself that produces this result, by continuously making the organisational functions of a considerable number of entrepreneurs socially superfluous and simultaneously "eliminating these 'superfluous elements' from the immediate operations of the economic life" (Bukharin, 1927, p. 25).

Keynes himself, some years later, referring to the effects on consumption of a change in the wage-unit, explicitly dealt with distribution of a given real income between *entrepreneurs* and *rentiers* (see Keynes, 1936/2013, pp. 92, 262). In this context, he identified the rentier class with creditors who have a remuneration that is contractually fixed in terms of money – i.e. *interest earners* – and pointed out that "interest rewards no genuine sacrifice, any more than does the rent of land" (Keynes, 1936/2013, p. 376).

Thus, following the traditional neoclassical approach, Keynes held that the owner of money capital can obtain interest insofar as, like land, it is scarce.

However, he deemed, there are no intrinsic reasons for scarcity of money capital in the long run.

Consequently, he believed that rentiers, unlike entrepreneurs, could sooner or later quietly disappear (see Keynes, 1936/2013, p. 221). In fact, discussing the possible "euthanasia of the rentier", defined as the "euthanasia of the cumulative oppressive power of the capitalist to exploit the scarcity-value of capital", due, in turn, to an increase in the stock of capital up to a point where its marginal efficiency is very low, Keynes explicitly defined the rentier as a "functionless investor" (Keynes, 1936/2013, p. 376).

In the context of this reasoning, Keynes also clearly distinguished the figure of the *rentier* from that of the *financier*, who was by contrast characterised by "intelligence and determination and executive skill" like the entrepreneur and therefore deserving of adequate remuneration for services rendered (see Keynes, 1936/2013, pp. 375–377).

Thus, in accordance with the meaning of the term "rentier" we find in this economic literature, we can simply define "financial rent" as the income of the rentier. Unlike Keynes, however, we include in this income dividends and capital gains, too, because, although they are not fixed in monetary terms like interest, today the risk associated with them is often more akin to gambling risk than to business risk. According to Engels, in fact, the capitalist class, in the age of large joint-stock corporations, "has no further social function than that of pocketing dividends, tearing off coupons, and gambling on the Stock Exchange, where the different capitalists despoil one another of their capital" (Engels, 1878/1987, p. 265). And gambling is traditionally a typical activity of the leisure classes who have no direct relation to production.

Moreover, while in the past rentiers were mainly the owners of gilt-edged securities, such as national bonds and other types of safe bonds, today they are mostly the clients of mutual funds, hedge funds and other financial intermediaries that form the core of the shadow banking system. All these intermediaries, in fact, create the illusion of separating return from risk by means of elaborate financial instruments that promise to offer protection against the volatility of the underlying assets.

Monopoly capital, corporate control and the evolution of large industrial holding companies

Therefore, networks of corporate control by financial institutions are hardly new. A century ago, many Marxist theorists described "finance capitalism" as a new system in which banks controlled large NFCs. This was, according to them, the main result of the advent of large-scale production and centralisation processes due to the creation of cartels and trusts in which the professional managers at the top of large corporations faced banks as their own controllers. In other words, it is the very process of concentration and centralisation of capital that prompts financial forms of control.

Engels, while commenting on some of Marx's statements concerning what the formation of joint-stock companies involved – gathered in the third volume of Capital – already highlighted that, since Marx had written them, "new forms of industrial organisation have been developed, [...] representing the second and third degree of joint-stock company" (Marx, 1894/1991, pp. 568–569). These new forms were to concentrate the entire production of a branch of industry into "one big joint-stock company with a unified management", where the technical management of the reunified individual plants under a single control often remains in the same hands as before, "but financial control is concentrated in the hands of the general management" (Marx, 1894/1991, pp. 568–569).

Thus, in tandem with the development of the industrial giant corporations, financial control has become the main and most efficient way of managing the giant multi-unit industrial organisations.

Hobson, Lenin and Bukharin were among the first to draw attention to the "holding system" in which a "mother" company can control several subsidiaries owning only a share of their capital. The "daughter companies", in turn, can control other subsidiaries in the same way, and so on. By means of this control structure, it is possible to control vast areas of production and commerce with a relatively small amount of capital.

Moreover, a change in control strategy links to changes in international competition. Financial control, in fact, is essential in the context of national markets dominated by large corporations, too. However, international competition enhances this tendency because it requires more flexibility than strict control.

Today, large industrial holding companies are economic institutions that play a major role in the resource allocation process in many industrialised market economies and dominate the world market scene unchallenged with powerful multi-corporate combines relying on the holding company institution to control their intermarket network.

Holding companies, of course, should not be confused with the legal entities that proliferate in tax havens whose only function is to organise tax evasion across national borders. The large holding company is an economic institution through which industrial groups manage multi-company systems. It is more typical in some European countries – such as Belgium and France – and Japan than in the United States, where, for both legal and managerial reasons, the giant integrated multiunit enterprise rose to dominance. However, both the giant American integrated multiunit companies and the large European and Japanese holding companies are capitalist institutions that internalise allocation decisions on a massive scale, substituting a visible hand for the invisible one of the market. Extrapolating to the large holding companies what Marx already said about the socialisation process achieved by joint-stock companies, we can say that they are "the abolition of capital as private property within the confines of the capitalist mode of production itself" (Marx, 1894/1991, p. 567).

Thus, holding companies and intermarket combines play a crucial role in the most basic sectors of the economy outside the United States and large holding companies are effectively financial institutions that manage a portfolio of shares in order to control the companies in which they hold a share. It is only the struggle for corporate control that differentiates them from other financial institutions. Holding companies, therefore, are no more than financial institutions whose activities are mainly directed towards control over the capital management function.

Control of a "daughter" company by a holding company means that the latter must have representation on the board of directors or a significant share of votes in the shareholders' meeting in order to effectively monitor and influence the top management of the subsidiary. This type of control is obviously a different governance mechanism from that of *the market for corporate control* – apparently preferred by the protagonists of the "shareholder revolution" in the United States – but it is not, by its very nature, necessarily less oriented towards maximising the subsidiary's profits. Strategic considerations related to positioning in a particular sector and market may come into play more easily, but flexibility in changing subsidiaries still puts them in competition with each other when ensuring maximum profitability for the parent company.

Today, large holding companies usually control complex intermarket networks which may consist of more than a hundred companies, as is the case with Berkshire Hathaway. However, many subsidiaries are only indirectly controlled through intermediate sub-holding companies. This indirect participation allows the "mother" holding company to control a pyramid structure of companies and some of the subsidiaries may also be among the largest corporations in an economy.

Thus, when the first layer of controlled companies is composed of sub-holding companies, the "mother" holding company can control a very impressive quantity of assets. In principle, there is no limit to the extent of control and nothing would prevent a company from controlling the entire asset structure of an economy. However, given that the shareholding threshold for securing control may vary due to the actions of competing holding companies, this outcome is very unlikely in the real world which is characterised by fierce oligopolistic competition.

Nevertheless, the business of many of them ranges from the utility and energy sectors to retail, insurance, finance and other services, and of course various manufacturing sectors. Chandler and Mazlish (2005) report a famous UN statement from just over 20 years ago that "of the 100 entities with the largest GNP, about half were multinational corporations". In other words, roughly 50 large multinational corporations are larger economic entities than at least 120 nation states and the largest holding companies show revenues comparable with the GDP of developed countries, such as Portugal (see Table 3.1).

Thus, according to Chandler and Mazlish (2005), giant multinational corporations are becoming the new *Leviathan* that is capable of having a decisive

Table 3.1 Top holding companies and conglomerates in the world (2022)

Rank	*Company Name*	*Revenue*	*Headquarter Location*
1	Berkshire Hathaway	$276B	Omaha, United States
2	Alphabet	$258B	Mountain View, United States
3	Reliance Industries	$183B	Mumbai, India
4	Sinochem	$156B	Beijing, China
5	Bajaj Holdings & Investment	$150B	Akurdi, India
6	Vitol	$140B	Geneva, Switzerland
7	EXOR	$140B	Amsterdam, Netherlands
8	Walgreens Boots Alliance	$135B	Deerfield, United States
9	Mitsubishi Corporation	$130B	Tokyo, Japan
10	Alibaba Group	$128B	Hangzhou, China

Source: Datanize.

impact on almost every sphere of modern life, from decision-making in every socio-economic field to the very future of nation states and their alliances.

However, above all, large holding companies are living proof that forms of financial organisation can be very efficient tools for implementing and extending a comprehensive system of corporate control on a global scale.

Financial institutions, however, are able to gain and hold such control insofar as they issue securities to buy and hold "substantial" blocks of stocks – i.e. controlling interest – in operating companies and other holding companies. They therefore need a capital market setting to function on a large scale. Consequently, the expansion of financial markets and financial activities are not, by their very nature, at odds with the expansion of big business, but can, on the contrary, be a powerful lever for it.

Holding companies are in all respects financial institutions that issue financial claims to hold claims in other companies. They usually offer savers a substitution of the securities of the controlled companies for the holding companies' own securities. In doing so, the holding companies act in the capital market as financial intermediaries between savers and investors for long-term financial assets and by doing so, they function formally as a closed-end mutual fund. The only difference is that they strive to take control of corporate decision-making, whereas mutual funds may not be willing to do so (see Daems, 1978).

Moreover, large conglomerates often diversify business risk by participating in many different markets. In doing so, their top management actually act as financial investors who manage a financial portfolio. It is precisely this type of behaviour that ultimately defines the true intrinsic characteristic of the financialisation of NFCs.

In conclusion, following Marxist approaches, the financialisation of NFCs can be seen not as a historical accident, but, on the contrary, as the necessary development of capitalist accumulation according to its own laws of motion.

This, of course, does not mean that it cannot be a problem for the evolution of social welfare in developed countries. It can, in fact, dramatically change the ways in which traditional economic policies work and their effectiveness, as we shall see more fully in Chapter 7. This simply means that the financialisation of NFCs is closely linked to the very nature of the capital circuit described by Marx and the role played by credit within it, as we will try to show in the next chapter.

Notes

1 Other interesting observations on the rise of the joint-stock company and its managerial apparatus, as well as the role of the stock exchange and the banks, had also been dealt with briefly in Engel's *Anti-Dühring* (1878/ 1987, pp. 264–266) .
2 Bukharin's book on *Imperialism and World Economy* (Bukharin, 1917/1929) was really written in 1915 although it was only published in 1917. Lenin wrote a preface to it in December 1915 which was not rediscovered and published until 1927. The dating of Lenin's preface, therefore, establishes that Bukharin's work probably came before Lenin's and influenced it (see Brewer, 1990).
3 Considering the different items that surplus value is divided into is only important if the distribution of its components among different economic agents affects the rate of accumulation since too much surplus value is eventually consumed in luxury goods instead of being capitalised.
4 In "Some Theoretical Implications", the missing chapter of Monopoly Capital, published in the July–August 2012 issue of Monthly Review, the authors showed their broad agreement with Sraffa's idea that wages may include a share of surplus product (see Baran and Sweezy, 2012; Foster, 2012, 2014).
5 For the role of "Warfare" in sustaining the effective demand in the US monopoly capitalism, see also Braverman (1974).

References

Alchian, A. A. (2008). "Rent". In: *The New Palgrave Dictionary of Economics. Volume 7.* New York: Macmillan Publishers, pp. 90–3.

Baran, P. and Sweezy, P. M. (1966). *Monopoly Capital. An Essay on the American Economic and Social Order.* New York: Monthly Review Press.

Baran, P. and Sweezy, P. M. (2012). "Some Theoretical Implications". *Monthly Review,* 64 (3): 24–59.

Brandeis, L. D. (1914). *Other People's Money. And How the Bankers Use It.* New York: Frederick A. Stokes Company Publishers.

Braverman, H. (1974). *Labor and Monopoly Capital. The Degradation of Work in the Twentieth Century.* New York: Monthly Review Press.

Brewer, A. (1990). *Marxist Theories of Imperialism. A Critical Survey.* London and New York: Routledge.

Brown, M. B. (1972). "A Critique of Marxist Theories of Imperialism". In: Owen, R. and Sutcliffe, B. (eds.), *Studies in the Theory of Imperialism.* London: Longman Group Limited, pp. 35–70.

Bukharin, N. I. (1917/1929). *Imperialism and World Economy.* London: Martin Lawrence Limited.

Bukharin, N. I. (1927). *The Economic Theory of the Leisure Class.* New York: International Publishers.

Chandler, A. D. and Mazlish, B. (2005). *Leviathans. Multinational Corporations and the New Global History.* Cambridge: Cambridge University Press.

Daems, H. (1978). *The Holding Company and Corporate Control.* Leiden and Boston, MA: Martinus Nijhoff Social Sciences Division.

Davis, G. F. (2008). "A New Finance Capitalism? Mutual Funds and Ownership Re-Concentration in the United States". *European Management Review*, 5, 11–21.

Dutta, S. (2021). "Laws of Concentration and Centralization of Capital: A Modern Review". *Cambridge Open Engage*. doi:10.33774/coe-2021-qxgvs

Engels, F. (1878/1987). "Anti-Dühring". In: Marx K. and Engels F., *Marx & Engels Collected Works*. Vol 25. London: Lawrence & Wishart, pp. 5–309.

Epstein, G. A. (2005). "Introduction: Financialization and the World Economy". In: Epstein, G. A. (ed.), *Financialization and the World Economy.* Cheltenham and Northampton, MA: Edward Elgar Publishing Ltd, pp. 3–16.

Fine, B. (2014). "Financialization from a Marxist Perspective". *International Journal of Political Economy*, 42 (4): 47–66.

Foster, J. B. (2012). "A Missing Chapter of Monopoly Capital: Introduction to Baran and Sweezy's 'Some Theoretical Implications'". *Monthly Review*, 64 (3): 3–23.

Foster, J. B. (2014). *The Theory of Monopoly Capitalism. An Elaboration of Marxian Political Economy.* New York: Monthly Review Press.

Glyn, A. (2006). *Capitalism Unleashed. Finance, Globalization, and Welfare.* New York: Oxford University Press.

Hilferding, R. (1910/1981). *Finance Capital. A Study of the Latest Phase of Capitalist Development.* London: Routledge.

Hobson, J. A. (1891/1992). "Can England Keep Her Trade?". In: Hobson, J. A., *Writings on Imperialism and Internationalism.* New York and London: Routledge, pp. 1–11.

Hobson, J. A. (1902/2005). *Imperialism: A Study.* New York: Cosimo.

Kemp, T. (1972). "The Marxist Theory of Imperialism". In: Owen, R. and Sutcliffe, B. (eds.), *Studies in the Theory of Imperialism.* London: Longman Group Limited, pp. 15–34.

Keynes, J. M. (1936/2013). *The General Theory of Employment, Interest and Money. The Collected Writings of John Maynard Keynes.* Volume VII. Cambridge: Cambridge University Press.

Lenin, V. I. (1916/1974). "Imperialism, the Highest Stage of Capitalism. A Popular Outline". In: Lenin, V. I., *Collected Works.* Volume 22. December 1915 – July 1916. Moscow: Progress Publishers, pp. 185–304.

Luxemburg, R. (1913/2003). *The Accumulation of Capital.* London: Routledge

Magdoff, F. and Foster, J. B. (2014). "Stagnation and Financialization: The Nature of the Contradiction". *Monthly Review*, 66 (1): 1–24.

Magdoff, H. and Sweezy, P. M. (1987). *Stagnation and the Financial Explosion.* New York: Monthly Review Press.

Marx, K. (1867/1990). *Capital.* Volume I. London: Penguin Books.

Marx, K. (1885/1992). *Capital.* Volume II. London: Penguin Books.

Marx, K. (1894/1991). *Capital.* Volume III. London: Penguin Books.

Mattick, P. (1978). "Monopoly Capital". In: Mattick, P., *Anti-Bolshevik Communism.* London: Merlin Press, pp. 187–209.

Mills, C. W. (1956). *The Power Elite.* New York: Oxford University Press.

Palley, T. L. (2012). *From Financial Crisis to Stagnation. The Destruction of Shared Prosperity and the Role of Economics.* Cambridge: Cambridge University Press.

Pollin, R. (2007). "Resurrection of the Rentier". *New Left Review*, 46: 140–53.

Quadrio-Curzio, A. (1998). "Rent". In: Kurz H. D. and Salvadori, N. (eds.), *The Elgar Companion to Classical Economics (L-Z)*. Cheltenham, and Northampton, MA: Edward Elgar, pp. 289–93.

Ramsay, G. B. (1836). *Essay on the Distribution of Wealth*. Edinburgh and London: Adam and Charles Black.

Sau, R. (1979). "On the Laws of Concentration and Centralization of Capital". *Social Scientist*, 8 (3): 3–14.

Sombart, W. (1913). *Der Bourgeois*. München and Leipzig: Duncker & Humblot.

Sweezy, P. M. (1941). "The Decline of the Investment Banker", *The Antioch Review*, 1 (1): 63–68.

Sweezy, P. M. (1942/1946). *The Theory of Capitalist Development. Principles of Marxian Political Economy*. London: Dennis Dobson Limited.

Sweezy, P. M. (1956). "Power Elite or Ruling Class?". *Monthly Review Pamphlet Series*, 13: 138–50.

Sweezy, P. M. and Magdoff, H. (1972). *The Dynamics of U.S. Capitalism. Corporate Structure, Inflation, Credit, Gold and the Dollar.* New York: Monthly Review Press.

4 Interest-bearing capital vs industrial capital

Money capital and productive capital

According to Marx, as we know, the circuit of capital, in its pure state,[1] comprises three fundamental stages: M–C–M', where M is the initial value of money capital, C is the value of commodities in which M is transformed by means of a simply act of commodities circulation and M' denotes an increase in money capital value as the result of acquiring surplus value in the form of unpaid labour.

In this formula, money is the independent expression of a sum of value that, on the basis of capitalist production, can be transformed into capital – i.e. "self-valorising value capable of increasing itself" (Marx, 1894/1991, p. 459). This means, of course, that Marx's theory of capital accumulation is intrinsically a monetary theory, in which money is not a veil but a main character (see Mandel, 1990).

Thus, according to Marx, capital always starts its circulation process as a sum of value at its highest level of abstraction – i.e. money capital or, as we would say in modern terms, financial capital. Money capital, according to Marx, is indeed financial capital to all intents and purposes and by its very nature.

The entire circuit of capital itself appears to be a circuit of money capital due to the fact that the latter constitutes both its point of departure and its point of return. Indeed, in this circuit, money plays the role of the independent form of appearance of the exchange value of commodities, the attainment of which is the true aim of all capitalist production processes.

However, according to Marx's theory, in order to valorise itself by adding unpaid labour to its initial value, this money capital has to go through the process of commodity production. Money capital has to transform itself into productive capital – i.e. means of production and wages – to produce commodities that embody – thanks to *surplus labour* – a greater value than the original money capital. However, money capital is, by its very nature, indifferent to the specific use-values it has to produce and sell in order to complete its circuit. In fact, for money capital, the time spent in the sphere of use-values is an inconvenient deviation from its true final aim – i.e. self-valorisation – which must be circumvented as soon as possible. From the point

DOI: 10.4324/9781003223221-5

of view of any capitalist, the production process simply appears as an "unavoidable middle term, a necessary evil for the purpose of money-making" (Marx, 1885/1992, p. 137). This "explains why all nations characterised by the capitalist mode of production are periodically seized by fits of giddiness in which they try to accomplish the money-making without the mediation of the production process" (Marx, 1885/1992, p. 137). In other words, this explains the perpetual tendency of capitalism towards financialisation!

However, according to Marx, on the basis of capitalist production money receives an additional *use-value* – namely "the ability to function as capital" (Marx, 1894/1991, p. 459). And, as potential capital, every sum of money becomes a commodity of a special kind that can be sold – i.e. lent, in accordance with the usual legal arrangements in modern societies – to some particular buyers – namely *functioning capitalists*. The use-value of this peculiar commodity, of course, consists in the profit that it can produce when transformed into productive or commercial capital.

Every owner of money as potential capital can lend it over a certain span of time to a functioning capitalist, who can actually use it as productive or commercial capital that results in the capacity to produce profit. The functioning capitalist, then, pays the lender a share of the profit produced, as the use-value of the original lent sum used by him as productive capital. And, according to Marx, it is exactly this share of the profit of the functioning capitalist that is usually called *interest*. At the aggregate level, therefore, interest is nothing but a part of unpaid labour – i.e. social surplus value.

Following Smith's classical approach, Marx did not hold the view that the rate of interest is the same as the rate of profit or the entire income of capital, as in current mainstream economics. According to him, interest is only part of the profit seen as surplus value, a part that is, in turn, determined only by competition between lenders and borrowers.

However, this competition is characterised by the market structure of the financial intermediation and the market power of the participants, both on the lender and on the borrower side.

This may sound odd if you think of interest rate as the price of loanable funds under perfect competition, as mainstream economic thinking usually does. Yet, the view that the term structure of interest rates is determined only by adding liquidity and risk premiums to a risk free rate tightly controlled by the central banks is the result of abstracting from any possible market power in money markets other than that by the central banks themselves. Neoclassical theory, therefore, can identify the interest rate with the marginal profit rate only as a consequence of the hypothesis of perfect competition in the market of loanable funds, thanks to which the interest rate can be assumed to always reach its upper marginal limit.

Marx, however, splits total profit – i.e. total surplus value – into two parts: *entrepreneurial profit*, which accrues to functioning capitalists, and *interest*, which, in turn, accrues to money capitalists who limit themselves to lending money capital to the former.

Within the social relations that characterise the capitalist mode of production, money gives its owner the power to draw interest only because its use by the functioning capitalist can produce profit. In point of fact, the very ethical acceptance of the payment of interest consists in the fact that it arises from the current relations of production as their natural consequence. The legal forms of the contracts between lenders and borrowers, which can only be enforced by the state laws, are justified just so long as their content corresponds to the economic laws of the capitalist mode of production and is adequate to them.

However, at the aggregate level, the capital function of money really works on average if and only if it is eventually spent as investment demand – i.e. purchase of means of production – in any part of the economic system.

Nevertheless, insofar as the legal owners of money either spend it for their private consumption or hoard it, this money cannot be spent as capital by a functioning capitalist. In point of fact, it is the lender who originally spends a sum of money as *interest-bearing capital*, transferring it to a functioning capitalist. Thus, as far as loanable funds alone are concerned, borrowers can only function as capitalists because lenders – i.e. money capital owners – turn liquid funds over to them as interest-bearing capital. In other words, financial investment decisions by money-owners affect capital accumulation!

Thus, according to Marx there are two focus points in the circuit of interest-bearing capital in its ordinary form. The first is the characteristic feature of its circulation process. The second is the specific way it is sold as a commodity – i.e. *lent* instead of being spent or hoarded.

In fact, with regard to interest-bearing capital, the first spending act of money is not a stage in the circuit of capital in its pure and abstract form. The latter really begins only when it is spent by the functioning capitalist. Thus, the first spending act in the money capital circuit is simply a transfer of money from the lender to the borrower.

The circuit of interest-bearing capital is thus:

$$M - M - C - M' - M' \tag{4.1}$$

In Marx's circulation formula there are consequently two movements *in duplicate*: the expenditure of the money as capital and its reflux as realised capital ($M' = M + \Delta M$).

The double expenditure of the money as capital, first by the creditor and then by the functioning capitalist, is matched by its double reflux as valorised value, first to the functioning capitalist and then to the interest-bearing capital owner. However, ΔM for the interest-bearing capital owner does not amount to the whole profit, but simply the part of it that is transformed into interest.

Thus, the vicissitudes of money as interest-bearing capital are quite different from those of money for expenditure on goods and services. The owner of money as interest-bearing capital, in fact, parts with it to a functioning capitalist as value that possesses the use-value of creating profit and has eventually to go back to the person who originally spent it as a loan. Thus, this money comes out of the possession of its initial owner only temporarily, with the provision that it has to return to its starting point after a certain period of time as "realised capital" – i.e. capital that has implemented its use-value of producing surplus value. It is neither definitively given out as money nor as a commodity, nor exchanged for a commodity.

However, when we consider the reproduction process of interest-bearing capital as a whole, we simply find that an initial sum of money is given out and it goes back after a given period with a surplus value. This sum of money is maintained and increased in the course of this cyclical movement and can go through the same process once again. And it is only in this capacity that it is lent out as money capital.

Thus, according to Marx the legal form of lending results from the fact that money as capital becomes itself a commodity, whose use-value consists in the profit that it can produce when transformed into productive or commercial capital. However, it is only as the result of the entire circulation process, when it goes back to its owner as valorised value, that the original sum of money shows its true nature as capital money. When it goes back to its initial point, nevertheless, the mediation of all the circulation process – that is, the production process that valorised it – has already disappeared and the money capital owner can be quite unaware of it. From the viewpoint of its owners, the circuit of interest-bearing capital appears to be just as M–M'. This abbreviated circuit is exactly what is generally believed to be the new system of "profits without investment" prevailing in finance-dominated capitalism!

Interest-bearing capital, therefore, appears to its owners "as money breeding money" or "self-valorizing value" by its very nature and capacity (see Marx, 1885/1992, pp. 138, 185, 234 and 291). From this viewpoint, ΔM no longer bears any marks of its origin as a mere share of social surplus value.

The production process carried out by the functioning capitalist thanks to the loan of interest-bearing capital is usually taken into account by the lender only insofar as it is a security on his loan. And this feature of interest-bearing capital circuit is precisely one of the major components of the "psychology of the rentier" we will consider in more detail in the next chapter.

According to current mainstream economics, of course, this attitude of interest-bearing capital owners is not a problem at all. It is the invisible hand of the loanable funds market that, through movements in the equilibrium interest rate, encourages them, seen as mere savers, to meet the needs of companies regardless of their selfish and utilitarian interests.

Marx, however, although holding that the level of the interest rate is determined by the free interplay of supply and demand between lenders and borrowers, believed the balance point cannot be explained by any inner economic relation, as in the case of commodity prices, which are instead governed by the law of value. According to Marx, therefore, when it is only competition as such that determines the level of an economic variable, this determination can only be intrinsically accidental.

And a similar argument could also be made on the basis of Keynes' theory of purely monetary determination of the interest rate, because even in this case there is no guarantee that changes in the interest rate will bring saving and investment decisions into balance.

Furthermore, if we consider the entire circular movement of interest-bearing capital, the starting point appears at the same time as the point of return, where money returns as valorised value. Insofar as we take this point as an imaginary point of repose, interest-bearing capital as well as money capital in general – as stock variables – appear as withdrawn from circulation of real goods and services. At this point in the money capital circuit, therefore, money simply appears as capital either in its relation to the capitalist himself or as a key phase in the overall process of capitalist reproduction, depending on whether we consider things from a subjective or objective point of view. If, however, the point of repose were not imaginary but real, then money capital would become hoarding – i.e. demand for money for precautionary or speculative purposes, as we will see in more detail in Chapter 6. In any case, corporate cash holdings remain money capital to all intents and purposes and as such can, in turn, be transformed into interest-bearing capital or, more generally, into financial capital.

The role of credit in capitalist production

Credit makes its appearance in the commodity circulation process whenever a commodity can be sold and paid for at a later date (see Hilferding, 1910/1981, p. 60). When this happens, the seller immediately becomes a lender and the buyer a borrower and, as a result of the temporal decoupling of sale and payment, money itself acquires a new function as a means of payment.

According to both Marx and Hilferding, commercial credit is nothing more than the creation of *credit money* – i.e. endogenous money – arising on the basis of direct relations between industrial and commercial capitalists,[2] which is in any case subject to the same laws that generally regulate the amount of money in circulation. It represents the way in which money supply adjusts to the demand for it, determined, in turn, by the needs of the circulation of commodities and the timing in the realisation process of commodities value in a market economy. In so far as credit consists exclusively of commercial credit, its changes do not depend on changes in the rate of interest (see Hilferding, 1910/1981, p. 83).

The quantity of means of payment commercial credit can generate is determined, all other things being equal, only by the aggregate value of the commodities produced. Credit money supply is, therefore, limited from above by the value of potential product divided by the velocity of circulation of money, according to the following formula (see Hilferding, 1910/1981, p. 47):

$$M = \frac{total\ value\ of\ commodities}{velocity\ of\ circulation\ of\ money} \tag{4.2}$$

Bearing in mind here that the expression "total value of commodities" means the sum of the prices for the quantities of commodities produced, the above formula appears to coincide with the equation of the *quantity theory of money*. However, in this theory, the equation is used to conclude that, given the velocity of circulation of money – determined by institutional arrangements – and the quantity of commodities – brought about in real terms by the balance between supply and demand in both the goods and labour markets – the monetary prices of goods must rise or fall in direct proportion to the supply of money. Thus, the quantity theory of money really is a theory of monetary prices.

Hilferding, in contrast, merely argues that the above equation determines the amount of money required to satisfy the needs of the circulation of commodities actually produced. He, indeed, following Marx's theory, holds the view that the value of commodity money equals on average the labour time required to produce it. Money prices, therefore, are just the expression of the exchange value of commodities in terms of the commodity money. According to the Marxian labour theory of value, the proportion at which a commodity can be exchanged for money ultimately depends on the ratio between the labour time embodied in one unit of the commodity and the labour time embodied in one unit of the commodity money.

According to Marx's theory, therefore, in monetary systems where only commodity money is used, changes in the needs of the circulation of commodities have to lead to changes in hoarding money. These, however, actually change the velocity of circulation of available money and are in stark contrast to the quantity theory of money which, not by chance, assumes the possession of idle cash to be irrational and pathological. As we will see in more detail in Chapter 6, hoarding money, on the contrary, is central in Marx's theory of crises.

In monetary systems characterised by the exclusive use of token money, the needs of circulation could adapt to the quantity of money exogenously established by the issuing banks through changes in average money prices, in accordance with the quantity theory hypothesis, if and only if the velocity of circulation of money were constant. Yet once again this would imply that changes in cash reserves are in no way conceivable. Thus, changes in the quantity of money, according to Marx's theory, have in itself no systematic effect on the value of money (see Foley, 1986, p. 25).

In any case, in real economies in which credit money complements both commodity money and token money, the problem of adapting the means of payment to the needs of the circulation of commodities actually becomes an issue of credit adjustments.

However, credits and debts generated by commercial credit largely balance each other out. Thus, commercial credit actually creates currency when its notes, in turn, serve as a means of circulation and a means of payment (see Hilferding, 1910/1981, p. 83). Yet, this presupposes a fiduciary relation between all the private participants in the commercial circuit. Private credit money, indeed, in contrast to legal tender, is not guaranteed by the state, but by private agents only (see Hilferding, 1910/1981, p. 62).

It is precisely for this reason that bank credit has tended to progressively replace private bills of exchange in the circulation of commodities, thanks to the greater trust generated in people by the banks' liabilities. The banknote is nothing more than a banker's bill of exchange which is accepted with greater trust than other bills of exchange. However, banknotes and bank deposits are ultimately secured by private claims. Therefore, the supply of banknotes and bank deposits are bounded above by the number of private promises of future payments which, in turn, depend on mere expectations of future cash flows (see Hilferding, 1910/1981, pp. 84–85).

However, according to Marx and Hilferding, *capital credit* – also called *production credit*, due to the fact that it is channelled into financing new investments – is a completely different thing. It is the transformation of temporarily idle cash holdings into interest-bearing capital. While commercial and bank credit – as *circulation credit* – are determined by the needs of the circulation of commodities – and thus adjust to the demand for it – capital credit, as a mere transfer of purchasing power from one economic agent to another, is limited from above by the cash surpluses generated in the process of circulation of capital. In modern terms, capital credit turns out to be constrained on the supply side. Since money capital is "seeking investment" by its very nature (see Marx, 1885/1992, pp. 363 and 367), it is idle money capital amounts that play the leading active role in determining the overall volume of credit on the supply side.

Of course, in an economy with a developed credit system, intermediated by a banking sector that, according to Marx (1894/1991, pp. 594–606), adds *banking capital* – consisting of its customers' deposits and banknotes – to its own *invested capital*, any new investment demand that is not accompanied by any additional saving can be met by bank loans that temporarily exceed *ex-ante* saving decisions. In this case, the new investment demand will eventually be financed by credit money, created, directly or indirectly, through IOUs on future profit. Thus, supply side constraints on previously accumulated capital money cannot be considered as definitively limiting future capital accumulation.

According to Schumpeter (1923/1939, p. 111), in a market economy, granting entrepreneurs additional means of payment created *ad hoc* by the banks – i.e. bank credit for new investment – is equivalent to the command by the central authority in a centrally planned economy. Indeed, if this type of central authority, which controls all productive sectors, wanted to make new investment, all it would have to do is order the managers of the capital goods sectors to give a part of their current product to the sectors that have to make new productive investments. In market economies, however, due to the fact that the new means of production are privately owned and have to be purchased in the respective markets, the command has to be substituted by the creation by the banks of new means of payment based on the banks' reputation itself. The bank's liabilities have, in turn, to be secured by correct expectations about the future ability of borrowing entrepreneurs to produce and realise sufficient value to repay debts and interest. This means that the banks, with their own *invested capital*, act as guarantors of the entrepreneurs' expected future income, facilitating an intertemporal exchange between current capital goods and future income.

The intertemporal social budget constraint the banks should guarantee, however, is usually temporarily violated in the upward phases of the business cycle in contexts that sees excessive expectations taking shape, but only by creating at the same time the conditions for violent readjustment processes consisting of crises.

Moreover, if savers are owners of interest-bearing capital and the lack of saving is consequent to the decision to spend part of the interest on their money capital on luxury goods, then, without any excess of production capacity, the total demand for goods and means of production will exceed supply. Consequently, according to Wicksell (1906/1978, pp. 159–208), excessive bank lending will produce inflation and forced saving. And the financial sector is always in the forefront in calling for decisive action against inflation, because unpredictable high inflation can cause decrease in the real value of financial assets. In fact, while well-informed speculators respond favourably to the volatility they can exploit, the financial sector overall is much more comfortable with macroeconomic stability, and, from this viewpoint, there is no difference in interests between finance and the big non-financial firms.

This approach gives due recognition to an intertemporal macroeconomic constraint, in sharp contrast to the idea of *ex-novo* generation of credit by the banks which characterises the modern money circuit theories. The intertemporal budget constraint that emerges from this relation is an attractor that can be temporarily violated, but only by accumulating tension and triggering more or less violent readjustment dynamics – i.e. monetary or financial crises.

However, according to Marx and Hilferding, capital credit represents first and foremost the transformation of idle money into active money capital – i.e. financing of productive investment. In social contexts that see other property owning classes alongside the capitalists, part of this hoarded money will consist of their saving funds. Yet the largest part will be represented by depreciation funds and other forms of cash reserves necessary for the circuit of capital (see Hilferding, 1910/1981, p. 90) and, as we will see in more detail in Chapter 6, today most private savings are made and managed directly by NFCs.

According to Marx and Hilferding, the circuit of capital is simply the movement of capital value through a series of physical metamorphoses that take place over a finite span of time – i.e. the *rotation period* – consisting of a proper production period and two circulation periods – an initial one, corresponding to the time required to purchase the means of production and labour-power, and a final one, corresponding to the sale of commodities. In the cyclical reproduction of this circuit, money capital is the necessary stage between the realisation of the exchange value of commodities and the reinvestment of depreciation funds and surplus for a new turnover on the same or a larger scale. As such, money capital must be considered a flow. However, it can also be considered a stock insofar as we measure it as the total amount of capital existing in money form at a given time.

Thus, the money capital that is released at the end of the turnover period, as the result of the realisation of the exchange value of commodities, may have to remain idle, in the form of cash holdings, for a number of reasons. The first is the excess of the circulation period over the production period. This makes the availability of liquid funds necessary in order to start a new production cycle before having recovered the capital invested in the previous cycle (see Marx, 1885/1992, pp. 351–355; Hilferding, 1910/1981, pp. 71–72). The second cause is the need for a fund for wages and other forms of working capital. The third is the need for sinking funds to replace fixed capital after a certain number of turnovers. The fourth, in the case of self-financing, is the need to achieve a critical mass of money capital for new investments. With the development of large-scale industry, moreover, the last two reasons tend to increase the need for liquidity over time, due to the progressive growth of both the mass of and the time required to implement fixed assets.

Changes in average corporate liquidity, however, are due to changes in the turnover time of capital which, in turn, are induced by changes in technology, scale of production, length of the working day and also in the organic composition of capital (see Marx, 1885/1992, pp. 388–393).

However, "since profit originates in production and is only realised in circulation, there is a never-ending search for ways and means of converting the greatest possible amount of capital into production capital" (Hilferding, 1910/1981, p. 77). Thus, cash holding is generally only a necessary evil for companies and should theoretically be minimised or, if possible, eliminated completely.

Money capital periodically released in the turnover of any individual capital, as a result of the realisation of the exchange value of commodities, can function as money capital in the turnover of another capital thanks to the credit system (see Hilferding, 1910/1981, pp. 79–80). Yet, however, it is also possible to reduce cash holdings by resorting to credit. Thus, as money to all intents and purposes, idle money capital of some capitalists can enter into credit relations, transforming itself into *production credit*, i.e. money capital that is lent to other capitalists to the extent that the latter can secure the loan through the future profits they can obtain from the advanced money capital (see Hilferding, 1910/1981, p. 69). It is idle money capital lent to a *functioning capitalist* who is able to transform it into *productive capital* – i.e. into a source of new surplus value.

Moreover, all the changes in the need for cash holdings exert an immediate effect on supply and demand in the money markets (see Hilferding, 1910/1981, pp. 75–81). In particular, any reduction in the period of turnover of capital generates excess cash, which increases the supply of liquid funds to the money market.

In bank-oriented financial systems, the transfer of idle liquid funds from one company to another is usually intermediated by banks. Idle money capital, as bank deposits, is therefore transformed into *banking capital* (see Marx, 1894/1991, p. 531).

However, in market-oriented financial systems, this transfer can be intermediated by the capital markets and financial institutions operating in them. This, of course, appears as an increasing financialisation of some NFCs.

Fictitious capital and the promoter's profit

The progressive transformation of money capital into capital credit leads, through the creation of the joint-stock company, to a qualitative reversal of the relationship between money capital itself and productive capital. The productive capital invested in a corporation becomes pure money capital for its legal owners, i.e. shareholders (see Hilferding, 1910/1981, p. 107). This means that the money capital invested in industrial corporations works out for its owners like interest-bearing capital.

The form of interest-bearing capital assumed by equity capital likens dividends to the interest paid on a loan of equal value. However, because the rate of profit is larger than the interest rate, capitalisation of expected future profits is larger than the exchange value of the capital goods of the corporation. This larger value is exactly what Marx and Hilferding called *fictitious capital.*

This value was called *fictitious* since it is completely independent of the exchange value of productive capital which produces profits (see Marx, 1894/1991, pp. 525–542; Hilferding, 1910/1981, pp. 113–122). Once a share is issued, it has nothing more to do with the life cycle of the productive capital it represents and, vice versa, the vicissitudes of the shares in capital markets have no influence on the rotation of the productive capital they represent.

Fictitious capital is therefore nothing but the present value of the future surplus value that the shareholder will able to appropriate over time due to his claim on the profit deriving from a given productive capital. However, in capitalist societies, this claim is actually exchangeable on the stock exchange for money and other claims, and takes on an autonomous existence, standing alongside the productive capital on which it ultimately depends. However, this claim is nothing more than the price of the bear's skin before one has killed the beast, with the risk that in the meantime it is the "Bear" that will bankrupt the shareholder! Indeed, it only takes one overnight change in business expectations for the fictitious capital to contract or even dissolve instantaneously.

Fictitious capital, nevertheless, unlike productive capital, is a very liquid asset. It can be quickly exchanged for money in the stock market. This gives it a status which is quite similar to that of money capital itself.

Thus, due to competition between money capital owners, the rate of return on equity will tend to be equal to the average interest rate plus an average risk premium. Under free competition between money capitalists, indeed, this value is the attractor around which the ratio between dividends and share value has to gravitate.

Thus, due to the emergence of the organisational form of the joint-stock company, the capital owned by most of the shareholders does not expect to receive the average rate of profit at all, but is content with a little more than the average rate of interest. This implies that the average *rate of entrepreneurial profit* – accounted for as the ratio between corporate profits net of dividends, on the one hand, and capital owned by the controlling group on the other – is much higher than it would be if all the capital were owned directly by the controlling group. However, the resulting increase in entrepreneurial profit can only be retained by the controlling group as increased corporate savings, which, when reinvested, will, in turn, generate capital gains for shareholders.

Hilferding called *promoter's profit* the balance between the share capital of a corporation and the exchange value of capital goods actually invested in it. This profit arises from the mere transformation of industrial capital into stock capital – i.e. a special form of money capital. However, it can be immediately appropriated by the primary issuer of the shares, which, in the context of the *hausbank system* prevailing in Germany in Hilferding's time, was generally a large investment bank. The banks, indeed, anticipated the funds for industrial capital of the joint-stock companies in which they were the major shareholders and then refinanced themselves by issuing the shares on the stock exchange, making profit on the difference between the fictitious capital and the exchange value of the industrial capital actually invested in the firms.

During the life of a joint-stock company, the difference between the value embedded in its productive capital and its share capital can continually vary independently of changes in the company's profit and solely as a function of changes in the average interest rate. The same multiplier effect that inflates the value of fictitious capital relative to that of productive capital also makes share prices much more volatile than the underlying fundamentals, although the former ultimately depend on the latter.

However, the expansion of fictitious capital in the capitalist economies, as a result of the expansion of joint-stock companies and their growth, also generates effects on the demand for money. Financial trading, in fact, generates demand for money for financial transactions which is in addition to that deriving from the needs of the circulation of commodities (see Hilferding, 1910/1981, p. 113). Moreover, financial trading also enhances speculative demand for money which equals hoarding in creating lacks of effective demand.

The demand for money for financial transactions increases with the volume of fictitious capital, albeit to a less than proportional extent, due to the marketability of the securities themselves – i.e. their degree of liquidity – and the possibility of direct compensation between them in the course of financial transactions. However, the credit money that may satisfy this increasing demand for money for financial transactions is no longer backed by the value of commodities, as in the case of commercial credit. It is only secured by the value of shares – i.e. the value of the fictitious capital resulting from the capitalisation of expected future profits. This implies, on the one hand, a higher degree of uncertainty of the credit guarantee – due to the high volatility of the value of fictitious capital – and, on the other hand, the fact that the credit money for financial transactions is in fact a new form of capital credit – i.e. credit for financial investment – based on betting on future contingencies.

However, as far as capital credit is fuelled by idle money capital, credit for financial investments is both an indirect way of channelling this capital into financial uses and a new way of keeping it, at an aggregate level, in liquid form.

Shadow banking and capitalist production

The progressive rise of market-oriented financial intermediation since the mid-1980s has profoundly changed some traditional aspects of the credit system in many advanced countries. The most significant result of this evolution, particularly in market-oriented Anglo-Saxon financial systems, has been the rise of the so-called "shadow banking system", which has been playing an increasingly crucial role in the credit system since the early 2000s (see Pozsar, 2008, 2018; Adrian and Shin, 2009; Acharya et al., 2010; Gorton and Metrick, 2010, 2012; Stein, 2010; Gennaioli et al., 2013; Nijs, 2020).

The term "shadow banking" was first coined by McCulley (2007) to refer to the business of all financial intermediaries that carry out typical banking operations – such as maturity, credit and liquidity transformation – and rival traditional deposit banks, but do not have direct access to central bank money supply or public sector credit guarantees and, above all, are not subject to any banking supervision (see Adrian and Ashcraft, 2016). This type of financial intermediation, therefore, is very vulnerable to crises of confidence which can produce phenomena analogous to the runs that affected traditional banks in their early days before the introduction of legal deposit insurance systems and strict banking supervision (see Stein, 2010).

Thus, "shadow banks" are nothing but specialised financial intermediaries such as money market mutual funds, credit hedge funds, structured investment vehicles (SIVs), asset-backed commercial paper (ABCP) conduits, securities lenders, limited-purpose finance companies (LPFCs), and also, in the United States, the government-sponsored enterprises (GSEs) which convert risky, long-term assets into short-term, money-like liabilities. In this way they usually provide "short-term safe debt" to both financial and non-financial corporations which need to invest their large cash holdings in short-term and liquid form (see Pozsar et al., 2010).

Thus, shadow banks, like traditional deposit banks, are nothing more than institutions that transform idle money capital into short-term, liquid interest-bearing capital, albeit through innovative financial instruments.

The "shadow banking system" is the network of all such specialised financial institutions interconnected along complex chains of intermediation, in turn, implemented through a wide range of securitisation and secured funding techniques, such as ABCP, asset-backed securities (ABS), collateralised debt obligations (CDO) and repurchase agreements (see Pozsar, 2008; Pozsar et al., 2010).

The development of all such innovative financial instruments has its roots in the rising interest rates of the late 1970s and 1980s, due to which the deposit banks faced increasing competition from interest-bearing services offered by some non-bank financial institutions, such as money market mutual funds. At that time, deposit banks were also prohibited from providing services such as insurance and securities underwriting by a strict banking legislation that was the legacy of the financial distress of the 1930s. All this contributed to weakening their capability to compete with new financial intermediaries. The banks, therefore, looked for a way to finance themselves with cheaper liabilities than bank deposits and found it in the securitisation of their loans. The banks sold securities backed by their loans to other financial investors through subsidiaries called Special Purpose Vehicles (SPVs) – which usually do not appear on the balance sheet of the parent company – to which they had previously transferred their non-marketable assets and associated risks in exchange for cash (see Pozsar, 2008; Pozsar et al., 2010).

Securitisation was such a successful innovation that it quickly spread to other non-bank institutions such as large NFCs that offered consumer credit to their customers. Finally, with the development of further techniques to reduce the risk of securities, it became the core business of some specialised financial intermediaries.

Short-term debt securities provided by shadow banks, however, were only considered "safe" due to sophisticated insurance techniques against idiosyncratic risk which in 2007–2008 proved to be completely incapable of coping with systemic risk (see Gennaioli et al., 2013).

The shadow banking system, therefore, became notorious in the late 2000s for its shameful role in creating the main conditions for the subprime mortgage crisis of 2007 – i.e. cheap credit and lax lending standards that fuelled a housing bubble and were dramatically vulnerable to a moderate interest rate increase by the FED. The financial crisis of 2007–2008 itself was eventually considered by some analysts to be nothing more than a "run on shadow banking", triggering a broad debate on possible ways to effectively regulate the new sector (see Roubini, 2008; Haltom, 2010; Stein, 2010; Gorton and Metrick, 2012).

However, shadow banking remains a vital component of today's financial system, with no more regulation than before the crisis of 2007–2008, but perhaps just more caution taken by the players themselves.

In any case, securitisation and secured funding techniques are simply new ways of creating fictitious capital. Securitisation is in fact the practice of pooling various types of non-marketable contractual debt and selling to third-party financial investors – i.e. money capital owners seeking short-term financial investment – securities backed by the cash flows associated with the pool of original debts. These securities, however, are only backed by expectations on the payments of the collateral debt which may prove unfounded at any time. Nevertheless, such securities assume an autonomous existence alongside the original debt, although they remain dependent on the successful performance of all payments relating to it. These securities are in fact immediately exchangeable on the financial and over-the-counter markets for cash and other claims, and can also be pooled again to serve as collateral for further securities. This produces not a simple duplication – as in the case of share capital standing alongside productive capital – but a potentially endless multiplication. This is, in a nutshell, the basic mechanism that produced what, immediately after the outbreak of the subprime mortgage crisis in 2007, was termed "junk bonds" – i.e. securities for which it was suddenly impossible to formulate rational expectations about their future cash flows and whose present value vanished instantly.

When credit money, whatever its form, sees its fiduciary value disappear, a vacuum is also created in the circulation of commodities and "the *horror vacui* requires that it be filled at all costs" (Hilferding, 1910/1981, p. 66). "When this happens it is a perfectly rational policy to expand the circulation of state paper money or the bank notes of the central bank, the credit of which has not been impaired" (Hilferding, 1910/1981, p. 66). In fact, this was the inevitable conclusion of the "run on shadow banking" in 2007–2008 too, with the pressing need for huge injections of legal money by states and central banks in order to counter the crisis.

However, according to Marx, it is precisely with the development of interest-bearing capital and the credit system that "all capital seems to be duplicated, and at some points triplicated, by the various ways in which the same capital, or even the same claim, appears in various hands in different guises" (Marx, 1894/1991, p. 601). From Marx's viewpoint, therefore, the shadow banking system does not seem to represent anything really new under the sky of the capitalist mode of production.

Shadow banking is only the supreme manifestation of the fact that credit money can be created as securities backed by securities, from which a monetary and financial crisis can suddenly arise at any time with devastating effects, producing a global recession. The credit chain may, in fact, abruptly collapse at any time, turning into a chain of bankruptcies if payment on the due date is not made in any of its links.

Thus, in the shadow banking system there is nothing fundamentally different from what has always characterised the supply of credit money, except for a rising illusion that credit risk could be eliminated through the ingenuity of new financial architectures.

The real novelty of this additional credit system is that for a long time it mainly served to fuel consumer credit, supporting private demand in the face of falling wages and increasing job insecurity, which, in turn, were the consequences of the increased class conflict between capitalists and workers aimed at improving the profitability of capital.

Moreover, from the early 2000s onwards, the idle money capital mobilised through this new credit channels came, directly or indirectly, mainly from the NFCs, which, as we will see in more detail in Chapter 6, had started to turn into net lenders and short-term financial investors.

Notes

1 This means we abstract "from all aspects that have nothing to do with the change and constitution of the forms as such" (Marx, 1885/1992, p. 109) and assume for the sake of simplicity that commodities are sold at their values (embodied labour), ignoring any changes of prices that may occur in the course of the cyclical process, also because of implementation of a uniform rate of profit.

2 The main initial instruments of *circulation credit*, from a historical point of view, are bills of exchange which are added to commodity money as credit money.

References

Acharya, V., Schnabl, P. and Suarez, G. (2010). "Securitisation without Risk Transfer". *NBER Working Paper*, 15730.

Adrian, T. and Ashcraft, A. B. (2016). "Shadow Banking: A Review of the Literature". In: Jones, G. (ed.), *Banking Crises. Perspectives from The New Palgrave Dictionary*. Basingstoke: Palgrave Macmillan, pp. 282–315.

Adrian, T. and Shin, H. S. (2009). "The Shadow Banking System: Implications for Financial Regulation". *Banque de France Financial Stability Review*, 13: 1–10.

Foley, D. K. (1986). *Understanding Capital. Marx's Economic Theory*. Cambridge, MA and London: Harvard University Press.

Gennaioli, N., Shleifer, A. and Vishny, R. (2013). "A Model of Shadow Banking". *Journal of Finance*, 68 (4): 1331–63.

Gorton, G. and Metrick, A. (2010). "Regulating the Shadow Banking System". *Brookings Paper on Economic Activity*, Fall: 261–312.

Gorton, G. and Metrick, A. (2012). "Securitised Banking and the Run on Repo". *Journal of Financial Economics*, 104 (3): 425–51.

Haltom, R. C. (2010). "Out from the Shadows. The Run on Shadow Banking and a Framework for Reform". *Region Focus*, 2010: Q3 : 22–25.

Hilferding, R. (1910/1981). *Finance Capital. A Study of the Latest Phase of Capitalist Development*. London: Routledge.

Mandel, E. (1990). "Introduction by Ernest Mandel". In: Marx, K., *Capital*. Volume I. London: Penguin Books, pp. 11–86.

Marx, K. (1885/1992). *Capital*. Volume II. London: Penguin Books.

Marx, K. (1894/1991). *Capital*. Volume III. London: Penguin Books.

McCulley, P. (2007). "Teton Reflections". *PIMCO Global Central Bank Focus*.

Nijs, L. (2020). *The Handbook of Global Shadow Banking. Volume I. From Policy to Regulation*. Basingstoke: Palgrave Macmillan.

Pozsar, Z. (2008). "The Rise and Fall of the Shadow Banking System". *Regional Financial Review*, July 2008: 13–25.

Pozsar, Z. (2018). "Shadow Banking: A View from the USA". In: Nesvetailova, A. (ed.), *Shadow Banking. Scope, Origins and Theories*. London and New York: Routledge, pp. 19–24.

Pozsar, Z., Adrian, T., Ashcraft, A. and Boesky, H. (2010). "Shadow Banking". *Federal Reserve Bank of New York Staff Report*, 458.

Roubini, N. (2008). "The Shadow Banking System Is Unravelling". *Financial Times*, September 21.

Schumpeter, J. A. (1923/1939). *Business Cycle. A Theoretical, Historical and Statistical Analysis of the Capitalist Process*. New York and London: McGraw-Hill.

Stein, J. 2010. "Securitisation, Shadow Banking, and Financial Fragility". *Daedalus*, 139 (4): 41–51.

Wicksell, K. (1906/1978). *Lectures on Political Economy. Volume Two. Money*. Fairfield, CT: Augustus M. Kelley Publishers.

5 Financial rentiers and the revenant conflict between rent and profit

The conflict between rent and profit in classical political economy

As was effectively brought to light by Sraffa and his pupils' works, the English classical economists' approach to political economy was "founded on the notion of the surplus of which the community can dispose out of its production beyond what is physically necessary for reproduction, i.e. the replacement of the means of production and the subsistence of workers" (Garegnani, 2018, p. 618). This classical approach also provided the analytical starting point for Marx's successive "critique of political economy".

The determination of the share of the product other than wages as "surplus" – i.e. a residuum – is logically based on the possibility of determining social product and the real wage prior to this share (see Garegnani, 1984). This, of course, leads back to issues related to the classical economists' theory of value as opposed to the later marginalist one. However, in short, taking the social product as given, the quantity of the social product retained by the workers was fixed, according to Ricardo, as well as Quesnay and the Physiocrats before him, by their "subsistence" level, determined by historical and social conditions. The surplus, then, jointly constitutes the income of capitalists and landowners – i.e. the owners of the means of production – in the form of profits on capital and land rents, respectively. Finally, by defining the proper laws of rent determination, profit could, in turn, be inferred as the ultimate residuum.

In classical political economy, moreover, capital accumulation is determined by the use of the social surplus. This use, however, in turn, depends on the surplus distribution among the different social classes that own the means of production. In fact, in Ricardo's opinion, while capitalists usually reinvest the greater part of their income, favouring the growth of production capacity of the economic system, landlords tend to consume their income in luxuries. Consequently, Ricardo was explicitly in favour of a portion as near as possible to the capitalists rather than to the landlords, in order to favour the growth of the nations' social welfare.

Thus, in the classical approach, growth theory was closely connected both to the evolution of the social surplus over time and with its distribution among

DOI: 10.4324/9781003223221-6

the profits and rents – i.e. the distribution of the social surplus between the different social classes and their inner fractions.

Ricardo, following West and Malthus, explained the existence of rent on the basis of the differences in soil fertility alone – i.e. exclusively as *differential rent*. He did not explicitly link rent to private landed property and "the monopoly of disposing of particular portions of the globe as exclusive spheres of their private will to the exclusion of all others", as did Marx (1894/1991, p. 752) after him when he talked about *absolute rent*.

On the basis of his view of rent, however, Ricardo held that the growth of production, driven by capital accumulation itself, tended to increase the share of land rents within the surplus due to the dynamics of diminishing returns in an agriculture increasingly forced to spread on marginal land. This increasing absorption of surplus by rent, utilised by landowners only in their luxury consumption, implied, in turn, that capital accumulation and economic growth, without adequate technical progress in agriculture, would inexorably tend to slow down and finally come to a halt. In this respect, Ricardo was among the first to argue that economic growth must sooner or later come to a halt because of the scarcity of natural resources (see Blaug, 1985).

However, as far as the issues we are dealing with are concerned, Ricardo's theory clearly shows the vision of a structural conflict between rent and profit in the sharing of the social surplus that may lead to a halt of capital accumulation on the supply side due to a reduction of the funds available for new productive investments.

Malthus, on the contrary, believed that an adequate level of effective demand, able to counteract the underconsumption tendencies of the capitalist economy, was only possible, thanks to the existence of a stratum of "unproductive consumers" who buy goods without producing them (see Pullen, 2008). These unproductive consumers, according to him, mainly included service providers – such as civil servants, military personnel and clergymen – but could also include landowners and people who make a living from investing their savings in the public debt – i.e. the idle rich.

Indeed, Malthus was among the first to highlight the "realisation problem" of product value as opposed to the classical problem of adequate funds for capital accumulation, inaugurating, together with Sismondi, the theoretical strand of "underconsumption". He found the main solution to the "realisation problem" in the improvement of "unproductive consumption" – no matter whether generated by the state, the church or by the idle rich.

However, this anticipatory concern of his for the problems of effective demand was largely ignored for more than a century by most other classical economists who argued that the purchasing power generated in the production process would be sufficient for all products to be sold, according to the so-called *Say's Law* or *Mill's Principle*. It was only with the experience of the Great Depression of the 1930s that Keynes was able to challenge this widespread belief and recover Malthus' view of the merits of social classes and other agents – such as the state – who do not encourage saving and support large private and public unproductive consumption (see Pullen, 2008).

Many Ricardian authors, in particular, criticised Malthus' view and contested, from a capitalist point of view, the supposed positive function of unproductive consumers in general and landlords in particular. The derision of Malthus' thesis by an anonymous Ricardian economist, quoted by Marx in his *Surplus Theories*, was that, if the problem is to sell goods in order to make a profit, "it never can answer to part with that amount of money for nothing, to another person, that he may bring it back to you, and buy your goods with it" (Marx, 1861–1863/1989, p. 251).

This ironic paraphrase of Malthus' thinking conveys well the mood of capitalists at that time who viewed land rent and taxes as an illicit appropriation of a share of the surplus that should be theirs alone. It is no coincidence that Marx regarded this dispute between Ricardian and Malthusian views as an ideological conflict between the representatives of the interests of capitalists and the representatives of the interests of landowners. According to Marx, in fact, "a portion of the surplus-value that capital produces falls to the share of the landowner" (Marx, 1894/1991, p. 751). Therefore, the conflict between the two classes is self-evident.

However, already during this debate, the possible analogy between land rent and interest on capital came to the fore. As was highlighted by Marx, the interest paid by the borrower of the money capital is just like the ground rent that the capitalist pays to the landowner. Both are only contractually fixed sums of money to acquire the right to use some means of production (see Marx, 1894/1991, p. 755).

Some authors, either as representatives of the interests of landed property against the attacks of the economists representing the interests of capitalists, or as promoters of a more general harmony between the owners of the means of production, tended to equate land rent and interest and aimed to dilute the antagonism between landowners and capitalists. Just as in the early days of capitalism, when land ownership was the main form of ownership of the means of production, bourgeois economists such as North, Locke and Turgot presented interest on capital as being analogous to land rent in order to avoid charges of usury (see Marx, 1894/1991, pp. 759–760).

Land rent, however, shows formal similarity with interest in another way, too. It presents itself as "a certain sum of money that the landowner draws each year from leasing out a piece of the earth" (Marx, 1894/1991, p. 760). Hence, due to the fact that any particular monetary income can be capitalised, it "can be considered as the interest on an imaginary capital" (Marx, 1894/1991, p. 760) and, in capitalist economies, it is precisely the capitalisation of land rent that determines the purchase price of land and transforms land ownership into an equivalent of capital ownership. However, the capitalisation of expected future cash flows is precisely what determines the wealth of shareholders and bondholders too, just as it is capitalisation that determines, as we have seen, "fictitious capital" in financialised economies.

However, as Marx pointed out, to regard land rent as a form of interest on land capital is to ignore the real social nature of the former and "cannot but lead to the most peculiar and incorrect conclusions" (Marx, 1894/1991, p. 761). Nevertheless, interest, like rent, is in conflict with the profit of enterprise because, as we have seen in the previous chapter, there is a permanent dispute between the owners of money capital and the owners of real capital in the appropriation of the surplus that will be produced through the latter.

What is argued about interest can of course be extended to "financial rent" more generally. In Chapter 3, we defined "financial rent" as the income of "financial rentiers", composed of interest, dividends and capital gains. Of course, in accordance with the view of classical economists, interest and dividends are parts of profit by definition. Yet, capital gains too, if they are realised, absorb savings of other economic agents or part of the industrial profit of issuing corporations and are to be considered shares of social surplus.

Financial rent, however, is not the income of a particular social class in the Marxist sense – as in the case of land rent. It is the income of a subgroup of the capitalist class that can only take on certain psychological and behavioural aspects of the old landed aristocracy. Bond coupons and distributed profits are certainly – like land rent – a share of the social surplus taken away from the corporate profit. But they can only be effectively removed from the accumulation process if they are not transformed into new interest-bearing capital – i.e. only if they are completely consumed in luxury consumption. In this case, however, they can support effective demand, thus effectively reducing the extent of the "realisation problem".

Financial rent and accumulation of capital

What is therefore the possible role of "financial rentiers" in the process of capital accumulation? Does their peculiar social psychology – well described by Bukharin – have an effect on the tendency towards stagnation that has characterised Western economies in recent decades, as some literature on financialisation assumes?

Indeed, as we have seen in Chapter 3, those who today can be defined as financial rentiers largely consist of the clients of pension and mutual funds, edge funds and other institutional investors – i.e. the "shadow investment banking system". Thus, if these agents were to behave like landlords, consuming all their income in luxuries, then, according to the classical economists' analysis of the conflict between profit and land rent, we could say that the higher their income would be, the smaller the share of social surplus devoted to investment. However, according to Malthus, they could be supporters of effective demand which was so dear to Keynesian economists.

Keynes, however, held that "the effect of the transfer from entrepreneurs to rentiers is more open to doubt" (Keynes, 1936/2013, p. 262). Nevertheless, he thought that:

> if rentiers represent on the whole the richer section of the community and those whose standard of life is least flexible, then the effect of this also will be unfavourable. What the net result will be on a balance of considerations, we can only guess. Probably it is more likely to be adverse than favourable.
>
> (Keynes, 1936/2013, p. 262)

Keynes' doubts were probably mainly influenced by the priority he gave to the demand side over the supply side in his analysis. Keynes, in fact, held that the rentier was less prone to spend than the entrepreneur (see Keynes, 1936/2013, p. 290), because he probably considered the rentier to be a high-income consumer with a low marginal propensity to consume.

The propensity to consume, nevertheless, is only an empirical psychological concept which has no theoretical foundations outside the marginalist theory of decreasing marginal utility. Actually, it bears the hallmark of the historical experience of the increasing thrift of the capitalist class in the early times of capitalist development. However, the very thrift of the early capitalist class was nothing more than a result of free competition, which spurred capitalists to reinvest surplus value in order to accumulate capital and gain advantages, through increasing economies of scale, over their competitors, while historical experience shows that there was no limit to the luxury spending of the aristocracy in the *ancién regime*.

Thus, with this being the case, a change in the psychology of surplus takers – transformed into financial rentiers – may increase their marginal propensity to consume, weakening Keynes' qualms.

As we have seen in Chapter 3, Bukharin believed that the new rentier class was parasitical by its very nature and ruled by a peculiar "psychology of pure consumption" which arose directly from its "social being".

This psychology influences even their scientific thought – i.e. "the points of view from which reality is viewed and later logically manipulated" (Bukharin, 1927, p. 25). Indeed, Bukharin argued that marginalism itself embraced the psychology of rentiers when it first highlighted the point of view of consumption. Just as mercantilism, which arose in the golden age of commercial capital, was characterised by considering all economic phenomena from the point of view of exchange, and classical political economy, which arose at a time when capital had become the organiser of production, essentially considered economic problems from the point of view of production, so marginalism, which arose in the period of social affirmation of the rentier, found its main task in solving the consumer problem.

From this point of view, we could say that the intertemporal choice model, which is the foundation of modern financial economics, offers the way to describe financial decisions from the standpoint of financial rentiers. But we could, conversely, also say that financial economics models are a fair way to describe the psychology and subsequent behaviour of financial rentiers.

In any case, in accordance with Marx's reproduction schemes, if "consuming rentiers" are concerned only with their own luxuries and tend to consume all their income just as the landlords once did, the larger their share of the social surplus, the closer the economic system must come to conditions of simple reproduction, in which, by definition, surplus value is entirely converted into consumption by the capitalist class. If it were possible to stretch this situation to its absolute limit – i.e. if all surplus takers were rentiers and all the social surplus was consumed in luxury goods – then the economic system would be precisely under the conditions of simple reproduction, according to the Marxian definition.

Under simple reproduction conditions, with the proviso that the correct proportions between the capital goods sector and the consumer goods sector be respected, effective demand problems should not arise (see Kalecki, 1967/1971, pp. 148–150). Nevertheless, under the competitive conditions of the capitalist mode of production in general, and especially under the competitive conditions of monopoly capitalism, these corrected proportions are by no means guaranteed.

However, as long as even a small portion of social surplus is diverted from consumption – i.e. is saved – there is no guarantee of avoiding the "realisation problem" or lack of effective demand. After all, during most of the 19th and 20th centuries, even though in advanced countries a large part of growing profits enhanced real capital accumulation, much of the rest still went into the luxuries of the non-working classes. This way of utilising the surplus still proved an inadequate way to maintain full employment and full utilisation of productive capacity.

Thus, only the total consumption of social surplus can theoretically avoid the "realisation problem" by guaranteeing the conditions of simple reproduction. However, this would also imply a halt in capital accumulation. In point of fact, simple reproduction is a stationary state like that predicted by the classical economists as a consequence of the erosion of profit by land rent. Nevertheless, under monopolistic competition, a continuous, albeit attenuated, incentive to increase labour productivity in order to expand the rate of exploitation always remains and increasing labour productivity in stationary economic systems creates serious problems with regard to full employment and securing a subsistence income for workers, unless the exceeding workforce finds employment as servants of the owning classes.

Indeed, under simple reproduction conditions, not even exogenous stimuluses to growth are possible. Government spending financed in a balanced budget would only transform private consumption into collective consumption. No Keynesian deficit-financed government demand could promote growth because the propensity to consume would equal one and the Keynesian multiplier – in a closed economy – would lose all mathematical meaning so that the level of the national product could no longer be determined on the demand side. The same would be true in an open economy because imports would be strictly determined by exports and could not be an increasing function of income. Thus, no marginal propensity to import could play any role in the Keynesian multiplier, but, above all, if the correct proportions between the capital goods sector and the consumer goods sector were respected, there would be no production of new capital goods to support growth.

However, even if we disregard extreme and paradoxical situations, the scarcity of savings, which could result from massive consumption of social surplus in luxury goods, would induce, in the absence of expansionary monetary policies, a credit crunch and a dramatic rise in interest rates, which, in turn, would weaken the financial sustainability of public debt. This effect could be mitigated only if the interest rate influenced the intertemporal choices and savings of rentiers, as assumed by mainstream economists but denied by Keynesian economists. Or, from a more genuine Keynesian viewpoint, it could be countered only by expansionary monetary policies. In this case, however, the end result would be pure debt monetisation, which, especially in conditions of monopolistic competition, could lead to predominantly inflationary effects or balance of payments deficits, generating stagflation or monetary turbulence.

The only solution could be a state intervention that withdraws a portion of the social surplus, taxing financial rents, and transforms it directly into new productive investments to absorb the excess workforce – implementing a sort of "forced saving" within society – or, alternatively, uses it as subsidies for the unemployed – fostering a more equitable distribution of income.

Nevertheless, even Keynes guessed that a community equipped with modern technical resources, and whose population was not increasing rapidly, would attain "the conditions of a quasi-stationary community" within a single generation, but only because of its ability "to bring down the marginal efficiency of capital in equilibrium approximately to zero", and producing thereby "the euthanasia of the rentier" (Keynes, 1936/2013, pp. 220–221). Once again, the logical conclusion reached by Keynes depends strictly on his hypothesis of a parametric marginal propensity to save which increases as income rises. In fact, in order to guarantee conditions of full employment, as income and the marginal propensity to save increase, investments must grow at a rate equal to that of savings. This is only possible if the interest rate gradually decreases until it reaches zero, thanks to the open market operations carried out by the central banks.

Of course, the rentier Keynes thought of – who may be destined to disappear due to the zero risk-free interest rate – is the one who lives on bond coupons and not on distributed profits and capital gains on shares. However, if distributed profits may well be governed by interest rates since they compete directly with interest, capital gains on shares are ultimately determined by the average rate of profit and will not disappear as long as the economy is capitalist.

In any case, an empirical test of these two opposing hypotheses on rentiers' behaviour could lie in analysing the trend of the ratio of wealth effect to the component of profit share constituted by net property income. The wealth effect, in fact, can be viewed as a proxy of the stimulus to luxury consumption by financial asset appreciation (see Magdoff and Foster, 2014), which is closely connected, in turn, to the dynamics of both dividends and interest. Profit share, in turn, modifying the approach chosen by Epstein and Jayadev (2005), can be split between the share of retained earnings and the share of net property income – i.e. rentiers' income (see Duenhaupt, 2012).

Massive use of financial rents for luxury consumption is compatible with capital accumulation and growth only if financial rents are a limited proportion of social surplus. However, in a world in which there is a clear separation between capital ownership and corporate control, this could only happen if profits were not fully distributed – i.e. if there were substantial corporate savings. Thus, clear evidence of a growing tendency of financial rentiers to consume their rents entirely can be found in an increasing role played by corporate savings in the formation of national savings and a symmetric reduction in the share of household savings. As we will see more clearly in the next chapter, there is clear evidence that this is happening in developed countries.

However, from the supply side viewpoint that characterised classical and Marxian political economy, if there is any analogy between financial rent and classical land rent, the former can mainly obstruct the industrial profit as a first mover of capital accumulation and economic growth, just as land rent did according to classical economists. We can therefore suppose that increase in the "rentier share" of social surplus can shift a growing part of the latter towards the consumption of luxury goods, reducing the share devoted to new productive investments and capital accumulation.

Moreover, since the part of surplus value that belongs to the "functioning capitalists" – i.e. the firms – is determined by the general rate of interest that is presupposed in advance, before the production process begins, the redistribution of surplus value between financial rentiers and functioning capitalists can reduce corporate profitability and have significant effects on growth rates, inducing stagnation trends, as in the stationary state predicted by the classical economists. Thus, the structural relationship between interest-bearing capital and industrial capital, analysed in the previous chapter, can help us find some answers because most of the current trends in the use of financial rents are strictly inherent to the evolution of the credit system, regardless of the forms of regulation applied to it.

In the same way, the reshaping of these basic tendencies in the context of the shadow banking system, which has been developed as a result of the financial deregulation processes of the last 30 years, probably played a major role in creating the main premises for the financial crisis of 2007–2008.

Financial rent and economic stagnation

There is, therefore, probably a link between the financialisation of Western economies and their current structural crises. However, it would be a mistake to think that there is a one-way cause-and-effect relationship, i.e. the rise to dominance of money capital has halted economic growth and generated stagnation.

Many neo-Marxist scholars, in fact, insist on the reverse causal direction. According to them, it is the long-term trend towards stagnation of monopoly capitalism that improved the primacy of finance. The latter, in turn, acted on the cause, reinforcing the paralysis of Western economies, but we must not lose sight of the original causal sequence if the aim is to promote adequate political intervention (see Arlacchi, 2018).

According to Sweezy (1980), for example, financialisation in the United States was the direct consequence of its structural crisis, which, in the context of the Keynesian policies then in vogue, eventually took the form of stagflation in the 1970s. The short-term solution to stagflation was immediate new increase in government demand through massive expansion of militarisation, which was in fact called the "Second Cold War". Yet, the latter was not in itself sufficient to revive the accumulation process.

The only other major potential stimulus was to favour an expansion of finance, insurance and real estate sectors, which could stimulate the system by partially absorbing excess money capital. Thus, over the 1990s, a financial explosion occurred that represented a qualitative change in the operation of the American economic system, and which Sweezy called "the financialization of the capital accumulation process" (see Magdoff and Foster, 2014).

Sweezy's thesis seems, at first sight, very similar to the one prevailing in the current literature on financialisation. However, some of its features may reverse the interpretation of causal relations that tends to prevail today.

According to Sweezy, in fact, to examine the relation between stagnation and financialisation, we have to start from the dynamics of accumulation of capital. Doing so, we could discover that the real initial problem for the United States, as well as most of the Western economies, is that they had in reality been caught in a long-term crisis of capital accumulation since the 1970s (see Sweezy, 1980). And, from the standpoint of theory of monopoly capitalism (see Baran and Sweezy, 1966), the tendency to stagnation of all the advanced countries depends on the general inability of monopoly capitalism to absorb the enormous surplus generated within production.

American neo-Marxists' theory is a Marxist one insofar as it traces the dynamics of capitalist development back to the process of capital accumulation. However, it even shows considerable influence by Michal Kalecki and Josef Steindl, not to mention Hansen's stagnationist approach (see Sweezy, 1980). Like most of today's theorists of the "secular stagnation" – such as Summers – the immediate cause of the slowdown in the growth process of the advanced countries is found in a high propensity to save accompanied by a low propensity to invest (see Magdoff and Sweezy, 1987). However, many American neo-Marxists, as well as Kalecki and Steindl themselves, also thought that this immediate cause was only the final effect of more profound structural transformations not solely due to demographic and technological dynamics.

Thus, the "line of thought" American neo-Marxists follow is an "over-accumulation" – i.e. underconsumption – theory that is quite controversial from an orthodox Marxist viewpoint (see Fine, 2009). According to this line of thought, under monopoly capitalism, there is a growing tendency for more surplus value to be produced than can find profitable investment outlets. The main result is a slowdown in the rate of growth of output and income, with rising unemployment and falling rates of utilisation of production capacity, which, in turn, put an added damper on investment and economic growth.

However, in this approach, as we saw in Chapter 3, the main reason for overaccumulation is the process of concentration and centralisation of production. Thus, the more monopolistic the economy proves, the stronger is the tendency to stagnation. This means that today "stagnation is the norm, good times the exception" (Sweezy, 1980). Consequently, what needs to be explained theoretically are not periods of economic crisis and slow growth, but rather "periods of sustained expansion" (Sweezy, 1980).

Thus, according to Sweezy (1980), the shortage of real investment outlets increasingly pushed the surplus capital available to corporations and the assets of American households alike into financial channels in pursuit of speculative opportunities unrelated to real production.

Financial intermediaries coped with this increased speculative demand by supplying new ingenious financial instruments such as repackaged futures, options, derivatives and money-market schemes, which were leveraged by growing debt on the part of the poorest households. And the Federal Reserve System only took on its institutional role as a lender of last resort, with a view to intervening quickly, whenever the system seemed to be in danger of a credit crunch or financial collapse.

The new financial architecture was then rapidly globalised and soon began to take on a logic of its own, eventually dominating production itself.

From this viewpoint, therefore, financialisation is seen as being no accident, but as a structural consequence of the development of capitalism in its monopolistic phase. In contrast to more recent interpretations of financialisation, in fact, while Sweezy blames financial liberalisation, he sees this political action as simply the reaction of the superstructure to the structural tendencies of monopoly capitalism, in an attempt to curb or postpone the crisis.

Magdoff and Sweezy (1987), however, immediately argued that the "financial explosion" was a qualitatively new historical development – since never before had a major financial expansion occurred under conditions of economic slowdown and on such lasting bases. According to them, therefore, a huge "financial superstructure" was emerging on top of the productive base of the monopoly capitalism, which could work for a long time, prospering while real production continued to stagnate.

The wealth effect, in fact, produced a favourable impact on the productive sector that went beyond the growing demand deriving from the value added created within the financial sector as a simple service provider sector. Increase in personal debt was moreover added to the wealth effect, in contrast to the stagnating real income for most workers. In this way, debt became one of the major supports for economic growth, increasing from about 150% of GDP in 1980 to over 350% of GDP just before the financial crisis of 2007–2008 (see Magdoff and Foster, 2014).

Thus, according to Sweezy and Magdoff (1972, 1983), the expansion of debt leverage to cope with an increasing demand for speculative instruments, which was totally disproportionate to the dynamics of the underlying real economy, constituted the very essence of the financialisation process in the United States. However, in this context, financialisation can work as a way to counteract stagnation insofar as it is propelled by financial bubbles, which lead, in turn, to periodic financial crises, but it eventually intensifies the structural crisis of the system without removing its root causes.

In this general explanatory framework, Sweezy and Magdoff (1983) also argued that financialisation of the economy is at odds with capital accumulation because trading absorbs money capital that could otherwise be used for productive investment.

This observation, as we have already pointed out in Chapter 1, may seem unconventional at first sight, because in reality, speculation in securities, as well as mergers and acquisitions of existing companies, does not necessarily divert capital from productive investments. Even though the purchase of financial securities can be alternative to physical investment at the level of a single economic agent, at the macroeconomic level, in fact, the phenomenon shows a clear *fallacy of composition* (see Tobin, 1997). All purchases of securities do is transfer money from buyers to sellers and the final macroeconomic effect depends only on what the sellers then do with the money they receive.

The money used to buy existing assets is, of course, money capital for the buyer that is transformed into real assets that were previously owned by other capitalists. This kind of transaction can, of course, be a way of increasing productive capital at the level of a single company, but it does not increase productive capacity at the macroeconomic level. What occurs is only a symmetrical change in the portfolio compositions of different groups of capitalists. The final result at the macroeconomic level depends on whether the transferred money capital will sooner or later be transformed into productive capital – i.e. capital goods – within one accounting year. However, it is also true that, if the initial money capital continued to change hands repeatedly for more than one accounting year, then it would basically remain trapped in the circulation process as money for financial transactions or speculation and, at the macroeconomic level, would cause, on the one hand, an increase in the demand for money – i.e. hoarding – and, on the other hand, lack of investment.

Sweezy and Magdoff, therefore, simply highlighted a potential conflict between productive and financial capital – i.e. between the underlying productive base of the economy and its financial superstructure – which may or may not occur depending on how money capital owners behave. However, the behaviour of these economic agents, in turn, depends on the structural conditions of the social and economic system.

In the earlier days of industrial capitalism, most production was carried on by small competitive proprietorships or partnerships and the financial superstructure was relatively insignificant. But as from the end of the 19th century, with the spread of big corporations as the typical form of firms, the composition of the capitalist economy underwent a qualitative transformation. The growing issuance of corporate securities encouraged the development of organised stock and bond markets, brokerage houses and new forms of banking. And, as we saw, this development usually boosts the increase in the number of rentiers, too.

People who had risen to the top of the capitalist hierarchy of wealth and power in those years were, not by chance, defined by Veblen as *captains of finance*, who can be assimilated to Keynes' *financiers*.

After the financial crisis of 1929 and the subsequent Great Depression, the expansion of the financial sector proceeded less rapidly in the period of sustained economic growth after the Second World War, although there was a real proliferation of new kinds of financial institutions and instruments along with growing speculation. Most of the developments of the time in the field of corporate finance and banking were really significant, although largely ignored by economic theory and relegated to the status of mere case studies of "applied economics", with partial exceptions in the case of Keynes and Minsky and a new wave of intensification of financial and speculative activities could already be registered from the second half of the 1960s onwards (see Sawyer, 2014).

Sweezy and Magdoff, therefore, back in the early 1980s argued that a large, increasing part of money capital in advanced economies was not directly transformed into productive capital, but was usually used to buy interest-bearing or dividend-yielding financial instruments (see Sweezy and Magdoff, 1983). According to them, it is only an axiom of theoretical orthodoxy that the sellers of these instruments were themselves productive capitalists who use the proceeds to expand their real capital, transferring to the buyers part of their profits in the form of interest and dividends. Indeed, in modern credit systems, money capitalists and rentiers are offered a huge variety of financial instruments other than traditional shares and bonds to choose from – such as certificates of deposit, money-market funds, options, futures and so on – and there is no guarantee that the money invested in any of these instruments will be transformed, directly or indirectly, into real capital accumulation.

Sweezy and Magdoff's main thesis, therefore, is that in this context some part of money capital may remain in the form of transaction or speculative money circulating in the financial sector, fuelling financial bubbles which increasingly take on a life of their own. In other words, it simply feeds the "pot" in the rentiers' games of chance.

However, according to Sweezy and Magdoff, the division of the economy into productive and financial sectors, which, as we saw, characterises the rise of the rentier mindset, also has its real roots in the introduction of the legal form of the public limited company, closely connected to the development of monopoly capital. In fact, this legal form allows a number of investors to start a business together without putting their personal assets at risk. Moreover, the corporation legally owns the real assets, while its stockholders only own shares in it. Corporations can then freely sell their assets on the one hand, while on the other hand the shareholders can freely sell their pieces of paper. Moreover, if organised securities markets exist, corporate securities acquire the attribute of liquidity, which the physical assets of corporations by their very nature could never have. Thus, the legal form of the corporation is the basis for the separation of money capital holders and functioning real capital.

A second crucial step is the legal possibility for corporations to have the power to own the securities of other corporations. Historically, as we have seen, this gave rise to *holding companies*, whose main purpose is to own the stocks of other corporations, in a theoretically endless chain, in order to obtain corporate control in wide sectors of activities. However, this strategic instrument within monopoly capital competition also ended up by exponentially increasing the number and volume of financial transactions without any addition to the underlying productive base at the bottom of the pyramid. Thus, the financial sector, although established for other purposes, progressively expanded in size and influence, boosting the purchase and sale of securities on credit, the development of options and futures markets, the multiplication of specialised financial intermediaries and stimulating corporate mergers and acquisitions.

Furthermore, most of the large corporations which are officially classified as "non-financial" are in reality engaged in financial operations such as buying and selling securities and other existing assets, borrowing and lending money, and so forth. Non-financial corporations, moreover, hold large amounts of cash for both productive and financial operations and, in deciding how to invest these funds, they are guided by criteria of profitability, security, liquidity and so forth. They are, in other words, money capitalists as well as productive capitalists, and fuel the games of the financial sector.

Thus, to conclude, on the basis of all the previous considerations, we can say that financial rents, as we have defined them, can only conflict with capital accumulation in two ways: by increasing luxury consumption, which, in turn, reduces the share of social surplus devoted to capital accumulation, and by creating new demand for money for financial transactions and speculative purposes.

The first way would be theoretically sustainable in the context of a simple reproduction scheme as long as the correct proportions between the capital goods sectors and the consumer goods sectors were respected and labour productivity were kept constant. However, of course, under the competitive conditions of the capitalist mode of production in general, and especially under the competitive conditions of monopoly capitalism, both these corrected proportions and constant labour productivity are by no means guaranteed and the problem of making productivity growth, slowing accumulation and full employment compatible remains unsolved and troubling.

The second way is even more destabilising and could only be countered by financial regulations similar to those in force during the post-war period. But these are now radically at odds with the rules of current globalisation.

Furthermore, the analyses of stagnation phenomena produced by neo-Marxists like Sweezy and Magdoff highlight a series of very interesting features of modern economic systems.

If, in accordance with Steindl's thesis (see Steindl, 1976, 1990), internal accumulation is the first mover of corporate investment for the large multinational corporations that characterise today's world economy, and this produces investment-seeking surplus value, the investment alternatives available for NFCs can play a fundamental role in determining the growth rate in a single national economic system. In fact, the possibilities for foreign investments, both direct and financial, may decrease the domestic accumulation rate. But also financial bubbles booming in secondary or derivatives markets can produce new interest-bearing forms of liquidity holdings for corporations, which can be viable alternatives to reinvesting profits in production plants and machinery in periods of high uncertainty. And the expansion of consumer credit or public debt can play the same role.

As we have seen in the previous chapters, today most of these different kinds of alternatives to domestic production investment are exactly what is collected together under the single label of "financialisation of NFCs" which also underlines the transformation of production capital into "finance capital" – analogous, in many respects, to interest-bearing or dividend-yielding capital – and the parallel transformation of a growing proportion of capitalists into pure financial rentiers.

However, these financial investment alternatives can also offer a rapid way to take part in the accumulation process of regions of the world with greater rates of profit owing to very low wages. In fact, at the macroeconomic level, if the average profitability in closed economies can only affect capital movements from one sector to another, in direct or financial form, but cannot account for the absolute level of real investment, in open economies the differences in average profitability between different countries can matter, reducing capital sources for real investment in one country by means of capital transfers, in direct or financial forms, towards other countries.

Moreover, in the corporations' portfolio choices, as well as the rates of return, the liquidity degree of the assets can also be a very important determinant, in close connection with business fluctuations. Thus, the corporations' portfolio choices also depend largely on the degree of uncertainty in their economic environment, which can lead to hoarding – ultimately the real prime mover of decreasing aggregate investment.

References

Arlacchi, P. (2018), *I padroni della finanza mondiale: Lo strapotere che ci minaccia e i contromovimenti che lo combattono*. Milan: Chiarelettere.

Baran, P. and Sweezy, P. M. (1966). *Monopoly Capital. An Essay on the American Economic and Social Order*. New York: Monthly Review Press.

Blaug, M. (1985). *Economic Theory in Retrospect*. Cambridge: Cambridge University Press.

Bukharin, N. I. (1927). *The Economic Theory of the Leisure Class*. New York: International Publishers.

Duenhaupt, P. (2012). "Financialization and the Rentier Income Share. Evidence from the USA and Germany". *International Review of Applied Economics*, 26 (4): 465–487.

Epstein, G. and Jayadev, A. (2005). "The Rise of Rentier Incomes in OECD Countries: Financialization, Central Bank Policy, and Labor Solidarity". In: Epstein, G. A. (ed.), *Financialization and the World Economy*. Cheltenham and Northampton, MA: Edward Elgar Publishing Ltd, pp. 46–74.

Fine, B. (2009). "Enigma in the Origins of Paul Sweezy's Political Economy". *Review of Political Economy*, 21 (1): 157–161.

Garegnani, P. (1984). "Value and Distribution in the Classical Economists and Marx". *Oxford Economic Papers, New Series*, 36 (2): 291–325.

Garegnani, P. (2018). "On the Labour Theory of Value in Marx and in the Marxist Tradition". *Review of Political Economy*, 30 (4): 618–42.

Kalecki, M. (1967/1971). *Selected Essays on the Dynamics of the Capitalist Economy. 1933–1970*. Cambridge: Cambridge University Press.

Keynes, J. M. (1936/2013). *The General Theory of Employment, Interest and Money. The Collected Writings of John Maynard Keynes*. Volume VII. Cambridge: Cambridge University Press.

Magdoff, F. and Foster, J. B. (2014). "Stagnation and Financialization: The Nature of the Contradiction". *Monthly Review*, 66 (1): 1–24.

Magdoff, H. and Sweezy, P. M. (1987). *Stagnation and the financial explosion*. New York: Monthly Review Press.

Marx, K. (1861–1863/1989). "Economic Works, 1861–1863". In: Marx, K. and Engels, F., *Collected Works*. Volume 32. New York: International Publishers, pp. 7–543.

Marx, K. (1894/1991). *Capital*. Volume III. London: Penguin Books.

Pullen, J. M. (2008). "Malthus, Thomas Robert (1766–1834)". In: Durlauf, S. N. and Blume, L. E. (eds.), *The New Palgrave Dictionary of Economics*. Second edition. Volume 5. Basingstoke: Palgrave Macmillan, pp. 250–58.

Sawyer, M. (2014). "What is Financialization?". *International Journal of Political Economy*, 42 (4): 5–18.

Steindl, J. (1976). *Maturity and Stagnation in American Capitalism*. New York: Monthly Review Press.

Steindl, J. (1990). *Economic Papers. 1941–88*. New York: Palgrave Macmillan.

Sweezy, P. M. (1980). "The Crisis of American Capitalism". *Monthly Review*, 32 (5): 1–13.

Sweezy, P.M and Magdoff, H. (1972). *The Dynamics of U.S. Capitalism. Corporate Structure, Inflation, Credit, Gold and the Dollar*. New York: Monthly Review Press.

Sweezy, P. M. and Magdoff, H. (1983). "Production and Finance". *Monthly Review*, 35 (1): 1–13.

Tobin, J. (1997). "Comment". In: Pollin, R. (ed.), *The Macroeconomics of Savings, Finance and Investment*. Ann Arbor: University of Michigan Press, pp. 299–304.

6 Corporate saving glut and liquidity holding

Hoarding and economic crises

Today, most economists fairly agree that capitalist economic systems must grow to be healthy, and that growth depends on the relation between savings and investment decisions. But only a few economists, generally heterodox, recognise that this relation is the result of the inherent dynamic of capitalistic accumulation.

The classical economists dealt with accumulation of capital as the process through which the wealth of nations grows. But they concentrated their attention on the effects of accumulation without considering the reasons for it, because they were convinced that in capitalist economies, there was a "natural" tendency to invest all that is saved (see Sardone, 1994). In this perspective, there was no need for a specific theory of investment as a major component of the aggregate demand (see Magdoff and Sweezy, 1987).

In fact, during the childhood of capitalism, when aggregate capital stock was built up from scratch, capital accumulation appeared to be virtually unlimited. All savings seemed to be devoted to investment, and growth seemed to be interrupted only by financial strains and sectoral disproportionalities between demand and supply. Crises and depressions were seen as spontaneous transitional ways to eliminate these temporary disequilibria and resume the normal course of capital accumulation (see Magdoff and Sweezy, 1987).

However, the capitalist accumulation process has typically been characterised by long booms that give way to more or less long downturns with economic crises being the passages that normally occur between these two kinds of phases following the typical pattern in capitalist accumulation. Every economic crisis, moreover, also manifests itself first and foremost as a financial crisis (see Shaikh, 2016), so that the latter often appears as the primary cause of the subsequent imbalances and turbulence. According to Kenneth Galbraith, for example, the Great Depression of the 1930s, although preceded by evident financial speculation leading to the stock market crash of 1929, was actually generated by the poor and fragile state of the real economy in 1929 (see Galbraith, 1955). In this scenario, according to most economists, it

DOI: 10.4324/9781003223221-7

is the logic of non-financial profit that seems to drive the recurrent pattern (see Shaikh, 2016). In other words, it is the expected profitability of new investments, compared with both what is considered the normal rate of profit and the interest rate, that determines the proportion of the social surplus that is reinvested, promoting capital accumulation.

In Marx's economic theory, however, capital accumulation is driven not only by profit, but also by competition which forces individual capitalists to invest in order to survive in the market, utilising dynamic economies of scale, increasing returns, technical innovations and progressive mechanisation to defend and expand their market share. Thus, Marx never regarded the accumulation of capital as a smooth and orderly process, developing in the context of regular business cycles, but as a chaotic process determined by the contradictions continually generated by the anarchy of the capitalist market. Nevertheless, he identified some basic structural tendencies of capitalism that inevitably lead to the genesis of crises and the momentary halting of the capital accumulation process.

Indeed, in Volume Two of the *Theories on Surplus Value*, Marx investigates the "abstract possibilities" or "abstract forms" of crisis (Marx, 1861–1863/1989, p. 140), underlining that *crisis potential* "can only emerge in the *circulation process* which is in itself also a *process of reproduction*" (Marx, 1861–1863/1989, p. 143).

According to Marx, the metamorphosis formula of the circulation of commodities itself, *C-M-C* (*Commodity-Money-Commodity*), contains, in fact, the germ of *the most abstract form of crisis*. In other words, "the possibility of crisis therefore lies solely in the separation of sale from purchase" (Marx, 1861–1863/1989, pp. 138–139).

Thus, according to him, a crucial stage in the potential crisis process is the possibility of subtracting money from circulation – i.e. liquidity holdings.

Of course, this is only

> the *most abstract form* of crisis, without content, without a compelling motivating factor. [...] The factors which turn this possibility of crisis into [an actual] crisis are not contained in this form itself; it only implies that *the* framework for a crisis exists. [...] These forms alone, therefore, do not explain why their crucial aspect becomes prominent and why the contradiction contained in them potentially becomes a real contradiction.
> (Marx, 1861–1863/1989, pp. 140–142)

However, in the sphere of the circulation of commodities, taken in itself, a break in the exchange process is unlikely and a pure matter of chance. Its only systematic cause can be found in *hoarding*, a common phenomenon in pre-capitalistic context, too, but generally operating on a small scale, with smooth dynamics over time, which cannot be held responsible for sudden and violent crises such as those experienced in the contemporary economy (see Sweezy, 1942/1946).

The true leap in quality occurs in the capitalist mode of production, with the transformation of the circulation formula from *C-M-C* to *M-C-M'* (*Money-Commodity-Money*), with *M'* greater than *M*. In this new kind of circulation – i.e. capital circulation – production is no longer aimed at consumption, but at capital valorisation. The capitalist's goal becomes increase in the value of his initial capital ($\Delta M = M' - M$), or better, its magnitude relative to the original amount of capital size ($\Delta M/M$). Thus, the goal of production becomes maximisation of the profit rate.

In this new context, *Say's law* no longer holds. The statement that supply creates its own demand has no general validity, even though it may still have local and contingent validity in the expansive phases of the cycle. In the depressive phases, the capacity of supply to create its own demand cannot be counted on since money, as capital, tends to crystallise in that form (hoarding), while waiting for the business cycle to bring about adequate conditions of returns on investments once again (see Sweezy, 1942/1946). In this way, hoarding is no longer psychological, fortuitous behaviour but a systematic phenomenon, closely connected with the dynamics of the capital valorisation conditions. According to Marx, the classical economists' lack of understanding of this crucial passage precluded an understanding of capitalist crisis.

The lack of effective demand, in this case, is a result of the very process of rotation of capital due to the decision, in some part of the economic system, to suspend momentarily reinvestment of the surplus value in new forms of productive capital, for many and varied reasons. It is not, then, the consequence of the short supply of money, however much hoarding of the monetary form of a part of the stock may hold back the process of metamorphosis of another part of it.

The second abstract form of crisis lies in the money function as a means of payment. This second form is, according to Marx, more "concrete" than the first, or more involved in the network of social connections that characterise a particular form of historically determined reality. In fact, the money function as a means of payment is in its fullness only in the context of a mature capitalist economy, with a fully developed credit system. In this kind of reality, a general crisis is "nothing other than the *possibility of crisis* described when dealing with money as a means of payment" (Marx, 1861–1863/1989, p. 142).

The relationship between these two abstract forms of crisis is thus the basis of the connection Marx believes to exist between the financial and real features of a crisis. In fact, the first form is possible without the second – i.e. "crises are possible without credit, without money functioning as a means of payment" (Marx, 1861–1863/1989, p. 144). The second form, instead, is not possible without the first – i.e. "without the separation between purchase and sale" (Marx, 1861–1863/1989, p. 144). The second form, in fact, is the *actual* form of money crises, which arise "from the *non-fulfilment of a whole series of payments*" (Marx, 1861–1863/1989, p. 144) – i.e. from the sudden break in the credit chain. However, credit crisis finds its triggering factor in – even temporary – blockage of the circulation of commodities, and therefore also of capital metamorphosis, although then becomes a potent multiplier of its initial mover. Every industrial and commercial crisis always manifests itself first and foremost as a monetary and financial crisis.

However, as striking as credit and monetary crises may be in their effects, they are not generally the first cause. In fact, Marx specifies that a money crisis "follows as a matter of course" when an industrial or commercial crisis occurs. Thus,

> in investigating why the general possibility of crisis becomes a reality, in investigating the conditions of crisis, it is therefore quite superfluous to concern oneself with the forms of crisis which arise out of the development of money as means of payment. This is precisely why economists like to suggest that this obvious form is the cause of crises.
>
> (Marx, 1861–1863/1989, pp. 144–145)

According to Marx, therefore, it is only "the superficiality of political economy" that leads to see the expansion and contraction of credit as the cause of the periodic fluctuations in the industrial cycle, while they are just "a mere symptom" of them (see Marx, 1867/1990, p. 786).

Even the first abstract form, however, cannot be considered the true cause of real crises. For this to turn into reality, a whole series of conditions are required which do not depend on the circulation of commodities alone (see Marx, 1867/1990, p. 209).

In Marx's works, moreover, there is no reference to the fact that the rate of profit can be a subjective incentive for accumulation of capital or play a role in changing aggregate investment decisions. When profits are squeezed by rising real wages in expansionary phases, if they become too low to adequately cover expected risk premiums, capitalists can obviously halt the process of new investment, holding liquidity in waiting for better times and thus effectively reducing effective demand and creating the conditions for a general crisis. The crisis, in turn, increases unemployment, which again drives down real wages and increases profits, allowing a new cycle of accumulation to begin. However, this sketch of Marxian cyclical dynamics is only driven by objective conditions and is not influenced by subjective expectations about normal profitability, as Sweezy (1942/1946) believed. Indeed, Sweezy's view is far more reminiscent of Keynes' view of normal interest rate level expectations that influence the speculators' demand for money.

Thus, according to Marx, the main potential cause of economic and financial crises is the hoarding of money – i.e. the withdrawal of money from the circulation process – which is the real cause of the lack of effective demand and the fallacy of *Say's law*. However, money hoarding is not seen as a pathological human behaviour, as assumed by many classical and neoclassical economists, but rather a phenomenon that is closely linked to certain physiological features of capital accumulation which can be more or less tempered by the presence of financial intermediaries and credit conditions.

Keynes, who, in turn, emphasised both the relevance of the demand for money in real economic equilibria and the fallacy of *Say's law*, attributed the effects on effective demand by the former to the changes in the money market interest rate alone, losing sight of a more direct effect of liquidity holding, based on simply stopping the process of surplus value circulation.

However, liquidity holding is most certainly a particular type of asset which, according to Tobin (1958), becomes part of what we call portfolio choices. Thus, changes in the liquidity holdings of any economic agent are, in a balanced budget, the result of their management of savings. Companies' liquidity holdings are also closely linked to their saving choices and the subsequent decisions on the allocation of savings to different alternative uses, based on their different rates of return.

Liquidity holding and corporate saving

Capital accumulation needs saving – i.e. "abstaining" from consumption. However, this is only possible for goods that are not necessities. Thus, saving must, by definition, be a portion of social surplus and can only be decided by its recipients. According to classical as well as Kaleckian and Marxist economists, therefore, the only source of saving is capitalists' profits because workers are forced to the subsistence level by competition in the labour market and landowners consume all their share of social surplus in luxury goods. However, in these analyses of social classes' behaviour, no distinction is usually made between corporate and personal capitalists' incomes.

Neoclassical economists, in turn, do not usually deal separately with the corporate saving because they assume that households, owning corporations, integrate corporate saving decisions in their own saving decision (see Jauch, 2012).

Keynes, too, following the functional neoclassical approach, did not distinguish between different social classes, but focused only on personal saving behaviour, with little attention paid to the saving behaviour of corporations, governments and other institutions (see Smith, 1963). He allowed himself only a passing remark that the saving motives of agents other than households were "largely analogous to, but not identical with, those actuating individuals" (Keynes, 1936/2013, p. 108). Thus, according to Johnson, Keynes' neglect of corporate savings was in full continuity with Marshallian economic analysis, and "reflects Marshall's inability to integrate the modern corporation into his system" (Johnson, 1961).

Corporate finance analysts have, however, always been well aware of the importance of corporate savings, but for a long time they only dealt with them as a source of funds for growing companies.

According to a scholastic economic view, based on the high abstraction level of basic economic models, enterprises should generally be net borrowers. In other words, they should raise funds on the market of loanable funds to invest in productive capital goods in order to obtain a stream of future cash flows through which they can repay the initially borrowed funds and the related interest. This does not, of course, exclude the possibility that at any point in time, for contingent reasons, some companies may be net lenders, but it does assume that, on average, there will always be many more companies raising funds than repaying them.

However, as we shall see in the following pages, since the mid-1990s, the non-financial sector has – on average – become a net lender in many advanced countries, shattering the certainties of common sense.

The lack of a genuine theory of corporate saving first became apparent in the United States in the late 1930s, when economists proved incapable of expressing the pros or cons for Roosevelt's proposal for a tax on undistributed surpluses (see Livermore, 1938). Moreover, in the 1930s and 1940s, corporations began to be viewed as specific institutional decision makers, with their own specific objective functions, who did not utilise marginal principles when making their investments (see Smith, 1963). The household sector, in turn, was progressively considered unable to completely pierce the "corporate veil" (see Poterba et al., 1987). Yet, this means that corporations can remain outside the schemes of intertemporal choice between present and future consumption. So, lower investment decisions do not necessarily become higher consumption decisions, but they may also generate liquidity holding and, consequently, a lack of effective demand.

Today, there is not even a comprehensive theory as to why companies hold cash and use it. This is probably due to the fact that corporate cash holding is a subject of corporate finance theory – which, according to Tirole (2006, p. 6), is still a young and unexplored field with no unified framework. The discrepancy of assumptions across different papers also makes it difficult to identify the key economic elements driving the analyses.

The "pecking-order hypothesis", which has received substantial empirical support, assumes that corporations have a preference ordering to finance their investments, moving from retained earnings to debt, hybrid securities and finally equity, due to the fact that internal finance does not suffer from the informational asymmetries associated with external finance (see Myers, 1984; Myers and Majluf, 1984). This may justify liquidity detention for short time periods in order to reach the critique mass for new investment.

However, holding cash or near-cash assets is generally expensive for companies, because it usually generates opportunity costs by providing zero returns or lower returns than productive or financial investments. Even if a company had no real or financial investment opportunities, the cash could be used to increase dividends or acquire other companies by transferring the cash from the corporate balance sheet to shareholders.

The cost to the firm of cash holding is the difference between the after-tax interest received from the cash or near-cash assets and the return on the productive investment of the same money. Since NFCs often have the ability to reinvest in their core business, a rough measure of the cost of holding cash is the difference between their return on equity (ROE) and the return available for the cash invested in the money market. ROE for industrial companies is also often well above money market returns, with an average spread reaching 20% after the economic crisis of 2007–2008. For NFCs, therefore, holding cash can result in a loss of up to 20% of potential returns (see Tambo and Theobald, 2017).

Cash holding decisions by companies also show a close connection with corporate governance features. According to "the free cash flow hypothesis", formulated by Jensen (1986) and Stulz (1990), shareholders should limit managers' access to free cash flow to mitigate agency conflicts. The pay-out policy, indeed, depends on the features of companies' governance and, with no control threat, it is difficult to lead self-interested managers to transfer cash reserves to shareholders as dividends.

In the early 2000s, some cross-country econometric analyses clearly showed that the larger the shareholders' rights, the lower the cash holdings (see Dittmar et al., 2003; Pinkowitz et al., 2003; Lins and Kalcheva, 2007). However, companies with weaker corporate governance may hold smaller cash reserves too because they usually choose to repurchase shares instead of increasing dividends in order to avoid future pay-out commitments (see Harford et al., 2008).

In any case, accumulating excess cash reserves gives flexibility to corporations' management. Companies with stronger governance tend to increase dividends, while those with a weaker governance prefer more flexible options, choosing to buy back shares in order to avoid commitment to keep stable future pay-outs.

However, the results of research by Harford, Mansib and Maxwell on the US companies appear to be inconsistent with the current view resulting from most international studies that as shareholders' rights increase, cash balances decrease. The authors, therefore, believe that the overall protection of shareholders' rights at the national level is probably more important than specific governance rules and practices at the company level.

Large, unused cash balances, moreover, are always a negative signal for markets and can promote proxy contests which are dangerous for the stability of managers' jobs (see Faleye, 2004). Thus, managers should prefer to convert cash into real assets relatively quickly in the context of weak governance, too.

However, this is a general rule that has found exceptions not only in times of economic and financial crises, but also in the years immediately preceding the crises. This once again supports the view that hoarding processes can play a major role in producing financial crises and some of their specific features.

Thus, it is not by chance that, while corporate saving and cash holding receive scant analytic attention today, whether in macroeconomic or microeconomic analysis frameworks, they saw a glorious period of analysis from the late 1920s to the early 1950s, immediately before, during and after the experience of the Great Depression.

Some views on corporate savings and liquidity holding around the Great Depression

Corporate savings and the cash balance policy of enterprises first attracted attention in the late 1920s, immediately before the Wall Street crash of 1929. Between 1922 and 1929, in fact, many large companies made deductions in excess of their investment needs (see Dobrovolsky, 1951), and utilised part of their previous accumulated cash balances to buy securities in the stock exchange market in order to profit from the high call loan rate. They were therefore accused of contributing to the boom on the stock exchange, but also of feeding the financial markets at the expense of the other markets (see Lutz, 1945).

During the period 1910–1919, corporate savings were estimated to account for 25% of total saving and 4% of the national income (see Knauth, 1922). They reached higher proportions during the 1920s and for the period 1916–1927 were estimated to account for 43.7% of total corporate net income (see Ebersole et al., 1929).

In December 1927, the *Federal Trade Commission*, in its *Report on Stock Dividends*, stated, in turn, that, for the period 1920–1926, in a sample of 566 large corporations, cash dividends had accounted for 35% of total corporate surplus, while stock dividends and undistributed profits had accounted for 24.8% and 40%, respectively (see Meech, 1928; Jewkes, 1931). The large corporations analysed, therefore, usually retained about two-thirds of their net income for their own growth or for outside investment in other concerns, as had already been pointed out by some analysts (see Kotany, 1922; Thorp, 1929).

However, for the years 1924–1928, in a larger sample of 2,046 manufacturing corporations, cash dividends paid out varied, year by year, from between 50% and 72% of net income (see Buchanan, 1938). The total amount reinvested during the five years within this broader sample of corporations was therefore only 33% of the net profit.

Corporate-retained earnings, of course, fell to a low ebb during the 1930s due to squeezed profits during recession, but again became a significant component of the total savings in the economy in the 1940s.

Thus, the American economic literature during the Great Depression not only began to deal with corporate saving as a conspicuous and increasing phenomenon, which was determining a very large share of national saving, but also underlined some evident cyclical determinants in its development. Above all, companies' cash holdings were the subject of heated debate, because, according to some economists, corporations held "idle" cash – i.e. cash balances in excess of current operation needs – which contributed to the stagnation of the economic system.

Jewkes (1931) was among the first economists to recognise the relevance of corporate saving as a major part of the aggregate national saving. He wrote a note in the *Quarterly Journal of Economics* about the influence that financial interests were able to exert on the American industrial structure, creating new concerns which were "too unwieldy" in size to be efficient.

He argued that the periods of cyclical economic expansion were likely to bring overexpansion, too, particularly because of the large corporations which were accumulating ample profits instead of distributing them to shareholders. Indeed, he supported the thesis that, since the early 1920s, corporate savings had become a major part of national saving, because it was usual for the large corporations to retain a good part of its net annual income and utilise it for its own expansion.

In accordance with Veblen (1904), Jewkes thought that the largest corporations were not the most efficient when measured by unit costs or rate of profit. So, according to him, the accumulation of corporate savings had a major role in the tendency for companies to grow beyond the optimum size, for raising capital in this way sidestepped the judgement of the financial markets about investment profitability.

With statistical data analysis, Jewkes found that corporate saving was prevailing in the largest companies. These savings took different forms. A corporation could accumulate profits to increase its physical assets without any change in its outstanding capital stock. But it could also issue stock dividends, and between 1920 and 1927, this kind of dividends represented about 50% of the total corporate savings.

The rate of growth of stock capitalisation in the sample of corporations analysed by the *Federal Trade Commission* in 1928 was greater for the small groups and tended to decline in the larger ones. According to Jewkes, this was evidence that greater size brought increased resistance to further stock expansion. But even though the largest corporations grew less than the smaller, they were equally inclined to use accumulated profits to provide the means for expansion. Thus, Jewkes supposed that in some cases stock dividends might merely represent a process of "watering" capital and not real savings. Indeed, corporations might transfer a part of corporate savings corresponding to stock dividends into the form of bonds, in which case the stock capitalisation did not coincide with increase in their material assets.

Furthermore, between 1920 and 1927, some corporations issued an amount of stock dividends greater than the actual increase in outstanding stock capitalisation. Jewkes explained this phenomenon assuming that in a period of depression following a period of prosperity, in which stock dividends were issued, corporations wrote down their stocks, following the reduction in their earnings.

Jewkes also thought that the practice of corporate saving was an automatic operation that drove the large corporations to move on to dimensions which were not justified at the level of efficiency. His opinions were shared by other economists, such as Weidenhammer (1933), who held the view that the tendency towards cartelisation and trustification, on the one hand, and the separation of ownership and management, on the other, represented two institutional factors that increased the probability of the faulty investment of corporate savings.

Means (1931), instead, criticised some conclusions reached by Jewkes in his note. He argued that Jewkes' figures exaggerated the amount of corporate savings because of an incorrect use of data reported by the *Federal Trade Commission*. Thus, the "total surplus" that remained undistributed in each period, which Jewkes had assumed to represent corporate savings, included surplus already accumulated at the beginning of the period as well as earnings made during the period. Therefore, the corporations analysed saved not 66% of their net income, but only 48% of it.

Furthermore, Means thought that this level of corporate saving was usual only for the corporations "which were very much above the average in prosperity", or roughly 5% of all corporations (see Means, 1931). He also thought that Jewkes failed to group together all the corporations with capital stock over ten million dollars, because corporations with about ten million of capital stock were small in comparison to modern big corporations and their performance was quite different from that of the latter. In 1920, according to the data of the *Federal Trade Commission*, only 30 corporations with capital stock of over 40 million dollars had issued 24.2% of all the stock dividends of the sample.

Furthermore, Means observed that the tendency of the rate of growth to decline as the size of company increases was refuted when the largest companies were separately dealt with. Indeed, the 30 largest corporations showed an average growth of 90%.

He also argued that studies of optimum size have dealt with the size of manufacturing or distributing units, not with the size of companies. Thus, there was no justification for applying conclusions based on the size of a productive unit to a corporation which may own a multitude of such units. Furthermore, he thought that it was quite possible for a corporation to grow so fast as to become inefficient; yet in this case, the result did not come from the size but rather from the hasty manner of reaching it. So, he thought that Jewkes could be right in supposing that the slower growth of the larger corporations showed incapacity to absorb additional capital at profitable rates, but, because the sample of the *Federal Trade Commission* included only corporations that have had earnings sufficient to warrant the declaration of stock dividends and, therefore, were far above the average in profit-making capacity, the slower growth could also be explained assuming that as corporations increase in size, they tend to become more stable.

Buchanan (1938), in turn, underlined that American corporations had the common practice of reinvesting a large part of their annual profits and raised the question as to whether or not this practice worked out in the interests of the shareholders. He also thought that the "marginal principle" of capital investment played little part in management decisions.

In fact, in accordance with this principle, managers should have been maximising the net returns through time to the shareholders and no part of the profits should have been reinvested inside the company unless the return on the increment of capital had been at least as large as could be on the same capital invested outside of the company. Yet, many evidences were quite different.

Buchanan argued that the major reason for which corporations did not pay as dividends the full amount of the profits was connected with the cash position of the company. However, insufficient cash did not explain dividends paid consistently below earnings over a period of years showing positive net earnings.

Thus, he thought that a more convincing motivation was that corporations wish to accumulate a surplus credit to face expected losses in subsequent periods without eating into the original paid-in capital. Yet, once again, to achieve a surplus credit by means of additional capital is against "marginal principle", unless this capital could earn as much within the corporation as elsewhere.

According to Buchanan, corporations can also reinvest a large part of their profits during expansion periods in order to stabilise their dividend rate through periods of prosperity and depression. However, to achieve this end, the reinvested profits must be kept in a relatively liquid form.

Buchanan underlined the fact that, at the time he was writing, many authors had already stressed the separation of ownership and control in large corporations. Thus, he believed that, under these conditions, there was no justification in assuming that dividend policy was primarily made in the interests of the shareholders. If the management group was a professional one, they would have a rather strong incentive to increase the size of the corporation, expecting their salaries to be proportional to it. If, however, the management group enjoyed a profit-sharing contract, it would have a direct incentive to increase the total investment under its control. Furthermore, the management could derive bigger "psychic income" from controlling a larger company. Thus, as can be seen, Buchanan was fully in line with the strand of literature on the "managerial revolution" that was emerging in those years in the United States and we critically analysed in Chapter 1.

According to him, in large corporations, the management had an interest in retaining as large a part of the profits of each period as was consistent with the shareholders' regular rate of return on their financial investment. During the 1920s, many corporations could save all profits and satisfy shareholders' regular stock dividends. Whether it is rational or irrational, to retain the profits depends on the marginal returns from increments of investment.

Furthermore, Buchanan thought that it might be usual for many corporations to end their life with a gradual process of disinvestment, retrieving as much as possible of the original shareholders' capital in the form of liquid assets.

He also attempted to apply the accepted economic principles of capital investment to the problem of dividend distribution. If dividend declarations by the boards of directors were made on this basis in expansion periods, then the directors should have estimated the returns on the additional investment in their companies to be at least equal to, or greater than, the rate of interest.

The empirical data suggested that during business expansion phases, almost all corporations followed the policy of paying out as dividends an amount less than their profits. This could mean that, on the basis of the theoretical mainstream, almost all the directors believed that the marginal productivity of capital in their companies exceeded the rate of interest. But Buchanan thought that this theoretical conclusion was open to suspicion, and insofar as this theoretical hypothesis failed to find confirmation, the result would be misdirection of capital investment.

Thus, he more reasonably believed that corporate directors did not usually consider the dividend policy in marginal terms at all. Habit and custom played a major part and had led directors generally to apply rules of thumb, relevant and useful in many cases, to almost all corporations.

He also believed that the reinvestment of profits in liquid assets during business expansion periods was nevertheless desirable since it could easily maintain the level of dividends during depression periods.

Some American views on corporate savings and cash holding in the 1940s

If in the 1920s and 1930s the American economic literature had underlined the importance of corporate saving as a major part of the aggregate national saving, viewing its growing role as a direct consequence of the separation of ownership and control in large corporations, in the 1940s, based on the experience of the Great Depression, it also focused on the possible connections between corporate savings and cash holdings, on the one hand, and business cycles on the other.

In the early 1940s, most of the analysts took it that corporate savings enabled firms to improve their financial strength during the periods of business expansion, increasing their power of resistance to the adverse events during the periods of business depression. Others, in contrast, contended that they tended to intensify the cyclical fluctuations.

Corporate savings according to Dobrovolsky

Dobrovolsky (1945), agreeing that corporate savings represent a major part of aggregate saving, observed that their effect on cyclical swings depends on their amount, the kind of assets in which they are invested and the dissavings made during depressions. Thus, according to him, not only analysis of the corporate propensity to save – i.e. the ratio of corporate saving to corporate net income – has considerable importance, yet all the factors involved in corporate saving decisions depend, on turn, on corporate governance.

Dobrovolsky set out to examine, on a theoretical plane, the economic significance of the surplus accumulation process during the periods of business expansion and that of the reverse process of corporate dissaving during the periods of business depression.

Starting from an evident Keynesian viewpoint, he believed that accumulation of corporate surpluses increases the aggregate saving and makes it more difficult to maintain economic equilibrium at a high-income level. Moreover, insofar as corporate savings lead to accumulating cash balances, they generate hoarding, contributing to diminish the effective demand. Yet also investment of the retained earnings in operating assets may jeopardise the economic equilibrium because of insufficient investment outlets for individual savings.

In those years, as we have seen, some economists thought that investment of retained funds could be "unwise" because not submitting competitive bids in the capital market enables the management to follow speculative or prestige motives, which can lead to social misallocation of economic resources. However, according to others, corporate savings gave management a greater scope in investing funds, enabling it to embark upon new projects with important technical improvements and innovations, which could not easily be financed with external funds. Furthermore, corporations may reinvest their earnings without as much concern for the rate of return as would be the case if the funds were raised from the capital market.

Dobrovolsky pointed out that the aggregate propensity to save would be lower if corporate net earnings were completely distributed among shareholders, because it is improbable that the greater income of the latter would be totally saved. But retained corporate earnings could also increase the propensity to invest, because managers, thanks to their better knowledge of market potentialities, may be able to find new investment opportunities that would not appear attractive enough to the financial markets. All this would mitigate conditions for disequilibrium between aggregate saving and investment.

Part of the dividends may obviously be hoarded by the stockholders, too. Yet, the major part may be spent on goods and services, contributing to the aggregate effective demand. Thus, according to Dobrovolsky, the only problem for a deficit of aggregate demand could arise from a policy of retention oriented to building up cash reserves.

Statistical evidence did not show any tendency to accumulate cash during the phases of economic expansion in the early decades of the 20th century. Instead, this tendency was evident in the periods of economic depression.

Furthermore, Dobrovolsky thought that the financial markets are subject to waves of excessive optimism as well as excessive pessimism. So financing corporations from the capital market does not eliminate misallocation of resources. The direct reinvestment of retained corporate earnings, instead, could implement a use of funds which would not find an outlet for them through the capital market. This could produce a greater degree of utilisation of resources rather than of their misallocation.

Thus, according to Dobrovolsky, the policy of retention of earnings may reduce aggregate demand over the expansion phase of the cycle but, on balance, it should not necessarily have an adverse influence.

During the downturns of the first decades of the 20th century, in most corporations, the accumulated undistributed earnings of the past years were reduced due to payments of dividends in excess of current earnings, or to compensate the current deficits. From 1929 to 1935, American corporations paid out 34.5 billion dollars in excess of their receipts for wages, taxes, dividends and other obligations. Defenders of this corporate policy claimed that this kind of dissaving in times of depression helped to maintain the aggregate volume of payments and to mitigate business contraction and unemployment. However, this fact also created the opinion that during the periods of depression, corporations were able to put into the economic system large amounts of cash over and above the amounts flowing into their cash accounts (see Dobrovolsky, 1945).

At the end of 1929, the aggregate amount of cash balances of non-financial corporations in the United States was 7.3 billion dollars, while at the end of 1935, it was 6.7 billion. Thus, payments exceeded receipts by 0.7 billion over this period. Usually, business enterprises can inject new cash into the economy without diminishing their cash balances, thanks to expanding bank loans. But from 1929 to 1935, American corporations also reduced their bank indebtedness and thus had to reduce their cash holding because of the excess of total costs plus dividends over total revenues.

The cash holding of an enterprise is merely the result of the difference between receipts and payments. Corporate dissaving, resulting from revenues insufficient to cover costs, may therefore be accompanied by an increase in corporate cash holdings – when cash receipts exceed cash payments – just as well as by a decrease in corporate cash holdings – when cash receipts fall short of cash payments. When the former case occurs, accumulation of cash goes on concurrently with partial dissipation of the fixed capital. When receipts fall off during a depression, corporations can sustain the level of payments by drawing on their cash holdings, selling marketable assets or borrowing new funds on the financial markets or from the banking system.

Payments in excess of current receipts depend on profit considerations. Yet even though most of corporations were choosing to operate in "deficit financing" to maintain the level of employment, they would need financial help from the government or the banking system, for the combined holdings of cash and marketable securities constitute only a small percentage of the total annual cash outflows. Furthermore, massive sales of corporate security portfolios within a short span of time would be impossible without organised intervention by the financial authorities. Moreover, during a depression, new borrowing on a large scale would not be available without a specific public policy of support.

In a depression period, payments are cut at the same rate as receipts fall off. At the outset, contractual obligations coming from the expansion period can partially be met by decreases in liquid assets. But progressively, the payments are usually rapidly adjusted to the falling receipts. Most large corporations remain in a strong liquid position, because their principal problem is to balance costs and revenues, and the former usually exceed the latter, even though payments and receipts are balanced, because of depreciations.

The replacement of fixed capital can be slowed down or temporarily interrupted without significant effects on the current production process. So corporations can maintain their other payments by cutting down the replacement of fixed capital and also in inventories.

Because depreciation accruals figure as a component of total costs, these can be reduced by diminishing the scale of production, but this will not necessarily entail a growth in profits. The loss can be the same whether the company maintains its previous scale of production or whether it stops production and dismisses all its workers.

If all variable costs involve cash outflows and the revenue coincides with cash inflows, then also the cash balance will be the same in both situations.

Obviously, corporations usually try to minimise their losses by fixing the level of production at some intermediate point between the original level and total suspension of the activities.

If corporations maintain the scale of production as before, but their fixed capital is undermaintained, then purchases from the capital goods industries are reduced. The resulting dissaving reduces effective demand at the expense of current production and employment.

In the 1940s, the statistical evidence showed a positive correlation between the amount of business dissaving and the amount of employment. Thus, Dobrovolsky's interpretation was that firms usually adjust the scale of production to the expected changes in demand for their products. When the demand was expected to fall, production was curtailed and employment and the flow of payments were consequently reduced, leading to a further decline in demand. As a result, both dissaving and unemployment were growing as the depression proceeded. When a new particular combination of factors produced a change in the direction of movement of the effective demand, the process was reversed. The level of production was adjusted upwards, generating increases in employment and the flow of payments so that demand was further stimulated, in a virtuous circle as recovery went on.

The question was whether the existence of corporate savings improved the ability of corporations to incur dissaving in bad years. Obviously, corporate saving may be of importance to this end only if it is kept as cash holding, because in this case it can be utilised to cover disbursement if the corporation is short of cash and decides to maintain its volume of production.

The importance of the surplus account could be analysed comparing two companies equal to each other in all respects except the proportion in equity of paid-in capital and corporate savings.

Ruggles (1939) deals with the case in which two companies start with equal amounts of capital, with no difference in the amount of outside financing, but one of them regularly saves part of its net earnings, while the other distributes all net earnings to shareholders. She argues that, after a certain period, the former will have better equipment and lower costs, and so will suffer less during a business depression. But this result depends on the inequality of the capital invested by the two firms at the end of the period considered, not the different structure of equity.

Dobrovolsky thought that in the real economy the younger and the smaller firms usually find it difficult to obtain external funds and, therefore, the companies which are able to save more of their profits are in a better position to grow, to improve the quality of their equipment and show better performance during the different phases of the business cycle than firms with a smaller saving capacity.

Furthermore, corporations with strong savings could enjoy a better credit standing and, therefore, it could be easier for them to obtain new funds from financial institutions.

According to Dobrovolsky, the case in which two companies are compared that have equal total equities but unequal savings has to be distinguished from the case in which two companies are compared that have equal capital stocks but different amounts of total equity, because of a difference in their corporate savings. Companies that have the same paid-in capital but a larger surplus than others would obviously be preferable customers.

Dobrovolsky observed that previously accumulated corporate savings were, as a rule, a necessary legal condition for the payment of dividends in profitless years. Dividends in such periods may or may not increase the aggregate flow of payments, depending on the source from which the funds are obtained. If they come from previous cash holdings, we may expect a favourable effect on the aggregate flow of payments. But if corporations pay dividends resorting to sales of securities that they hold in their portfolios, the effect may be different.

If securities were sold to subjects – individuals or firms – who would otherwise hoard the money, or if they were sold to banks against additional money, favourable effects would be expected. If, however, they were sold to operators in the place of goods or services, no significant effect could be expected.

If dividends were paid out by curtailing expenses for employment and downsizing fixed capital, then the effect would likely be unfavourable, because the stockholders would have less propensity to consume than the workers.

Dobrovolsky also underlined that during the depressions of the first decades of the 20th century, large corporations had accumulated large amounts of cash not required for current operations. They had, as a rule, reduced their operating assets but strengthened their liquidity holding. Therefore, their ability to distribute dividends in profitless years had not been maintained at the expense of other payments, thanks to these reserves.

Yet, the accumulation of inactive cash was intensified also in the absence of dividend distributions. Cash holdings, for example, may make it easier for corporations to continue production in depression periods despite losses. Sometimes, in a long-run strategic perspective, corporations may engage in operations whose immediate financial results do not even cover the variable costs. This kind of policy is certainly more probable if there are strong liquid reserves deriving from previous corporate savings.

Thus, according to Dobrovolsky, it seems that high corporate savings and accumulation of large cash holdings in periods of cyclical expansion had led to creating a buffer to sustain larger amounts of cash disbursement and of employment in periods of cyclical contraction.

But large amounts of cash remained inactive throughout the periods of depression. According to Dobrovolky, most of the large corporations came out of such periods with the surplus account still showing a very substantial credit balance and quite a strong liquidity position.

Dobrovolsky also wondered whether the financial interests of the shareholders are reconcilable with corporate saving and its use for production stabilisation purposes.

He observed that the economic literature on corporation finance had always emphasised that, the shareholders being the owners of the entire corporate net income, retention of part of the latter by the management deprives the shareholders of the right to decide for themselves the best allocation of the amounts concerned. Thus, some economists concluded that corporate saving was against the shareholders' interest, while others thought that the freedom of the board directors in employing these funds should be restricted.

Dobrovolsky thought that, while it is true that from a legal standpoint stockholders are the owners of the entire net income, there is no economic justification to identify their claims to the retained net income with the effective distributed parts of it. Indeed, he said, corporate net income is a return on the equity capital invested plus a reward of an entrepreneurial nature. The latter part is usually considered as a reward for organising and managing the business and for taking on risk. And, even though the issue is controversial, some argue that the entrepreneurial function is performed by the managers.

Dobrovolsky also underlines that in the early decades of the 20th century, there was a substantial difference between the behaviour of modern corporate shareholders and that of the proprietary capitalist-managers of non-corporate enterprises of the earlier phase of capitalism. He agreed with the view that the essence of the entrepreneurial function lies in active decision-making rather than passive responsibility-taking. Thus, he deemed that the typical behaviour of shareholders was radically different from that of managers, and therefore he agreed with Berle and Mean's idea that in the new century a new form of conflict had arisen between corporation "beneficial ownership" and "control". The shareholders kept only the "beneficial ownership", while "control" was "turned over by them to the directors and officers" (Dobrovolsky, 1945).

However, while Berle and Mean believed that "only a fair return to capital should be distributed to the 'owners'; while the remainder should go to the control as an inducement to the most efficient ultimate management" (Berle and Means, 1936, p. 344), Dobrovolsky pointed out that, according to the findings of the Cowles Commission, for a long time cash dividends on common stocks of American corporations had represented a yield considerably higher than that on corporate bonds. The ratio of cash dividend payments to stock prices, in fact, averaged 5% a year, against the average return from high grade bonds of about 4.2%.

This means that the owners of common stocks had been receiving as cash dividends not only a pure interest on the invested capital, but also a reward for the risk involved in the investment. Instead, the retained part of profits had not become income for the managers. Legal title to retained profits had remained with the shareholders, and the accumulation of surpluses provided an additional reward to them through appreciation of stock prices.

The first question was whether there was a definite pattern in the relationship between corporate net income and corporate savings. During the expansion phase of the 1920s corporation managers were believed to follow the rule of thumb that it was a sound principle of corporate finance to retain 50% of net income. This rule should have produced a well-defined and stable pattern of corporate saving. Yet, the data on manufacturing corporations indicated a different scenario.

The statistical data showed a fairly clear pattern between corporate net income and corporate savings. In general, greater corporate net income had been accompanied by greater dividends as well as greater savings, but the proportion of income retained had not been a fixed percentage, varying with the level of corporate income.

In fact, in the late 1930s, in some large corporations, retention of 30% of net income was consciously held to be an appropriate long-run policy.

Thus, the question arising immediately then was whether the variations in corporate savings were related to specific changes in business or financial conditions. It was important to understand to what extent these variations had been associated with changes in corporate profitability and in corporate investment.

Dobrovolsky notes that, in the short run, variations in net income were usually closely correlated with variations in the rate of return on capital invested. But in the long run, there was no close relation between the two.

Since external investors are usually greatly interested in the rate of return on their capital, the corporate ability to retain income depends on the ratio of its net income to the owners' capital.

Econometric analyses showed that corporations began to save when the rate of net income was about 5%, while they had a net dissaving below that level.

Above this level, a variation in the rate of net income of 1% was associated with a change of 0.8% in the same direction in the rate of corporate savings. So, while the corporate marginal propensity to save was stable, the proportion of corporate savings to net income varied with the level of the latter.

But over the period 1924–1943, there was no evidence of a long-run trend for the corporate "propensity to save", at each net income level, to increase or decrease.

Small declines in profitability in 1926 and 1927 determined pronounced reductions in the rate of corporate saving, while the considerable recovery of profitability in 1928 and 1929 produced relatively small improvement in the proportion of corporate savings to net income.

These movements may be partly accounted for by an increase in dividend requirements at the end of the 1920s. After a succession of good years, stock market prices were rising much more rapidly than profits, and distribution of a greater proportion of them among the shareholders was a way to offset the fast increase in the price-dividend ratio. But larger dividends were also possible because of a simultaneous relative decrease in the requirements for corporate accumulation of capital.

However, according to Dobrovolsky, also the managers had obtained advantages from the policy of corporate saving. They were provided with new financial resources avoiding the procedures needed for new external funds and without any agreement on the purposes for which they should be employed. Furthermore, in the case of losses connected to faulty investment, the use of internal funds produced a less unfavourable reaction on the part of creditors and shareholders.

Thus, Dobrovolsky believed that corporate saving shifted some benefits from the "beneficial ownership" to the "control group", as a consequence of the division of functions between these two groups of economic operators. Thus, according to him, it was more in keeping with the relationships within corporations.

Dobrovolsky concluded that, as long as the dividends paid were comparable with the return on senior securities, the policy corporate saving was not unfair to the shareholders. It could be unfair to them only if corporations made it a practice to maintain a larger volume of payments during the periods of depression, because such a practice might produce a reduction in surpluses and a greater loss of earning power at the end of such periods. Yet even in this case, he thought that this policy should be sustainable if at the end of the period the company was still able to bring a satisfactory return on the paid-in equity funds.

Cash holding according to Lutz

In the same years, another relevant contribution on these issues was provided by the book on *Corporate Cash Balances* by Friedrjch A. Lutz, which originated with a special enquiry under the *Financial Research Program's War Financing Project*. This research programme was stimulated by a spectacular growth in corporate cash balances since the outbreak of Second World War and had the task of analysing the significance of this phenomenon to the functioning of the financial system.

The work immediately found a connection with contemporary theories of the value of money and of the role of money in business fluctuations, looking for the role which the behaviour of cash balances of corporations could have in them.

In the United States, since the beginning of the war, bank business deposits had increased sharply. Between the end of 1939 and the end of 1944, the demand deposits of all the commercial banks increased by 120% and about 63% of them were held by domestic business enterprises, which indicated the great relevance of cash balances held by business sector.

Lutz underlined that cash balances give rise to at least two serious problems. First, they could affect the volume of payments and pose problems for monetary management. Second, they could have relevant implications for the financing of government expenses, because the greater their amount, the smaller the amount of government bonds that business bought.

Lutz's study set out to analyse how cash balances had actually behaved over the three decades from 1914 to 1943. It was based on annual financial statements of samples of manufacturing corporations in two size groups, large corporations, on the one hand, and medium-sized and small companies, on the other hand. The assets of the sample of large manufacturing corporations amounted to about 45% of the assets of all large manufacturing corporations in the United States.

Lutz attempted to discover whether there was a definite pattern in the behaviour of corporate cash balances over the period 1919–1939 and, if so, what were its determinants. To this end, he analysed cash balances plus marketable securities in relation to payments. He also studied the movements of corporate cash balances against changes in the total means of payment.

During the First World War, corporations bought marketable securities on a large scale, so that at the end of the war the liquidity position of large manufacturing corporations was higher than at the beginning. After the war, marketable securities continued to be a significant part of corporations' assets.

According to Lutz, all the large corporations utilised outside funds to finance their new investments during the boom that followed the war and in the 1920s large manufacturing corporations held no more cash than was required by their payments. Only in the depression years did the ratio of cash plus marketable securities to payments rise sharply. This ratio diminished from 1933 to 1937, and then rose again in 1938, because of a new business contraction.

Thus, according to Lutz, the ratio of cash plus marketable securities to payments shows a rise in periods of business contraction and a fall in periods of expansion as a rule. The movement of these free liquid funds showed an inverse correlation with the profit rate of the large corporations.

During the 1930s, the large manufacturing corporations held "free" liquid funds – i.e. funds not justified by the volume of their payments. Lutz therefore deduced that they "hoarded" money. The major reason for this accumulation of "free" funds during the early 1930s was that, at the end of the 1920s, the large corporations were largely independent of bank credit, so that their bank debts did not absorb the "surplus" cash originated through liquidation of inventories and receivables during the depression.

The situation had been totally different in 1921, when the large manufacturing corporations were heavily indebted to the banks. At that time, no "free" liquid funds made their appearance. This behaviour suggests that in a system in which companies are not largely indebted to the banks, business fluctuations may be reflected in a change in the velocity of circulation of firms' deposits.

The increase in cash holdings never absorbed more than 3.6% of the total cash receipts of the corporations, and the decrease never financed more than 2.7% of the cash payments. The cash balance was constantly fed on current account, by the difference between receipts from sales and operating expenditures. Instead, the cash receipts from sources other than sales – i.e. increases in funds from outside – were always less than the non-operating expenditures – i.e. dividends and expenditures on fixed equipment.

According to Lutz, during the period of depression in the 1930s, medium-sized and small corporations had a small increase in their cash holdings, because great losses and the retirement of bank debt absorbed the liquid funds that would otherwise have been accumulated. Thus in the 1930s, "hoarding" was mainly a phenomenon of large manufacturing corporations.

In periods of business contraction over the period 1914–1943, corporations' cash balances were fed by partial liquidation of inventories and receivables and by the postponement of replacements for fixed equipment. Most of the additional cash was paid out mainly through distribution of dividends.

As a consequence, in the 1930s, large manufacturing corporations' cash balances tended to rise in relation to other assets during periods of business contraction, and to fall during periods of expansion. However, in the same years, this cyclical pattern was not followed by the medium-sized and small manufacturing concerns.

The corporations' cash balances followed the general cyclical pattern shown by the total means of payment, so that the ratio of cash balances to the total means of payment was relatively stable.

Corporate savings during the Golden Age

The onset of the extraordinary post-war expansion phase reduced the focus on cyclical fluctuations and corporate behaviour in downturns. As we saw in Chapter 2, the gradual establishment of Keynesian approaches in economics also made a decisive contribution to a definitive dismantling of the business cycle paradigm previously prevailing in economic thought, while economists increasingly focused on equilibria with unemployment that cannot change endogenously.

Moreover, in the aftermath of the Second World War, for almost a quarter of a century, the US financial markets were the most developed and liquid in the world, while, although financial liberalisation was under way along with development throughout the rest of the OECD area, most other countries maintained strict financial controls (see Eichengreen, 2007).

In this global context, the United States turned out to be the "banker to the world" (see Despres et al., 1966), importing short-term capital while investing long-term capital abroad (see Eichengreen, 2000). In fact, under the new arrangements of the Bretton Woods System, the United States could take advantage of the dollar's prominent position in the world market by selling low-yielding debt securities abroad while making high-yielding foreign direct investments. In this way, the United States also became a supplier of financial services to the rest of the world. European firms, indeed, borrowed long-term capital from the United States because its capital markets were more efficient and interest rates were lower. On the contrary, many European net savers maintained short-term bank deposits in the US banks because of their higher returns (see Lamfalussy, 1968).

An increasingly developed banking intermediation also provided an alternative to securitised finance, at least until the late 1960s, when a new gravitational shift towards financial intermediation services re-emerged (see Sawyer, 2014). Debt capital also largely collected private saving deriving from the surplus wages, generated by the increase of wage-share in national income due to full-employment policies.

In the first three post-war decades, moreover, the *market for corporate control* was severely limited by the heavily restrictive financial regulation and capital flow control that were the legal heritage of the financial and real crises of the 1930s. However, this lack of control was quietly accepted by the small savers who demanded only liquidity for their assets and desired no commitment for their time and effort.

Nevertheless, in the 1950s and 1960s, large companies continued to favour a high degree of their financial independence through retained earnings (see Baran and Sweezy, 1966). As convenient as it might be to borrow from financial institutions and markets from a purely economic point of view, they strategically preferred to avoid excessive scrutiny by external financial institutions and shareholders.

Although the spreading of Keynes' view helped to divert attention away from savings decisions other than personal ones, in the 1960s, many neo-Keynesians took an intermediate position between Keynes and classical economists and began to deal with the aggregate saving function by assuming that, even though both workers and capitalists can save, the saving proportion of profits is higher than that of wages. Furthermore, as in the context of the modern corporation where not all profits are distributed as capitalists' personal income, some neo-Keynesian economists began to consider that profit retention within enterprises – i.e. corporate savings – is crucial to determining capital accumulation.

In some neo-Keynesian models, therefore, there was a progressive shift of emphasis from households to corporations when dealing with savings. This, of course, was also supported by the rise of the theories on the "managerial revolution" we dealt with in Chapter 1, and raised new concerns regarding corporate governance, as in the so-called "Managerialist Saving Function" (see Pitelis, 1987). However, according to this new approach, differential "saving propensities" between different types of household did not matter so much as differential "saving propensities" between households and corporations.

Kaldor considered the high saving propensity of incomes coming from profits as depending on the very nature of business income and not on the dimension of income or other peculiarities of the individuals who own capital (see Kaldor, 1966, p. 310). His view was justified by the very dilution of corporate ownership within the modern corporation system. Indeed, if shareholders, as pure financial rentiers, tend to consume an increasing part of their dividends and capital gains in luxury goods, then the aggregate propensity to save and the guarantee of capital accumulation will depend mainly on the propensity to save of the companies themselves (see Kaldor, 1966, p. 311).

This shift of emphasis to differential saving propensities between household income and corporate income also characterised the analyses of Galbraith (1967) and Marglin (1975), leading them to conclude that today's economy is characterised by "producers' sovereignty" rather than "consumers' sovereignty". In this scenario, the subset of capital owners that effectively control corporations saves in the form of corporate savings not only a portion of its own income, but also a portion of the income of the non-controlling subset of shareholders (see Pitelis, 1987).

Thus, despite the scant analytical attention paid by the mainstream economic literature to aspects of corporate savings, during the 1950s and 1960s, tax incentives were extensively used by the governments in the United Kingdom and the United States to reduce dividends and encourage corporate savings in the belief that this would increase investment spending (see Feldstein and Flemming, 1971; Feldstein, 1973). The US government, in particular, provided strong incentives for companies to save a substantial fraction of their income, taxing the capital gains that resulted from retained earnings at half of the personal income tax rate and only when realisation occurred, while dividends were taxed as personal income. In this way, the effective tax rate on retained earnings was very much less than the rate on dividends.

This tax incentive induced companies to increase the fraction of their total earnings they saved (see Brittain, 1966) so that in the 1960s, corporate-retained earnings became more than 50% of corporate net income and gross corporate savings exceeded 75% of corporate cash flow after tax. Total corporate saving rose to 52% of gross private saving and 40% of net private saving, accounting for a large portion of total investment (see Feldstein, 1973).

The rise in corporate saving, however, did not imply an equal rise in capital accumulation. This was explained as the effect of the reaction by shareholders who took corporate savings into account in making their individual saving decisions, reducing the level of their personal saving (see Feldstein, 1973).

NFC savings around the financial crisis of 2007–2008

According to the available OECD data, in the early 1970s, the US total corporate gross saving accounted on average for 42% of gross national saving.

However, NFC gross saving as a share of gross national saving started to increase significantly in the early 1980s, rising from 45% in 1980 to 66% in 2010 (see Figure 6.1). In the second decade of the 21st century, it then declined slightly, hovering around 50% for some years. In 2018, however, it rose again to 66%.

According to the available OECD time series, other advanced countries have shown similar trends since 1995 (see Figure 6.1). The United Kingdom and Japan even show higher amounts of the NFC gross saving as a share of gross national saving than the United States. NFC gross saving of the United Kingdom accounted for 67% of gross national saving in 1995 and rose to 85% in 2010. NFC gross saving of Japan accounted for 50% of gross national saving in 1995 and rose to 83% in 2013. The share of NFC gross saving in gross national saving of both countries shows a downward trend after these peaks, but, in the United Kingdom, it shows a new upward trend after 2018, rising again to 79% in 2020.

In this context, China is the exception. Although between 1995 and 2000, the ratio of NFC gross saving to national gross saving rose from 50% to 56%, it subsequently showed a downward trend, hovering around 40% in the end.

Despite the rise in their corporate savings, up until the early 1990s, NFCs in the advanced countries continued to be – on average – net borrowers, as common sense would expect. However, things were quickly changing.

Since 2001, the non-financial sector, just as in the years before the 1929 financial crisis, became a net lender in most G7 countries (see Figures 6.2–6.8).

In this context, the United States and Italy were partial exceptions, although for different reasons. In the United States, NFCs were net lenders only for very short periods – in 2005, 2009–2012 and 2018 – mainly in the proximity or the aftermath of the financial crisis (see Figure 6.2). The Italian

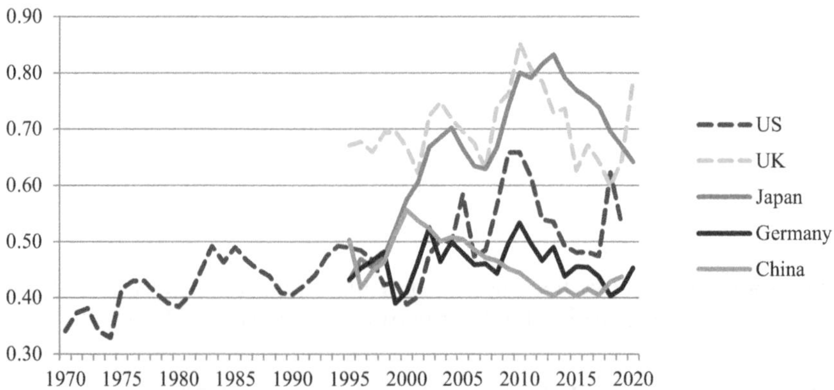

Figure 6.1 NFC gross saving as a share of gross national saving.
Source: OECD.

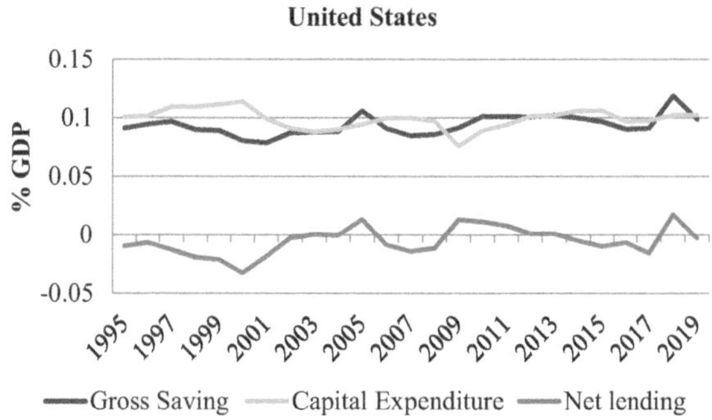

Figure 6.2 Gross saving, capital expenditure and net lending of NFCs as a share of GDP in the United States.

Source: OECD.

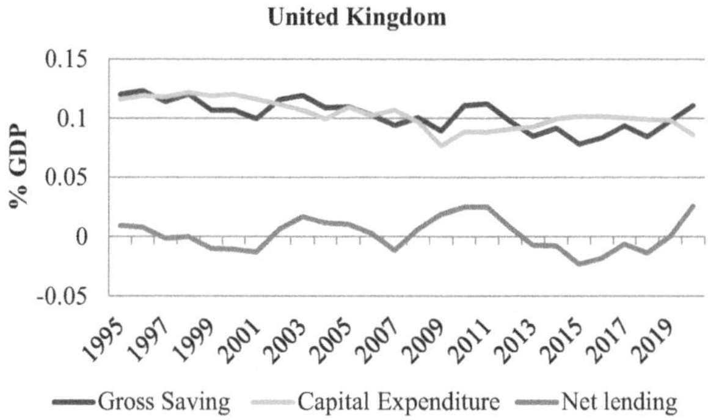

Figure 6.3 Gross saving, capital expenditure and net lending of NFCs as a share of GDP in the United Kingdom.

Source: OECD.

non-financial sector, mainly made up of SMEs, remained a net borrower throughout all of the first decade of the 2000s, but, in the end, also turned into a net lender after the euro crisis of 2011 (see Figure 6.8).

The Canadian and British non-financial sectors, however, remained net lenders for the entire first decade of the 21st century, turning to net borrower positions only after 2013 (see Figures 6.3 and 6.4). The French non-financial sector, in turn, although it was clearly a net lender in the early 2000s, quickly returned to a slight net borrower position after the 2007–2008 financial crisis (see Figure 6.7). In contrast, the German and Japanese non-financial sectors have remained decidedly net lenders (see Figures 6.5 and 6.6).

China's non-financial sector, however, was not affected at all by the phenomenon and neither were non-financial sectors in most emerging countries (see Figure 6.9).

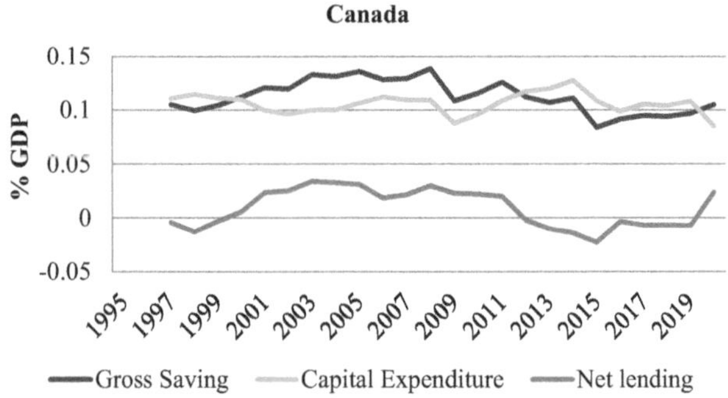

Figure 6.4 Gross saving, capital expenditure and net lending of NFCs as a share of GDP in Canada.

Source: OECD.

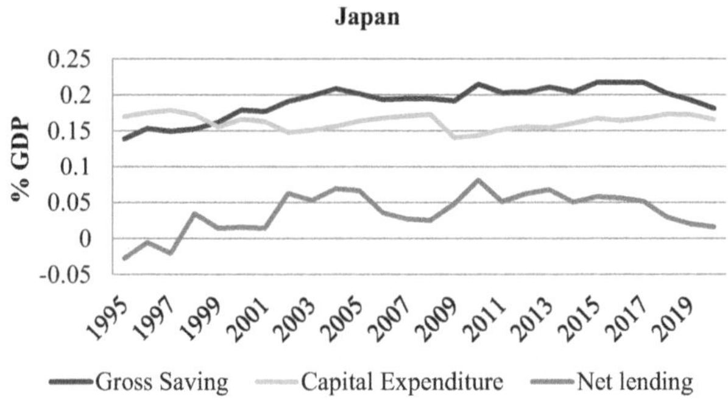

Figure 6.5 Gross saving, capital expenditure and net lending of NFCs as a share of GDP in Japan.

Source: OECD.

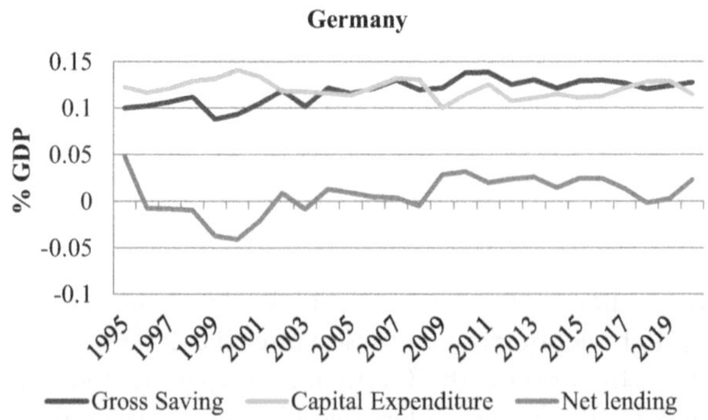

Figure 6.6 Gross saving, capital expenditure and net lending of NFCs as a share of GDP in Germany.

Source: OECD.

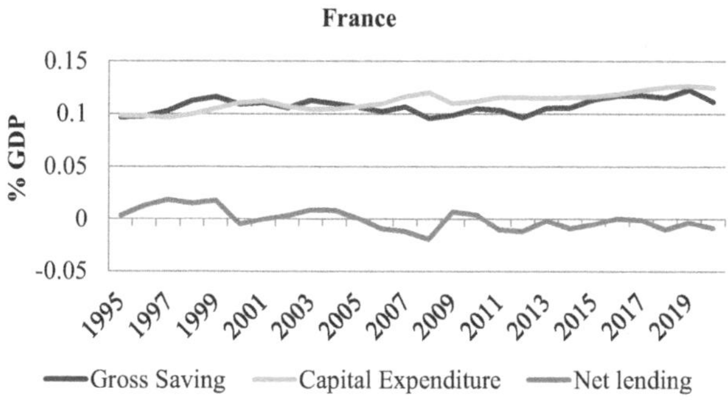

Figure 6.7 Gross saving, capital expenditure and net lending of NFCs as a share of GDP in France.

Source: OECD.

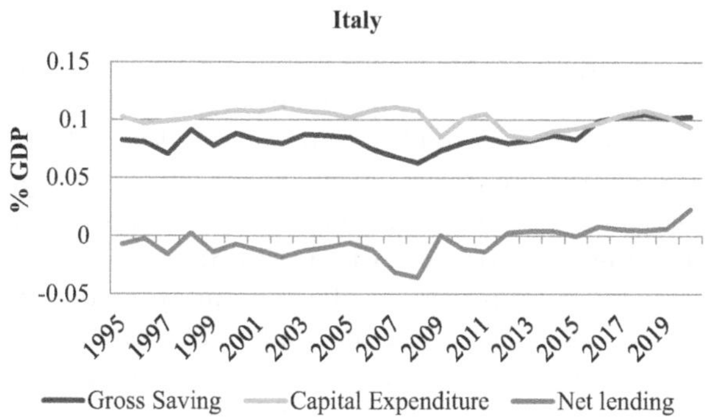

Figure 6.8 Gross saving, capital expenditure and net lending of NFCs as a share of GDP in Italy.

Source: OECD.

However, the rise in net lending is the result of two different tendencies: an increasing corporate saving share, on the one hand, and falling corporate investment, on the other (see Figures 6.2–6.9).

Over the last 20 years, in most advanced countries, rising corporate savings have been largely correlated with increasing profit shares – in turn, related to domestic wage moderation, lower interest rates and deleveraging of corporate balance sheets (see OECD, 2007; Karabarbounis and Neiman, 2013, 2014; Villani, 2021). Yet increasing profits from abroad, too, have probably played a major role. Cesaroni et al. (2018), through an econometric analysis, including 18 industrial countries over the period 1995–2014, found that corporate surpluses were structurally linked to net foreign direct investment.

The decline in real corporate investment relative to GDP, in turn, accounts for half of the increase in OECD aggregate corporate net lending over the period 2001–2005. The weakness in corporate investment, compared with

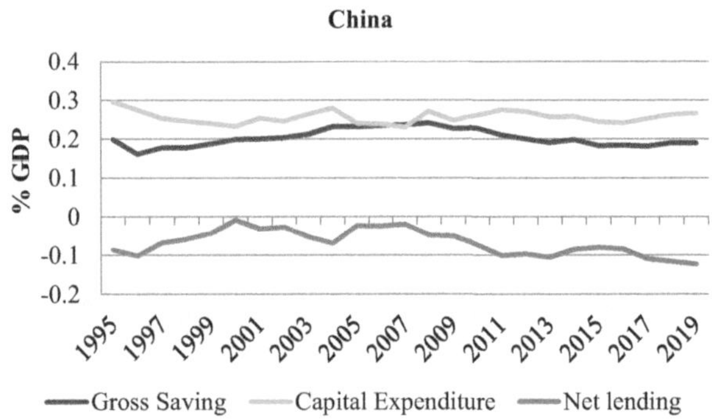

Figure 6.9 Gross saving, capital expenditure and net lending of NFCs as a share of GDP in China.

Source: OECD.

GDP, may be largely the consequence of the business cycle or the reaction to previous over-accumulation of capital during the bubble of the late 1990s. Yet, other causes, more structural in nature and thus longer lasting, have been detected in the progressive decline of the relative price of capital goods, in lower depreciation rates, in lower growth trends and, once again, increasing net foreign investment abroad (see Scarano, 2015).

Among the many reasons that have been found to account for the financial crisis of 2007–2008, one of the most interesting is, in our view, that of the "global saving glut", which, according to some privileged observers (see Greenspan, 2011), was the principal cause of the international imbalances that set off the crisis.

The concept of "global saving glut" had originally been defined by Ben Bernanke in March 2005, before the crisis, to denote the excess of saving over investment in the world economy, which was, according to him, lowering interest rates and encouraging risky financial investments (see Bernanke, 2005). However, the trend in the global saving rate had in fact been declining since the late 1970s, falling from 23% in 1970 to 19.6% in 2002, along the downward phase of a long-term cycle. When Bernanke identified the global saving glut phenomenon, the global saving rate had only temporarily risen above the average of the previous decades, but was still on a downward trend. Thus, no saving glut could really be attributed to an increase in the global saving rate above its long-term average (see Jauch, 2012).

In 2010, the McKinsey Global Institute, when decomposing savings of the world economy in their major institutional components (households, corporations and governments), stressed the increasing importance of the corporate sector in the global supply of loanable funds. Indeed, while household saving had been declining in developed countries, the corporate sector had increased its share in total saving worldwide, raising its own saving rate. About two-thirds of the supply of loanable funds in the capital markets of the developed countries eventually came from the corporate sector (see McKinsey Global Institute, 2010).

Thus, as early as 2005, *The Economist* argued that the saving glut highlighted by Bernanke was actually a "corporate saving glut" – i.e. a positive difference between undistributed profits and corporate capital expenditure – which was paradoxically transformed into net lending by the corporate sector (see The Economist, 2005).

From 2001 to 2005, the excess of gross saving over fixed investment in the OECD corporate sector was unusually large and rose more than the aggregate external surplus of the emerging market economies, driving the run-up in net lending and contributing to low global interest rates (see André et al., 2007; OECD, 2007). In this context, the financial sector was responsible for about 66% of the total increase in retained earnings, but, paradoxically, contributed less to the increase in net lending than the non-financial sector (see Loeys et al., 2005).

Since 2005, many research institutes pointed out the excess of corporate savings accounted during the early 2000s. In 2005, for example, a JPMorgan's research team showed that the increase in G6 corporate savings was about 5 times higher than the overall saving increase in emerging countries (see Loeys et al., 2005). In 2007, the OECD, in turn, pointed out that the increase in OECD corporate savings over the period 2001–2005 was 1.35 times the increase in total saving of all non-OECD countries (see Figure 6.10).

This level of corporate saving was immediately recognised as unprecedented and producing an economic result that, in the light of mainstream economic theory, was paradoxical: companies became net lenders against households that became net borrowers.

In the United States, most of the rising corporate savings were initially used to repay corporate debt accumulated during the 1990s. This prompted the hypothesis that deleveraging was one of the main reasons for the rise in corporate saving. Analysing the *net debt ratio* of American NFCs, Bates et al. (2009) found a "sharp secular decrease" in net debt, which, according to their analysis, was essentially fostered by the increase in cash holdings. However, according to Saibene (2019), there is no empirical evidence of a long-lasting strategy of deleveraging in the sample of American listed companies he analysed. And, indeed, in the early 2000s, the use of rising corporate savings quickly turned towards share buybacks (see Loeys et al., 2005). This kind of operation, involving an exchange of cash against equity, does not affect gross saving in national accounts and appears statistically as a use of corporate saving rather than a way of revealing it.

European companies, in turn, exhibited similar trends. However, in contrast to the US experience, in continental Europe, the household saving rate actually increased, probably for demographic reasons, but perhaps also because of new concerns about the future horizons generated by the EU's ongoing structural reforms (see Loeys et al., 2005).

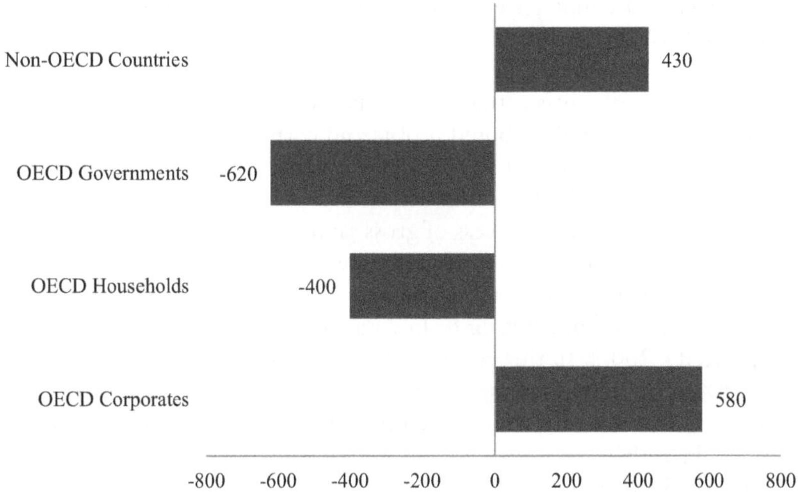

Figure 6.10 Changes in net lending between 2001 and 2005 ($ billion).
Source: OECD 2007.

An increase in corporate saving was also evident in the rapidly growing emerging market economies, although, in this case, this was predominantly explained on the basis of the liquid assets needed by credit-constrained firms (see Bacchetta and Benhima, 2015; Fan and Kalemli-Özcan, 2016). In the early 2000s, for example, Chinese companies saw their profits rise sharply in all production sectors and most of these increased profits were held as retained earnings with very low dividend distribution rates. However, in this case, the increase in corporate savings was largely used to expand productive investment in companies' core business.

Thus, the increase in corporate saving prior to the financial crisis of 2007–2008 was a widespread phenomenon worldwide and across sectors (see Scarano, 2015; Dao and Maggi, 2018; Saibene, 2019).

In the same period, the financial sector was a major contributor to the overall increase in corporate net lending, accounting for about 20% of the total, while the sector accounted for only 10% in terms of value added. However, before the financial crisis, in many countries, the increase in corporate net lending was significantly fed also by construction, real estate and the housing sectors, even though these drivers completely vanished with the burst of the real estate bubble.

Today, an extensive literature is available on the corporate saving glut and the resulting increase in the net lending position of NFCs. However, no comprehensive explanation for these phenomena has yet emerged.

The change in the corporate saving rate was initially interpreted as a short-term response to the previous over-investment in the 1990s, made in the context of a bubble in the stock markets of the developed countries and large capital inflows in the emerging countries prior to the Asian financial crisis. As a result, the corporate saving glut was initially dealt with only as a short-term anomaly – due to adjustments produced by previous exogenous shocks – and expected to disappear rapidly (see Loeys et al., 2005; IMF, 2006). Unfortunately, these views and expectations turned out to be wrong (see Cesaroni et al., 2018).

In fact, the net lending positions of NFCs persisted in most advanced countries even after the financial crisis of 2007–2008, albeit with some fluctuations (see Figures 6.2–6.8). This has led some analysts to believe that the phenomenon is actually a symptom of a new phase of "secular stagnation" (see Artica et al., 2017).

The IMF (2006) and André et al. (2007) were among the first to highlight a global increase in corporate saving relative to investment in advanced economies – which led to a simultaneous increase in NFCs' net lending position – pointing out the relevance of both cyclical and structural factors. The growing corporate saving glut was occurring both in countries that had previously experienced strong economic growth and in those showing very weak growth. However, by the early 2000s, most of these economies had been hit by the consequences of the bursting of the stock market bubble in the late 1990s, which had produced high levels of corporate debt (see IMF, 2006).

Moreover, according to the results of the panel regression analysis carried out by André et al., a decrease in the output gap of 1% generates an increase in corporate net lending of 0.5% of GDP. On the basis of this estimation, therefore, more than 25% of the increase in aggregate OECD corporate net lending between 2001 and 2005 could statistically be accounted for by the downturn of the cycle (see André et al., 2007).

However, according to both the IMF (2006) and André et al. (2007), the growth in corporate net lending could mainly be explained by a sudden and unexpected increase in corporate profitability – in turn, produced by a fall in taxes and interest rates, as well as by a fall in the price of capital goods – which lowered the cost of productive investment and therefore determined an automatic increase in corporate gross savings.

In 2007, the OECD distinguished between cyclical, transitory and trend drivers of corporate net lending, separating those which appeared to be common across most OECD countries from those which appeared to be country-specific (see OECD, 2007). This analysis showed that the large-scale expansion of corporate net lending was partly the transitory effect of two overlapping phenomena that simultaneously occurred in the financial sector, on the one hand, and in the non-financial sector on the other. In the former, net lending was mainly explained by short-term financial variables, such as decreasing interest rates and real house prices driven by the housing bubble. In the latter, net lending was mainly interpreted as partly due to the cyclical downturn since 2001. Cross-country differences in gross corporate savings were, in turn, explained as due to differences in gross operating surplus resulting from changes in profitability within sectors and not from a change in sectoral composition.

When analysing the role of NFC declining investment in enhancing corporate net lending in OECD countries, Gruber and Kamin (2015) also reached the conclusion that the amount of the latter was largely of cyclical nature.

In countries where the households' net lending position has remained positive, additional corporate net lending has produced a significant increase in overall private net lending. The national current account position, therefore, has ended up depending on the government's financial position alone. So, in the United Kingdom and the United States, government's net borrowing more than compensates for the private saving glut, producing a persistent current account deficit. In countries such as Germany, Japan, Korea and the Netherlands, however, where governments have not absorbed all the private saving glut, corporate net lending produces a persistent current account surplus (see IMF, 2017; Dao and Maggi, 2018).

Dao and Maggi (2018) also found a robust co-movement between the aggregate corporate net lending measured by national accounts and the firm level data of large listed companies. Among the companies analysed, those which show positive net lending are larger and more profitable than the others, engage strongly in R&D and have low effective tax rates due to their capacity to utilise complex international tax strategies. Saibene (2019), who analysed all NFCs listed in the US stock markets, also found that only the largest companies actually became net lenders, while small and R&D-intensive companies remained net borrowers. All this suggests that it is the saving-investment behaviour of large corporations which is the major mover of the trends in aggregate corporate net lending recorded by national accounts.

However, companies' net lending ultimately depends on the fact that the balance between increasing profits and decreasing productive investment is not distributed to shareholders. Over the last three decades, indeed, dividends did not increase in parallel with profits and in some cases fell relative to them. In point of fact, in the United States and Europe, over the period 1989–2003, fewer companies paid dividends, although those that paid some, paid more (see von Eije and Megginson, 2008).

Most often, the rising profits were transferred to the shareholders indirectly, through share buybacks. In the United States, according to some private datasets, share buybacks increased very rapidly over the period 2001–2005 (see OECD, 2007). There is some evidence that in the United Kingdom, too, share buybacks played a significant role. However, as we have seen, one usual good reason for increasing share buybacks is also cyclical in nature because they are a way to transfer extra funds to shareholders when profits are rising, avoiding cuts in dividends when profits subsequently drop. Therefore, massive share buybacks may be seen as a sign of a healthy current business with poor expectations for the future.

However, the corporate saving glut has often been consistently held in very liquid assets, such as currency, deposits and short-term debt (see OECD,

2007; Dao and Maggi, 2018). Thus, there is an evident connection between the corporate saving glut and corporate liquidity holding. However, what is the causal link?

The rise of NFC liquidity holdings

If growing corporate cash balances seem relatively trivial after the financial crisis of 2007–2008, its first seven years before the crisis were a warning sign, which, in 2012, led the business press to write about "hoard instinct" and "dead money" and to argue that corporations were driving a global shift to thrift (see The Economist, 2012; Wolf, 2015).

Dao and Maggi (2018), when analysing the co-movements of the empirical determinants of cash holdings and the net lending positions of companies in advanced countries, suggest that it was precisely the changes in demand for cash that drove the rise of corporate saving, with considerable implications also for the current account surpluses of some countries whose increase and persistence are mainly driven by non-financial sector cash holding.

However, since internal financing necessities should theoretically be the main drivers of companies' gross savings, it is crucial to understand why companies may reduce their pay-out ratios without increasing investment spending (see Jauch, 2012).

Liquidity holding is most certainly a buffer against sudden shocks to cash flows. All companies need liquidity to face shocks against which they are not completely hedged. Holding companies may, in particular, need to withstand several liquidity shocks deriving from the ample range of their controlled economic activities since they may forego profitable new investment opportunities if they were unable to liquidate their assets quickly (see Tirole, 2006). Thus, precautionary motives in uncertain and turbulent times are as good a reason for NFCs to hold cash or near-cash securities as to buy back shares and macroeconomic uncertainty has most likely played a major role in shaping companies' liquidity management over the last two decades (see Baum et al., 2009).

Indeed, since the bursting of the speculative bubble in the 1990s, uncertainty has come to dominate the global economic scene for non-financial sectors. After the financial crisis of 2007–2008, NFCs were certainly keen to accumulate larger cash balances to cope with the credit crunch. In the case of US corporations, furthermore, there were also tax incentives to repatriate cash from foreign subsidiaries at a time when most large companies were waiting to invest and make acquisitions due to uncertainty about profitability in the wake of the crisis. And, of course, all this can explain longer or shorter periods of unusual liquidity holding.

However, since 1995, NFCs in most G7 countries have held huge amounts of liquidity for long periods, all of which do not unequivocally qualify as downturns.

Nowadays, an extensive literature on corporate finance provides both evidence for and attempts to explain the rise in corporate cash holdings over the last two decades. This literature, unfortunately, is overwhelmingly focused on the United States. However, most analyses contrast with the possible view that companies may hold cash due to the lack of investment opportunities while several possible structural drivers have been identified.

Some analysts focus on the changes in institutional factors that affected the overall business environment. Foley et al. (2007), for example, highlight the role of tax-induced motive for cash holdings, while Azar et al. (2016) point out the changes in the costs of holding cash over time. When analysing cash holding over almost a century in the United States, Graham and Leary (2018) find that macroeconomic environmental conditions, such as profit opportunities and tax incentives, have had a significant role in determining cash holding in the US companies since 2000.

Armenter and Hnatkovska (2017), in turn, built a general equilibrium model to explain the rise in net lending of US corporations, where corporate saving is essentially led by the precautionary motive of accumulating financial assets and cash holdings to avoid potential financial constraints in the future.

The view that it is uncertainty and precautionary motives that lead to cash holding is also shared by Bates et al. (2018) who see them as the main determinants of an increase in the *shadow value* of cash holding, fully accepted and appreciated by shareholders themselves. However, according to Saibene (2019), there is no empirical evidence for the hypothesis of long-term precautionary motives for holding cash in the sample of US listed companies he analysed.

An alternative theoretical explanation was proposed by Chen et al. (2017), on the basis of another general equilibrium model, according to which it is essentially the decline in the prices of capital goods and real interest rates which reduces the amounts of corporate real investment and increases corporate savings, which are, in turn, used for share buybacks instead of dividend pay-out due to tax incentives.

However, many studies have also focused on the structural features of the new leading companies and their core business. According to Bates et al. (2009), the largest increase in liquidity holding occurred in companies with higher idiosyncratic risk, higher R&D expenditures and higher *Tobin's q*. Others scholars, in turn, have emphasised the role played by R&D, asserting that it encourages companies to move towards investment in intangible capital and reduces the proportion of tangible capital in the total assets when they go public (see Booth and Zhou, 2013; Graham and Leary, 2018; Begenau and Palazzo, 2021).

Thus, some economists have been spurred to focus on the possible role of intangible capital in itself. Falato et al. (2013), for example, argue that it is precisely the lack of pledgeability of intangible capital that, by reducing the external debt capacity of financially constrained innovative companies, prompts higher liquidity holdings to finance future investment opportunities. Other characteristics of intangible capital, such as its financing profile or its nature of capitalised costs, have also been pointed out by other economists as the main drivers of liquidity holding in innovating companies (see Ma et al., 2014; Döttling et al., 2016; Lyandres and Palazzo, 2016).

However, we believe that this is an explanation that may conceivably be adequate for companies such as Microsoft and Alphabet, which had, in 2020, huge cash reserves of around $134 billion and $122 billion, respectively (see Ross et al., 2022). However, current NFC liquidity is too large and widespread to be justified by innovating companies alone. In 2020, Ford, which is certainly not one of the most innovating corporations, had, for example, a huge cash balance of $46.4 billion, against a market capitalisation of just under $20 billion (see Ross et al., 2022, p. 646). If intangible capital really matters, it cannot only be traced back to the intangible results of R&D. In fact, it may also largely be made up of the mere capitalisation of future extra-profits which are more generally linked to the branding strategies of monopolistic competition between large multinational corporations.

Another strand of literature on liquidity holding also highlights the role played by increasing product market competition on a global scale which promotes higher cash holdings due to the need to rely on internal funds to finance future investment and gain strategic competitive edge (see Irvine and Pontiff, 2008; Della Seta, 2011; Ma et al., 2014; Morellec et al., 2014; Lyandres and Palazzo, 2016). In order to increase their market power, in fact, large corporations must pursue acquisitions as well as predatory practices which all need large cash balances and liquid assets holdings (see Saibene, 2019).

In any case, in the early 2000s, the corporate saving glut exceeded the increase in cash balances and also followed a path of risky financial investment, just as in the 1920s, helping to create the preconditions for the financial crisis of 2007–2008. Yet, over the last decade, too, in the advanced countries, NFCs have invested heavily in financial assets, making the boundaries between them and financial companies increasingly blurred.

Economic uncertainty undoubtedly may also affect holdings of non-currency financial assets, especially in less financially constrained companies. Financial assets, indeed, may be important components of corporate liquidity management of NFCs, which may hold them as precautionary saving (see Duchin et al., 2017). However, in addition to precautionary motives, trading and speculation may also be effective underlying reasons for companies to increase their holdings in non-currency financial assets (see Campbell and Kracaw, 1990; Ljungqvist, 1994; Huang et al., 2021). In other words, NFCs may increase their financial holdings not only to protect themselves from corporate liquidity crises, but also to improve the valorisation of shareholders' capital (see Huang et al., 2021).

Thus, if large NFCs gradually turn into large financial investors, they will be increasingly characterised by short-termism and need liquidity to guarantee flexibility to seize new financial investment opportunities. There is an evident trade-off between commitment and liquidity. Therefore, increasing cash holding by NFCs could also be the mere symptom of their progressive financialisation.

Post-Keynesians, too, deal with a possible connection between rising corporate net lending and financialisation (see Villani, 2021). However, in the context of this theoretical approach, in accordance with what we saw in Chapter 1, the main connection is identified exclusively in the alleged effects that financialisation – broadly understood as the rise to power of finance – may produce by depressing real investment against an increasing profit share. Once again, therefore, net lending seems to be explained as an automatic balance between rising profits and decreasing capital expenditure, with no explanation as to why the higher surpluses are not distributed to shareholders and are held in cash and liquid assets.

In any case, whatever their real reasons, huge increases in cash and near-cash holdings are actually hoarding which, as in Marx's theory of crisis, could be once again the first mover of decreasing aggregate investment that actually lies behind the multiform appearances of financialisation.

The huge rise of liquidity holding, moreover, calls into question the post-Keynesian view that today's NFCs are subjected to the tyranny of shareholders and financial markets. As we saw in Section "Liquidity Holding and Corporate Saving" indeed, shareholders should limit managers' access to free cash flow to mitigate agency conflicts, and large cash balances should be a negative signal for markets, unless the latter are fully aware of the *shadow value* of holding liquidity in a context of high macroeconomic uncertainty, as supposed by Bates et al. (2018).

Finally, what we have outlined in this chapter shows, in our view, the increasing role that large NFCs play in determining both the amounts of aggregate saving and their forms of utilisation in advanced countries. Today, therefore, large NFCs present themselves as the main actors in managing the relation between saving and investment which ends up being largely internalised within them.

Thus, if large NFCs are increasingly turning into large financial investors, the relationships between financial investment, real investment and cash holding become more and more a mere matter of their portfolio choices.

References

André, C. et al. (2007). "Corporate Net Lending: A Review of Recent Trends". *OECD Economics Department Working Papers*, 583, OECD Publishing.

Armenter, R. and Hnatkovska, V. (2017). "Taxes and Capital Structure: Understanding Firms Savings". *Journal of Monetary Economics*, 87: 13–33.

Artica, R. P., Brufman, L. and Martinez, L. B. (2017). "Delving into the Secular Stagnation Hypothesis: A Firm-Level Analysis of the Private Sector's Excess Savings in Advanced Economies". *Comparative Economic Studies*, 59 (1): 77 –106.

Azar, J., Kagy, J.-F. and Schmalz, M. C. (2016). "Can Changes in the Cost of Carry Explain the Dynamics of Corporate 'Cash' Holdings?" *Review of Financial Studies*, 29 (8): 2194–2240.

Bacchetta, P. and Benhima, K. (2015). "The Demand for Liquid Assets, Corporate Saving, and International Capital Flows". *Journal of the European Economic Association*, 13 (6): 1101–1135.

Baran, P. and Sweezy, P. M. (1966). *Monopoly Capital. An Essay on the American Economic and Social Order.* New York: Monthly Review Press.

Bates, T. W., Chang, C. H., and Chi, J. D. (2018). "Why Has the Value of Cash Increased over Time?". *Journal of Financial and Quantitative Analysis*, 53 (2): 749–787.

Bates, T. W., Kahle, K. M. and Stulz, R. M. (2009). "Why Do Us Firms Hold So Much More Cash Than They Used to?" *The Journal of Finance*, 64 (5): 1985–2021.

Baum, C. F., Caglayan, M., Ozkan, N. and Talavera, O. (2006). "The Impact of Macroeconomic Uncertainty on Cash Holdings for Non–Financial Firms". *Review of Financial Economics*, 15 (4): 289–304.

Begenau, J. and Palazzo, B. (2021). "Firm Selection and Corporate Cash Holdings". *Journal of Financial Economics*, 139 (3): 697–718.

Berle, A. A. Jr. and Means, G. C. (1936). *The Modern Corporation and Private Property.* New York: The Macmillan Company.

Bernanke, B. (2005). "The Global Saving Glut and the U.S. Current Account Deficit". Remarks by Governor Ben S. Bernanke at the Sandridge Lecture, Virginia Association of Economics, Richmond, Virginia.

Booth, L. D. and Zhou, J. (2013). "Increase in Cash Holdings: Pervasive or Sector-Specific?" *Frontiers in Finance and Economics*, 10 (2): 31–64.

Brittain, J.A. (1966). *Corporate dividend policy.* Washington, DC: The Brookings Institution.

Buchanan, S. (1938). "Theory and Practice in Dividend Distribution". *The Quarterly Journal of Economics*, 53 (1): 64–85.

Campbell, T. S. and Kracaw, W. A. (1990). "Corporate Risk Management and the Incentive Effects of Debt". *Journal of Finance*, 45 (5): 1673–1686.

Cesaroni, T., De Bonis, R. and Infante, L. (2018). "Firms' Financial Surpluses in Advanced Economies: The Role of Net Foreign Direct Investments". *LLEE Working Paper Series*, 137.

Chen, P., Karabarbounis, L. and Neiman, B. (2017). "The Global Rise of Corporate Saving". *Journal of Monetary Economics*, 89 (C): 1–19.

Dao, M. C. and Maggi, C. (2018). "The Rise in Corporate Saving and Cash Holding in Advanced Economies: Aggregate and Firm Level Trends". *IMF Working Papers*, 262.

Della Seta, M. (2011). "Cash and Competition", *SSRN Electronic Journal.* SSRN: https://ssrn.com/abstract=1808979 or http://dx.doi.org/10.2139/ssrn.1808979

Despres, E., Kindleberger, C. P. and Salant, W. S. (1966). *The Dollar and World Liquidity: A Minority View.* Washington, DC: Brookings Institution.

Dittmar, A., Mahrt-Smith, J. and Servaes, H. (2003). "International Corporate Governance and Corporate Cash Holdings". *Journal of Financial and Quantitative Analysis*, 38: 111–133.

Dobrovolsky, S. P. (1945). "Corporate Retained Earnings and Cyclical Fluctuations". *The American Economic Review*, 35 (4): 559–574.

Dobrovolsky, S. P. (1951). *Corporate Income Retention, 1915–43*, NBER.

Döttling, R., Ladika, T. and Perotti, E. C. (2016). "The (Self-) Funding of Intangibles". *Tinbergen Institute Discussion Papers*, 16–093/IV.

Duchin, R. A. N., Gilbert, T., Harford, J. and Hrdlicka, C. (2017). "Precautionary Savings with Risky Assets: When Cash Is Not Cash". *Journal of Finance*, 72 (2): 793–852.

Ebersole, J. F., Burr, S. S. and Peterson, G. M. (1929). "Income Forecasting by the Use of Statistics of Income Data". *Review of Economic Statistics*, 11 (4): 171–196.

The Economist (2005). "The Corporate Savings Glut". July 7th.

The Economist (2012). "Dead Money". November 3rd.

Eichengreen, B. (2000). "From Benign Neglect to Malignant Preoccupation: U.S. Balance-of-Payments Policy in the 1960s". *NBER Working Paper Series*, 7630.

Eichengreen, B. (2007). *Global Imbalances and the Lessons of Bretton Woods*. Cambridge, MA and London: The MIT Press.

Falato, A., Kadyrzhanova, D. and Sim, J. W. (2013). "Rising Intangible Capital, Shrinking Debt Capacity, and the US Corporate Savings Glut". In: *Finance Economics Discussion Series*. Washington, DC: Federal Reserve Board: 2013–2067.

Faleye, O. (2004). "Cash and Corporate Control". *Journal of Finance*, 59: 2041–2060.

Fan, J. and Kalemli-Özcan, S. (2016). "Emergence of Asia: Reforms, Corporate Savings, and Global Imbalances". *IMF Economic Review*, 64 (2): 239–267.

Feldstein, M. S. (1973). "Tax Incentives, Corporate Saving, and Capital Accumulation in the United States". *Journal of Public Economics*, 2 (2): 159–171.

Feldstein, M. S. and Flemming, J. S. (1971). "Tax Policy, Corporate Saving and Investment Behaviour in Britain". *The Review of Economic Studies*, 38 (4): 415–434.

Foley, C. F., Hartzell, J. C., Titman, S. and Twite, G. (2007). "Why do Firms Hold So Much Cash? A Tax-Based Explanation". *Journal of Financial Economics*, 86 (3): 579–607.

Galbraith, J. K. (1955). *The Great Crash. 1929*. London: Hamish Hamilton.

Galbraith, J. K. (1967). *The New Industrial State*. London: Penguin Books.

Graham, J. R. and Leary, M. T. (2018). "The Evolution of Corporate Cash". *Journal of Applied Corporate Finance*, 30 (4): 36–60.

Greenspan A. (2011). "Testimony to the Financial Crisis Inquiry Commission by Alan Greenspan". In: Dejuán, Ó., Febrero, E. and Marcuzzo, M. C. (eds.), *The First Great Recession of the 21st Century. Competing Explanations*. Cheltenham: Edward Elgar Publishing Limited, pp. 173–82.

Gruber, J. W. and Kamin, S. B. (2015). "The Corporate Saving Glut in the Aftermath of the Global Financial Crisis". *IMF Working Paper*, 1150.

Harford, J., Mansib, S. A. and Maxwell, W. F. (2008). "Corporate Governance and Firm Cash Holdings in the US". *Journal of Financial Economics*, 87: 535–555.

Huang, J., Luo, Y. and Peng, Y. (2021). "Corporate Financial Asset Holdings Under Economic Policy Uncertainty: Precautionary Saving or Speculating?" *International Review of Economics and Finance*, 76 (C): 1359–1378.

IMF (2006). "Awash with Cash: Why Are Corporate Savings So High?" *World Economic Outlook. Globalization and Inflation*. Washington, DC: International Monetary Fund.

IMF (2017). "External Sector Report". Washington, DC: International Monetary Fund.

Irvine, P. J. and Pontiff, J. (2009). "Idiosyncratic Return Volatility, Cash Flows, and Product Market Competition". *The Review of Financial Studies*, 22 (3): 1149–1177.

Jauch, S. (2012). "The Global Savings Glut, Corporate Savings and the Role of Share Repurchases". *Ludwig Maximilians Universitat Working Paper*.

Jensen, M. C. (1986). "Agency Cost of Free Cash Flow, Corporate Finance and Takeovers". *The American Economic Review*, 76 (2): 323–329.

Jewkes, J. (1931), "Stock Dividends in Large and Small Companies". *The Quarterly Journal of Economics*, 45 (2): 352–357.

Johnson, H. G. (1961). "The General Theory after Twenty-Five Years". *American Economic Review*, 51(2): 1–17.

Kaldor, N. (1966). "Marginal Productivity and Macro-Economic Theories of Distribution". *Review of Economic Studies*, 33 (4): 309–319.

Karabarbounis, L. and Neiman, B. (2013). "Declining Labor Shares and the Global Rise of Corporate Saving". *NBER Working Paper*, 18154.

Karabarbounis, L. and Neiman, B. (2014). "The Global Decline of the Labor Share". *The Quarterly Journal of Economics*, 129 (1): 61–103.

Keynes, J. M. (1936/2013). *The General Theory of Employment, Interest and Money. The Collected Writings of John Maynard Keynes.* Volume VII. Cambridge: Cambridge University Press.

Knauth, O. W. (1922). "The Place of Corporate Surplus in the National Income". *Journal of the American Statistical Association*, 18 (138): 157–166.

Kotany, L. (1922). "A Theory of Profit and Interest". *The Quarterly Journal of Economics*, 36 (3): 413–453.

Lamfalussy, A. (1968). *Les Marches financiers en Europe.* Paris: Presses Universitaires de France.

Lins, K. and Kalcheva, I. (2007). "International Evidence on Cash Holdings and Expected Managerial Agency Problems". *The Review of Financial Studies*, 20 (4): 1087–1112.

Livermore, S. (1938). "The Economics of Corporate Saving, by J. Ellwood Amos". *Journal of the American Statistical Association*, 33 (204): 781–782.

Ljungqvist, L. (1994). "Asymmetric Information: A Rationale for Corporate Speculation". *Journal of Financial Intermediation*, 3 (2): 188–203.

Loeys, J., Mackie, D., Meggyesi, P. and Panigirtzoglou, N. (2005). "Corporates Are Driving the Global Saving Glut". *JPMorgan Research.*

Lutz, F. A. (1945). *Corporate Cash Balances, 1914–43: Manufacturing and Trade.* New York: NBER.

Lyandres, E. and Palazzo, B. (2016). "Cash Holdings, Competition, and Innovation". *Journal of Financial and Quantitative Analysis*, 51 (6): 1823–1861.

Ma, L., Mello, A. S., and Wu, Y. (2014). "Industry Competition, Winner's Advantage, and Cash Holdings." *Working Paper*, University of Wisconsin–Madison.

Magdoff, H. and Sweezy, P. M. (1987). *Stagnation and the Financial Explosion.* New York: Monthly Review Press.

Marglin, S. (1975). "What Do Bosses Do? The Origins and Functions of Hierarchy in Capitalist Production. Part II". *Review of Radical Political Economics*, 7 (1): 20–37.

Marx, K. (1861–1863/1989). "Economic Works, 1861–1863". In: Marx, K. and Engels, F.), *Collected Works.* Volume 32. New York: International Publishers, pp. 7–543.

Marx, K. (1867/1990). *Capital.* Volume I. London: Penguin Books.

McKinsey Global Institute (2010). "Farewell to Cheap Capital? The Implications of Long-Term Shift in Global Investment and Saving". McKinsey and Company. https://www.mckinsey.com/industries/private-equity-and-principal-investors/our-insights/farewell-cheap-capital

Means, G. C. (1931), "Stock Dividends, Large Scale Business, and Corporate Savings – A Criticism". *The Quarterly Journal of Economics*, 45 (3): 536–540.

Meech, S. P. (1928), "Report of Federal Trade Commission on Stock Dividends". *The Journal of Business of the University of Chicago*, 1 (4): 485–488.

Morellec, E., Nikolov, B. and Zucchi, F. (2014). "Competition, Cash Holdings, and Financing Decisions". *Swiss Finance Institute Research Paper*, 13–72.

Myers, S. C. (1984). "The Capital Structure Puzzle". *The Journal of Finance*, 56: 575–592.

Myers, S. C. and Majluf, N. S. (1984). "Corporate Financing and Investment Decisions When Firms Have Information That Investors Do Not Have". *Journal of Financial Economics*, 13: 187–221.

OECD (2007). *Economic Outlook*, 82.

Pinkowitz, L. F., Stulz, R. M. and Williamson, R. G. (2003). "Do Firms in Countries with Poor Protection of Investor Rights Hold More Cash?" *SSRN Electronic Journal*. doi:10.2139/ssrn.476442.

Pitelis, C. (1987). *Corporate Capital. Control, Ownership, Saving and Crisis*. Cambridge: Cambridge University Press.

Poterba, J. M., Hall, R. E. and Hubbard, R. G. (1987). "Tax Policy and Corporate Saving". *Brookings Papers on Economic Activity*, 2: 455–15.

Ross, S. A., Westerfield, R. W. and Jordan, B. D. (2022). *Fundamentals of Corporate Finance*. New York: McGraw Hill.

Ruggles, C. G. (1939). "The Relation of Corporate Surpluses to Income and Employment". *The American Economic Review*, 29 (4): 724–733.

Saibene, G. (2019) "The Corporate Saving Glut". *Journal of Macroeconomics*, 62(C): 103076.

Sardone, C. (1994). "Accumulation". In: Arestis, P. and Sawyer, M. (eds.), *The Elgar Companion to Radical Political Economy*. Brookfield: Edward Elgar, pp. 1–5.

Sawyer, M. (2014). "What Is Financialization?" *International Journal of Political Economy*, 42 (4): 5–18.

Scarano, G. (2015). "Corporate Savings and the 2007–2009 Financial Crisis: A Warning for the European Banking Union". In: Calciano, F., Fiordelisi, F. and Scarano, G. (eds.), *The Restructuring of Banks and Financial Systems in the Euro Area and the Financing of SMEs*. London and New York: Palgrave Macmillan, pp. 175–87.

Shaikh, A. (2016). *Capitalism. Competition, Conflict, Crises*. New York: Oxford University Press.

Smith, D. C. (1963). "Corporate Saving Behaviour". *The Canadian Journal of Economics and Political Science*, 29 (3): 297–310.

Stulz, R. M. (1990). "Managerial Discretion and Optimal Financing policies". *Journal of Financial Economics*, 26 (1): 3–27.

Sweezy, P. M. (1942/1946). *The Theory of Capitalist Development. Principles of Marxian Political Economy*. London: Dennis Dobson Limited.

Tambo, O. and Theobald, S. (2017). *The Myth of Corporate Cash Hoarding*. Intellidex Research Report.

Tirole, J. (2006). *The Theory of Corporate Finance*. Princeton, NJ: Princeton University Press.

Thorp, W. L. (1929). "The Changing Structure of Industry". In: Committee on Recent Economic Changes of the President's Conference on Unemployment (ed.), *Recent Economic Changes in the United States*, Volume 1. New York and London: McGraw-Hill, pp. 167–218.

Tobin, J. (1958). "Liquidity Preference as Behavior towards Risk". *The Review of Economic Studies*, 25 (2): 65–86.

Veblen, T. (1904), *Theory of Business Enterprise*. New York: Charles Scribner's Sons.

Villani, D. (2021). "The Rise of Corporate Net Lending Among G7 Countries: A Firm-Level Analysis". *Review of Political Economy*, 33 (2): 212–235.

von Eije, H. E. and Megginson, W. (2008). "Dividends and Share Repurchases in the European Union". *Journal of Financial Economics*, 89 (2): 347–374.

Weidenhammer, R. (1933). "Causes and Repercussions of the Faulty Investment of Corporate Savings". *The American Economic Review*, 23 (1): 35–41.

Wolf, M. (2015). "Corporate Surpluses Are Contributing to the Savings Glut", *Financial Times*, November 17th.

7 Financialisation of NFCs, globalisation and growth

Investment choices and investment theories

As we have several times highlighted, capital accumulation is one of the major movers of economic growth and ultimately depends on the share of social surplus devoted to investment. In capitalist economic systems, moreover, profits are the main part of social surplus on the income distribution side, and thus they are also the most prominent source of potential investment in new capital goods.

Unfortunately, as we have seen, in the past 50 years, the investment/profits ratio has shown a declining trend. And since the late 1980s, NFCs, while reducing their accumulation of capital goods, have progressively increased their financial investment.

Thus, it becomes important to understand whether there is a connection between decreasing real investment and growing financialisation by NFCs. Unfortunately, the present investment theory is not particularly helpful in investigating this potential connection.

In fact, even though trends over time and volatility of aggregate investment in fixed capital should be central to understanding aggregate fluctuations in economic activities, investment theory shows some limitations in explaining these phenomena. Moreover, in the early 1960s, Jorgenson had already noted that there was a great gap between economic theory and econometric practice in the literature on business investment in fixed capital. Econometric models, indeed, merely find empirical correlations between aggregate investment and other economic variables, sometimes without any rigor in the underlying theoretical foundations (see Jorgenson, 1963).

Economists have long been trying to explain the aggregate investment demand empirically simply by using scale variables. The most famous attempt of this kind, as is well known, is the *accelerator model* by Clark (1917), built on the basis of the relation existing between the first differences of a simple fixed coefficient inverse production function. However, despite the empirical success of this model, since the late 1960s, there have been many attempts to introduce the cost of capital as an explanatory variable in econometric models specified starting from the optimisation problem of a perfectly competitive firm (see Hall and Jorgenson, 1967).

DOI: 10.4324/9781003223221-8

Meanwhile, other economists highlighted the predominance of liquidity variables over the interest rate for short-run investment, introducing elements of portfolio choices into investment theory (see Tinbergen, 1939; Meyer and Kuh, 1957). And capital goods were explicitly dealt with as a component of the corporate portfolio by Foley and Sidrauski in 1970, to model corporations' investment demand in the context of a general equilibrium framework (see Foley and Sidrauski, 1970).

Moreover, according to the Tobin approach, investment has been recognised as an increasing function of q – i.e. the ratio of the financial value of the firm to the market cost of its capital goods – which is, in fact, closely connected to the companies' rate of profit (see Brainard and Tobin, 1968; Tobin, 1969; Hayashi, 1982; Caballero, 1999).

Yet, very few models highlight the fact that investment in capital goods depends mainly on corporate savings decisions, which are, as we saw in the previous chapter, closely connected to the features of corporate governance and the forms of competition, and strategic competitive behaviours. And in most advanced economies, as we have seen, retained earnings constitute the dominant source of finance (see also Mayer, 1988; Allen and gale, 2000; Tirole, 2006; Shaikh, 2016).

Most models of investment decisions utilised in macroeconomic models, in fact, take free or perfect competition as explicit or implicit assumption. However, the oligopolistic structure of most real markets leads to corporate strategic behaviours that can produce very different results. Strategic decisions, connected with agency problems, can play a major role in producing financialisation and timing the rhythms of real investment. And, as we will see, free movements of capital, both short- and long-term, can, in turn, influence the portfolio choices which are at its core.

From a microeconomic point of view, neoclassical economists are accustomed to bringing together under the heading of real investment decision criteria all the rational choices that involve a trade-off between the present and the future (see Hirshleifer, 2008), with apparently no distinction between consumers' and firms' behaviour. In this way, investment is reduced to the problem of optimising consumption patterns over time. This obviously presupposes that all the economic agents can be reduced to consumers or their representatives, essentially because households are assumed to be the end owners of all the production factors and firms are viewed as mere agents.

Optimising consumption over time under conditions of uncertainty and the existence of capital markets is also what Fama and Miller maintain that the theory of finance is concerned with (see Fama and Miller, 1972). Thus, we could say that, according to the mainstream economic approach, the theory of finance is concerned with investment theory under conditions of uncertainty.

Of course, in this schematised picture of the economy, the relation between investment – simply seen as the amount of reduction in current consumption and, therefore, immediately identified with saving – and the market interest rate has to be governed by the consumers' structure of intertemporal preferences. Thus, assuming a universal psychological preference for the present on the part of consumers – i.e. households – investment will be an increasing function of the market interest rate, which is the average measure of this preference. Any decision to reduce current investment should automatically correspond to an increase in present consumption.

In the simplest models of investment decisions of this kind, it is usually assumed that, at every point in time, a firm has only two alternatives in utilising its net revenues. It can disburse them to its owners as income or invest them to produce a greater amount of net revenues at some future date. Thus, by reducing owners' current income at time *t* and investing its retained earnings, the firm can increase future income of the owners themselves. It is in this way that firms are no more than the simple agents for their owners' intertemporal consumption choices (see Branson, 1979).

However, in the economic literature, there are a number of models, both neoclassical and heterodox, in which the real investment decision-makers are firms that have no shareholders to satisfy (see Romer, 2012). In this case, the connection with intertemporal utility equilibrium is not so immediate. In fact, investment decisions follow from entrepreneurs' choices of techniques finalised to maximise their profit or, symmetrically, to minimise their production costs. The intertemporal utility equilibrium connected to them can still be demonstrated in the context of a general equilibrium scheme, thanks to the role played by market prices and interpretations of them in terms of utility.

According to Irving Fisher's neoclassical theory of capital, for example, firms should choose their production plans so as to maximise utility over time, and this, under certain conditions, would lead to maximisation of the net worth of the enterprise as the objective for optimal capital accumulation (see Jorgenson, 1963). However, this idea of firms maximising utility is the trivial result of the idea that market prices, at their equilibrium level, are measuring social marginal utilities. Thus, maximising the difference between revenues and costs – i.e. profit – equals maximising social utility. This final result, however, is no intentional outcome pursued by entrepreneurs, but only an impersonal effect achieved by the market's invisible hand.

However, the entrepreneurs' choices between present and future cannot be immediately described in terms of utility, because the latter is not the direct objective to be maximised by entrepreneurs.

According to Marx, for example, the capitalist mode of production is not governed at all by the satisfaction of human needs – i.e. the production of use-values – but by the aim of obtaining surplus value from the production process, realising it by finding markets for the commodities in which it is embedded, and adding it to the value of the advanced capital – immediately in the money form and then, if this is adequately profitable, as new means of production in order to have the process reproduced on a larger scale (see Mandel, 1990).

Nevertheless, also in a mainstream theoretical perspective, capital accumulation is the result of providing additional inputs – i.e. capital services – to the productive process, to maximise profit in accordance with given production functions. Yet, it is only the outcome of changes in techniques made by firms in response to changes in external decision parameters.

In neoclassical models in which the investment decision is the direct consequence of the entrepreneurs' choice of techniques, therefore, the interest rate is simply the price of utilising capital. Thus, its changes determine changes in the optimal technique chosen. If the interest rate goes down, then the choice moves towards more capital-intensive techniques, increasing the stock of capital desired and creating investment demand.

On this front, the main difference between neoclassical and neo-Ricardian models lies in attaining or not attaining *well-behaved* production functions that can guarantee optimal general equilibria. The Cambridge capital controversy, indeed, proved that there was no regular relation between the use of *jelly capital* – i.e. money capital – and labour productivity. Thus, in neo-Ricardian models, changes in the interest rate have effects on the choice of techniques by means of changes in income distribution that produce changes in the long-period prices. The changes of techniques that produce capital accumulation are still the consequence of minimising production costs; yet, the connection between the interest rate and the cost of utilising capital is more indirect (see Pasinetti, 1966).

In both these kinds of models, however, real investment, as accumulation of capital, is viewed as a passive behaviour, because it is only the result of firms adapting techniques to exogenous changes in market or social parameters.

Thus, real investment as a result of changes in the choice of techniques shows capital accumulation behaviour as a mere passive effect, led both by changes in technology and consumption preferences, as well as the relative availability of production factors in neoclassical models, and by changes in distributive variables and exogenous aggregate demand in neo-Ricardian, Keynesian and post-Keynesian models (see Crotty, 1992; Bonifati, 2016). However, this theoretical result is the consequence of the assumption of perfect or free competition, under which firms are aware they cannot modify their decision-making parameters.

Under oligopolistic competition hypothesises, things could be very different. In this case, firms could be following strategic behaviours aiming to gain key positions in the market for successive competition battles, such as a growing share of the total supply in specific production sectors. From this point of view, for example, firms could forgo present normal profit for greater expected future extra-profit, based on greater monopoly power. These kinds of strategic behaviour could, therefore, increase aggregate real investment as compared with equilibrium-saving decisions, producing disequilibria in the financial markets and pressures on interest rates, as was probably the case in Europe during the 1960s (see Lamfalussy, 1968).

A close connection between real investment and strategic behaviours clearly emerges from Shumpeter's analysis. According to his approach, in fact, capital accumulation is the consequence of "innovation" – i.e. the result of active strategies of reducing own production costs as compared with those of their competitors on the part of "entrepreneurs" – which are creative managers and capitalists or genial inventors well financed by forward-looking banks and other financial intermediaries. Thus, innovation appears as a series of creative actions by "enterprises" – i.e. innovative firms – intrinsically embodied in new investment goods, which push the economy out of its stationary equilibria, inducing adjustments in the choice of techniques, and then more investment, also in the non-innovative firms (see Schumpeter, 1923/1939).

From this point of view, capital accumulation is still connected with cost-minimising behaviours, but in a context of active and strategic competition for the conquest of dominant or monopolistic positions in the market, in order to make the highest possible extra-profit. There is no role played by the interest rate, apart from the risk premium required by financial operators, which could in some case discourage the entrepreneurs from seeking higher extra-profits.

Schumpeter is sometimes regarded as the major inheritor of the Marxian vision of capital accumulation and growth. However, Marx's conception of investment, as capital accumulation, is quite another issue, but very relevant to our task of analysis. According to Marx, in fact, capital accumulation is the mere result of the self-valorisation process of capital. If capital value is, by nature, in search of additional value, then the surplus value, which is of the same nature as the original capital value, will, in turn, be searching for its additional value. Thus, capital, by its very nature, organises a continuum process of self-valorisation that increases its value, until an overproduction crisis temporarily arrests it.

This conception, which might sound somewhat metaphysical to those who conceive of real investment only as a way to adapt production techniques to new market conditions, in fact fully complies with the "pursuit of shareholder value" principle, put in place by the managers of big corporations, who certainly cannot be suspected of being Marxists.

In Marx's works, moreover, as we saw in the previous chapter, there is no reference to the fact that the rate of profit can be a subjective incentive for accumulation of capital or play a role in changing aggregate investment decisions. According to him, the average rate of profit plays a role only in capitalist competition, stimulating movements of *money capital* – i.e. financial capital – from one productive branch to another and determining a redistribution of total surplus value proportionally to the *money capital* invested in capital goods and anticipated wages. Thus, different rates of profit in different productive branches can reduce real investment in those with the lowest rate, but increase it in those with the highest rate. Obviously, analogous movements of *money capital* can also occur between countries, financial branches or between real branches and financial branches. And Marx also thought the rising mass of profits that exceeds the possibilities for new industrial investment in periods of prosperity first accumulates as a huge mass of credit and then ends up by taking speculative paths, because, as we saw in Chapter 4, the production process usually appears only as "a necessary evil for the purpose of money-making", and at the first opportunity, "fits of giddiness" are unleashed in which capitalists "try to accomplish the money-making without the mediation of the production process" (Marx, 1885/1992, p. 137).

Financial investment and the term structure of interest rates

In neoclassical economics, the interest rate, at its equilibrium level, is not only a measure of the marginal intertemporal consumer preference, but also a measure of the marginal productivity of capital – i.e. the marginal rate of profit. Thus, investment quantity depends on capital profitability too, obviously compared with the available quantity of savings supplied which, in turn, depends on the intertemporal consumer preferences.

In recent years, after the financial crisis of 2007–2008, the idea is returning that the central banks have to influence market interest rates to drive them towards levels consistent with their best estimation of the equilibrium real interest rate – i.e. the *Wicksellian interest rate* (see Bernanke, 2015). Thus, according to mainstream approach, the objective conditions of the economic systems, and in particular return on capital invested, are again what ultimately determine the real rate of return for savers and financial investors.

This draws attention to the role of the interest rates as rate of return on financial assets. From this point of view, the term structure of interest rates is very important in determining portfolio choices, and then the alternative between financial and real investments.

In Keynes' theory, investment is the driving force of income levels and their fluctuations (see Minsky, 1975), and this, in turn, depends on the propensity to hoard, and therefore, on the monetary policy and expectations concerning yield of capital assets (see Keynes, 1937). Thus, Keynes' theory of investment connects the fluctuations of real investment to variables which are determined in the financial markets and primarily to the rate of interest (see Minsky, 1975). The monetary theory of the interest rate proposed by Keynes, in fact, underlined its meaning as required rate of return on financial investment. From this point of view, if speculators are not viewed as intrinsically different from other types of investors, the interest rate may be in competition with the expected rate of return on real investment – i.e. the rate of profit – within portfolio choices. New savings can be invested in a financial or real way depending on comparison between the interest rate on financial capital and the rate of profit with the risk premium deducted.

Thus, Keynes argued that even though aggregate saving depends essentially upon aggregate income level, the rate of interest plays a secondary role by influencing how economic agents allocate their savings among different potential shares of their portfolios.

Even though the Keynesian revolution was essentially focused on a short-period analysis, the key role it gave to investment stimulated new interest in accumulation theory. Many post-Keynesians authors, including Harrod, Domar, Robinson, Kahn and Kaldor, developed theories of accumulation starting precisely from Keynes' analysis.

Yet, some post-Keynesians developed their own analysis of accumulation by drawing also on classical political economy, reviving the connection between distribution and accumulation. Thus, most post-Keynesian analyses of accumulation ended up emphasising only two critical aspects of the economic system: the rate of investment which ensures steady growth with full employment and the strict relationship between capital accumulation and income distribution.

Kalecki, in turn, was the major exponent of a new synthesis between the Marxian and Keynesian approaches, autonomously arriving at some Keynesian results starting from the analysis of Marx and Luxemburg. And this different starting point led Kalecki to deal with an economic system characterised by oligopoly rather than free competition. Successively, Steindl followed Kalecki on this path, attributing to oligopolistic behaviour a strategic role in slowing down capital accumulation rate.

In all these post-Keynesian approaches, therefore, the interest rate ended up playing no role in explaining investment and capital accumulation.

Nevertheless, even though the interest rate in itself can play a minor role in determining real investment directly, if corporate managers act as financial investors, the term structure of interest rates could play a major role in determining investment in capital goods as a share of companies' portfolios. At this point, the way managers make their portfolio choices becomes crucial.

This issue, of course, may be closely connected to corporate governance problems, as we saw in Chapter 1. In fact, shareholders, as financial rentiers, tend to see NFCs as "portfolios" of liquid assets that their managers should continually be modifying to maximise the stock price at every point in time. If managers of NFCs are prompted to maximise "shareholder value" both by corporate governance rules and by appropriate systems of incentives, they should end up running their companies as financial portfolios and acting as financial investors. Consequently, the term structure of interest rates, or rather "the term structure of the rates of return", should play a major role in determining investment in capital goods as a share of companies' portfolios.

This structure will obviously depend on the available financial alternatives and the risk premiums that prevail in their markets. However, the "risk premiums" in imperfect markets are not necessarily the statistic measure of the riskiness of loans and contributions of capital, as the mainstream theory assumes, but can be, as we saw in Chapter 4, the result of power relations between financial capital and industrial capital, as held by the classical economists, Marx and Hilferding. In any case, the average rate of return on financial assets can be the measure of the comparative profitability in utilising capital in a financial or productive way.

From this point of view, the major variable in explaining investment decisions is not the interest rate on money markets, strictly controlled by central banks, but rather the average "risk premium" as a measure of the average profitability in financed real activities. This measure is closely correlated with Tobin's *q*.

Of course, at the macroeconomic level, in closed economies, the average profitability can only have effects on movement of capital from one sector to another, in direct or financial form, but cannot explain the absolute level of real investment. In open economies, however, the differences in average profitability between different countries can matter, reducing capital sources for real investment in one country by means of capital transfers, in direct or financial forms, towards other countries.

Moreover, in portfolio choices by corporations, in addition to the rates of return, the liquidity degree of the assets can also be a very important determinant which is closely linked to business fluctuations. Thus, portfolio choices by corporations also mainly depend on the uncertainty degree of their economic environment which can induce hoarding phenomena that are, ultimately, the real prime mover of decreasing aggregate investment.

Thus, the tendency to run NFCs as financial portfolios may not be the result of new forms of corporate governance and the pressure by new financial intermediaries at all, but, as we saw in Chapter 1, the traditional way to maximise equity capital self-valorisation in a new competitive environment and give new financial investment opportunities. This highlights other transformations of the capitalist system in the neoliberal era which have been all placed under the label of *globalisation*.

The contribution of free movement of capital

As everybody knows, there are a number of different ways to define globalisation, each of which underlines different aspects of a progressive worldwide integration process between people, companies and governments. However, here we prefer to focus our attention on its major economic features which can be summarised as a sustained move towards increasing liberalisation in trade and a progressive worldwide liberalisation of the movement of labour and capital.

So far, the movement of labour has only been liberalised on a very limited regional basis. As Hobson already highlighted by the end of the 19th century, in fact, labour shows a reluctance "to keep pace with the migration of capital" (Hobson, 1891/1992) just as free trade has been only partially implemented under the umbrella of the WTO, with many surviving, even though minimised, tariff regimes, and countless non-tariff barriers. Moreover, today these liberalisation processes appear to be running into a new series of problems.

At the moment, therefore, the main economic field of success of globalisation seems to be only the free movement of capital.

The unrestricted freedom of economic agents to transfer capital across national borders had long been a veritable dogma of liberal economic thinking. However, since the outbreak of the First World War and throughout the Great Depression, it was often violated in practice and its periodical suspension was long seen by economists as the necessary temporary consequence of extraordinary events and situations.

However, in the aftermath of Second World War, significant direct control over private capital movements, especially the so-called "hot money", was considered desirable by most countries not only for the early post-war years but also in the longer term. This widely accepted view was officially enshrined in the *Bretton Woods Fund Agreement* which explicitly recognised the right of each member country to control capital movements. Under certain circumstances, furthermore, the IMF could even make such controls compulsory as a condition for continuing to receive its financial support (see Eichengreen, 2007).

Thus, the post-war economic consensus for the control of capital movements represented a clear break with the past liberal orthodoxy.

This drastic doctrinal shift reflected a widespread disillusionment with the destabilising effects of these movements in the inter-war years. One of the main sources of international monetary and economic instability, in fact, had been the massive, over-reactive and unpredictable transfers of short-term funds – i.e. "hot money" – which benefited neither the giver nor the receiver. Nevertheless, in the inter-war period, even long-term foreign investment had been subject to erratic fluctuations and other dysfunctions which, in turn, led to the need for tighter controls, not so much with regard to its volume but to regularise its flow and improve its destination (see Bloomfield, 1946). The post-war international relations framework, moreover, was also designed on the basis of the protectionist world background that had arisen in the years of the Great Depression.

Thus, the years of the *Golden Age* were characterised by strict controls on international movements of capital. As we saw in Chapters 1 and 2, this feature has been considered by many post-Keynesian and neo-Marxist economists as a major component of the mode of regulation that guaranteed the long upward phase in those decades.

Eventually, however, in all advanced countries, the way out of the stagnation that occurred within the Bretton Woods institutional framework in the 1970s was sought in a new wave of expansion of free trade and capital mobility, in the hope that a larger free world market and wider investment opportunities would improve the profitability of large NFCs. The breakdown of the Bretton Woods agreements, moreover, also marked the end of US financial dominance, paving the way towards a more decentralised world system of capital movements.

However, unfortunately, today capital account liberalisation is the theoretical field where economics largely fails in explaining actual events in the real world.

According to neoclassical theory, free capital flows should only be a form of intertemporal trade and then their functioning rules should be no different from those of free trade. Thus, free flows of external capital should contribute to smoothing consumption and production paths, improving social welfare. However, in the real world, the result seems to be the exact opposite. Free movements of short-term capital, such as portfolio flows and short-term bank loans, have so far been related to a long series of serious economic and financial crises because of their volatility and exposure to surges in and sudden withdrawals from the financial markets.

Thus, successively to economic and financial crises in Asia, Latin America and Russia in the late 1990s, many economists underlined the possible dangerous effects of these kinds of capital movements for developing countries. Instead, long-term capital flows, such as FDI, were usually regarded as more positive for the long-term economic growth of developing countries, because they are generally more stable and can improve their production capacity and technology (see Stiglitz, 2002, 2004; Singh, 2007). Thus, the economic literature analysing the effects of liberalisation of capital flows on the developing countries usually highlights the difference between short-term and long-term flows.

However, free movement of capital can have significant effects on the developed economies, too, although in this case, the distinction between short-term and long-term capital flows can be less significant. Unfortunately, much less analysis has been dedicated to these effects, but they can play a major role in generating the present tendency to stagnation in this kind of economy.

Since money capital owners are in constant search of maximum surplus value, they prefer to invest their capital where wages are lowest since the rate of profit – which is the rate of return on real investment – depends on the difference between value added and wages. Yet, dividends on equity securities are directly proportional to this difference, too. Thus, under free movements of capital and wage differentials between different geographical areas – risk being equal – capital, in both real and financial forms, tends by nature to move from areas with higher wages to areas with lower wages.

If, in accordance with Steindl's thesis (see Steindl, 1976, 1990), internal accumulation is the first mover of corporate investment for the large multinational corporations that characterise today's world economy, and this produces investment-seeking surplus value, the investment alternatives available for NFCs on a global scale can play a fundamental role in determining the growth rate in a single national economic system. If real investment depends on the term structure of the rates of return over the full range of financial and real investment opportunities, then real investments in the developed countries also depend on the differential between their rates of returns and the rates of returns on real investments in the developing or emerging countries. Indeed, the possibilities for foreign investments may decrease the domestic accumulation rate of the developed countries, increasing their unemployment rates.

But above all, free movements of capital can also play a major role in financialisation of NFCs. In fact, the differential between the rates of returns on real investments in the developed countries and the rates of returns on real investments in the developing or emerging countries does not only act by means of FDI, but also by means of the possibility of financial investment in foreign securities, associated with real investment in foreign countries. Financial globalisation, multiplying the potential range of financial instruments available to big corporations' portfolios and creating new ways to indirectly access the high profits produced in the emergent markets, can therefore play a major role in changing the portfolio composition. Moreover, the managers of "financialised NFCs" can decide to substitute direct national real investments with financial investments in foreign corporations, thus also obtaining a greater liquidity for their portfolios.

However, this kind of investment does not necessarily have to go through the acquisition of equity, but can also be made by acquiring debt securities. Thus, decreasing capital controls can influence the very structure of countries' external liabilities, leading to substitution of FDI with equity inflows and external debt, which can, in turn, have a sizeable impact on the financial stability of debtor countries, significantly raising currency mismatch and making them more vulnerable to financial contagion (see OECD, 2012b).

Furthermore, financial investments by NFCs are usually very different from the traditional forms of takeover and corporate holding because their profitability depends not only on the ratio of profits to invested capital, but also on the terms of capitalisation of the expected future profits realised through the financial markets. Thus, the growing liquidity of NFCs' portfolios we highlighted in the previous chapter can contribute to heightening the usual volatility of the rates of return on financial assets as well as the vulnerability to contagion-induced financial shocks (see OECD, 2012a). Moreover, countries with a large financial sector have a riskier financial account structure, compared, for instance, with commodity-exporting countries, which show a safer financial account structure. And above all, free movements of short-term capital, such as portfolio flows and short-term bank loans, have so far been related to a long series of serious economic and financial crises because of their volatility and exposure to surges in and sudden withdrawals from the financial markets.

All this obviously increases the overall uncertainty of financial investment profitability itself. And this growing uncertainty, in turn, leads to a greater tendency to money hoarding by NFCs, which reduces the mass of real investment directly or indirectly financed by them.

An interpretation model

Summing up what we have dealt with throughout this book, we can say that a large number of different phenomena can play a role in changing corporate real investment decisions through several complex transmission mechanisms. For a clear understanding of the possible effects of financialisation on real investment in large NFCs, therefore, it may be useful to propose a model summarising the major connections previously examined (see Figure 7.1).

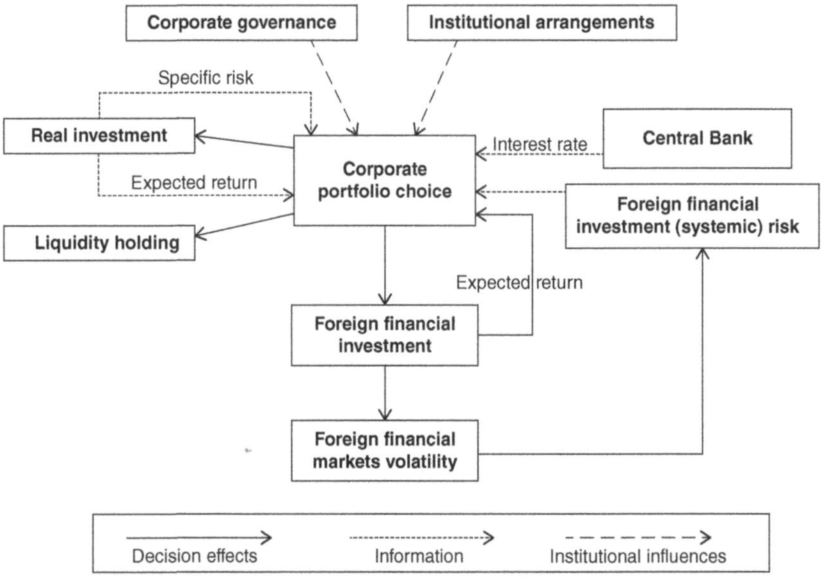

Figure 7.1 Flow-chart of the conceptual scheme of the model.

This is, of course, no macroeconomic model, but rather a "mesoeconomic" one, describing the aggregate behaviour of just a part of the productive system – i.e. the sector of the large or giant NFCs – even though this sector can produce major effects on the whole macroeconomic system. Like every model, moreover, it is a simplified description of the main links we can empirically observe in reality.

The first simplification, to remove the problem of fallacy of composition, is to assume a single corporate sector of a developed country that can financially invest only in the rest of the world. Inside the developed country, only real investment in capital goods is possible.

Let us assume, on the basis of the previous analysis, that corporate decision-makers behave like financial investors, managing their corporation as a financial portfolio. Under this assumption, the managers' objective function is to find the best combination of the expected rate of return and risk in the corporate portfolio, given their degree of risk aversion. If the managers are mere agents of the potential population of shareholders, we can assume that they have the average risk aversion that the financial markets show.

Let us also assume, for the sake of simplicity, that the aggregate corporate portfolio is composed of only three kinds of assets: liquidity, capital goods and foreign securities. Liquidity is no token money, but rather safe short-term securities, such as government bonds with a maturity of one year or less.

We will also assume that the three assets in the portfolio are gross substitutes, i.e. an increase in the rate of return of one asset raises its demand and lowers the demanded amount of the others (see Foley and Sidrauski, 1970). Decision-makers being risk-averters, if they face different and uncertain returns, they will then diversify their portfolios.

Thus, decisions on liquidity holding, real investments and foreign financial investments are the consequence of maximising the managers' objective function that takes as arguments – according to Markowitz's mean-variance portfolio theory – the expected return and risk of the corporate portfolio, under the constraint of their *efficient frontier.*

The foreign financial investment risk can be reduced to the foreign systemic risk because the optimal diversification of this part of the portfolio can theoretically eliminate its specific risk.

The flow of foreign financial investments, in turn, if they are massive, can produce increasing volatility in foreign financial markets over time, as we saw in the case of emerging countries. This increased volatility obviously results in an increasing level of uncertainty for the financial component of the portfolio, producing a higher demand for liquidity over time (see Figure 7.1).

In this scheme, it is evident that the quantity of real investment is a function of its expected return and risk, composed by the systemic risk within the developed countries plus its specific risk, compared with the systemic risk of foreign financial markets, the expected return on foreign financial investment and the interest rate applied by the central banks in developed countries that determines the risk-free rate in portfolio choice.

The corporate portfolio choice described in the previous scheme can be mathematised by means of a simple two-period optimisation model in which we assume that managers wish to maximise an objective function that depends only on date-1 expected portfolio return and risk. This kind of objective function, in fact, proves a good way to model the behaviour of managers that act as financial investors and operate in accordance with the current predominant financial rules.

Thus, the maximisation problem can be written as follows:

$$\max_{\boldsymbol{q} \in R^m} U\left(E\left(w_1\right), var\left(w_1\right)\right) \tag{7.1}$$

subject to:

$$w_0 = \boldsymbol{p}'\boldsymbol{q} \tag{7.2}$$
$$w_1 = \boldsymbol{x}'\boldsymbol{q} \tag{7.3}$$

where:

w_0 is the corporate wealth at date-0.
w_1 is the corporate wealth at date-1.
$\boldsymbol{x}$ is the payoff vector for the assets in the corporate portfolio at date-1.
$\boldsymbol{q}$ is the vector of quantities of the assets in the corporate portfolio.
$\boldsymbol{p}$ is the price vector of the assets in the corporate portfolio at date-0.

Let corporate choice space, as in the previous graphical scheme, comprise only three kinds of assets: liquidity, capital goods and foreign securities, respectively, denoted as 1, 2 and 3. Let asset 1 be risk-free, while assets 2 and 3 are obviously risky. Let $\boldsymbol{p} = (p_1, p_2, p_3)$ be the asset price vector at date-0 and $\boldsymbol{q} = (q_1, q_2, q_3)$ the vector of quantities of the assets in the corporate portfolio.

The initial corporate wealth will be:

$$w_0 = \boldsymbol{p}'\boldsymbol{q} = p_1q_1 + p_2q_2 + p_3q_3 \tag{7.4}$$

while the final wealth will be:

$$w_1 = \boldsymbol{x}'\boldsymbol{q} = x_1q_1 + x_2q_2 + x_3q_3 \tag{7.5}$$

where $\boldsymbol{x} = (x_1, x_2, x_3)$ is the vector of the payoffs for the different assets. Both x_2 and x_3 are obviously *state-contingent* variables, i.e. their values depend on the possible alternative *states of the world*.

If we define $R_i \equiv x_i/p_i$, the gross return obtained by investing in the ith asset, the rate of return of every asset will be $r_i = R_i - 1$. Accordingly, $r_1 = R_1 - 1$ will be the safe interest rate r_f, controlled by the central bank, while $r_2 = R_2 - 1$ is the rate of profit on capital goods.

Let us, to simplify successive notations, define the asset value vector $\boldsymbol{v} = (v_1, v_2, v_3)$, where $v_i = p_iq_i$. Thus, we can rewrite the final corporate wealth as follows:

$$w_1 = R_1v_1 + R_2v_2 + R_3v_3 \tag{7.6}$$

Combining Eqs. (7.6) and (7.4), we obtain:

$$w_1 = (R_2 - R_1)v_2 + (R_3 - R_1)v_3 + R_1w_0 \tag{7.7}$$

or, alternatively:

$$w_1 = (r_2 - r_f)v_2 + (r_3 - r_f)v_3 + R_1w_0 \tag{7.8}$$

The rates of return r_i on the risky assets can, of course, be treated as random variables, because they depend on *state-contingent* variables for which we assume a probability distribution can be defined. Accordingly, we can rewrite Eq. (7.8) as follows:

$$w_1 = \tilde{\boldsymbol{v}}'\left[E(\tilde{\boldsymbol{r}}) - \boldsymbol{1}_2 r_f\right] + \tilde{\boldsymbol{v}}'\left[\tilde{\boldsymbol{r}} - E(\tilde{\boldsymbol{r}})\right] + R_1w_0 \tag{7.9}$$

where $\tilde{\boldsymbol{v}} = (v_2, v_3)$, $\tilde{\boldsymbol{r}} = (r_2, r_3)$ and $\boldsymbol{1}_2$ is the 2×1 sum vector.

We can now use the decomposition, $E(\tilde{\boldsymbol{r}}) - r_f = \boldsymbol{B}\boldsymbol{u}$, where $\boldsymbol{B}$ is a $2 \times d$ "volatility" matrix, with $d \geq 2$, and $\boldsymbol{u}$ is a random vector with expectation zero and variance-covariance matrix equal to the identity matrix (see Mele, 2013).

By means of this decomposition, we can rewrite the budget constraint in Eq. (7.9) as follows:

$$w_1 = \tilde{\boldsymbol{v}}'\left[E(\tilde{\boldsymbol{r}}) - \mathbf{1}_2 r_f\right] + R_1 w_0 + \tilde{\boldsymbol{v}}'\mathbf{B}\boldsymbol{u} \tag{7.10}$$

Thus, the expected return and the variance of the portfolio value will, respectively, be:

$$E(w_1) = \tilde{\boldsymbol{v}}'\left[E(\tilde{\boldsymbol{r}}) - \mathbf{1}_2 r_f\right] + R_1 w_0 \tag{7.11}$$

$$var(w_1) = \sigma_p^2 = \tilde{\boldsymbol{v}}'\,\Sigma\,\tilde{\boldsymbol{v}} \tag{7.12}$$

where $\Sigma = \mathbf{BB}' = \left[\sigma_{ij}\right]$ is the covariance matrix.

If we assume that Σ has a full-rank and, as usual, $\sigma_i^2 > \sigma_j^2 \Rightarrow E(r_i) > E(r_j)$, then $r_f < min_j\left[E(r_j)\right]$.

If we also assume that managers maximise the expected return on corporate portfolio, given a level of variance of the portfolio's value amounting to $w_1^2\sigma_W^2$ – i.e. the level they could obtain with a perfectly diversified financial portfolio – then we can model their choice problem as follows:

$$\hat{\boldsymbol{v}}(\sigma_p) = \arg\max_{\tilde{\boldsymbol{v}} \in R^2} E(w_1) \tag{7.13}$$

subject to

$$\tilde{\boldsymbol{v}}'\,\Sigma\,\tilde{\boldsymbol{v}} = w_0^2\sigma_W^2 \tag{7.14}$$

The Lagrangian function for the constrained maximisation problem in (7.13) is as follows:

$$L(\tilde{\boldsymbol{v}},\lambda) = \tilde{\boldsymbol{v}}'\left[E(\tilde{\boldsymbol{r}}) - \mathbf{1}_2 r_f\right] + R_1 w_0 + \tilde{\boldsymbol{v}}'\boldsymbol{Bu} - \lambda\left(\tilde{\boldsymbol{v}}' BB'\tilde{\boldsymbol{v}} - \sigma_W^2\right) \tag{7.15}$$

Thus, the first-order conditions to maximise $L(\tilde{\boldsymbol{v}},\lambda)$ are:

$$\begin{cases} \hat{\boldsymbol{v}}(\sigma_p^2) = (2\lambda)^{-1}\Sigma^{-1}\left[E(\tilde{\boldsymbol{r}}) - \mathbf{1}_2 r_f\right] \\ \hat{\boldsymbol{v}}' BB'\hat{\boldsymbol{v}} = w_0\sigma_W^2 \end{cases} \tag{7.16}$$

If we substitute the first condition into the second, we obtain:

$$(2\lambda)^{-1} = \pm\frac{w_0\sigma_w}{\sqrt{\left[E(\tilde{\boldsymbol{r}}) - \mathbf{1}_2 r_f\right]'\Sigma^{-1}\left[E(\tilde{\boldsymbol{r}}) - \mathbf{1}_2 r_f\right]}} \tag{7.17}$$

where the square root argument in the denominator is none other than the portfolio *Sharpe ratio* (***S***) – i.e. the surplus rate of return of the portfolio over the rate of return of a risk-free asset divided by the variability (standard deviation) of returns. This index, in practice, is a measure of the portfolio risk premium per "unit" of risk.

Taking the positive solution of (7.17) to ensure efficiency and substituting it into the first condition, we obtain that the optimal combination of values of the risky assets in the corporate portfolio is given by:

$$\hat{\mathbf{v}}\left(\sigma_p^2\right) = \frac{\Sigma^{-1}\left[E(\tilde{r}) - \mathbf{1}_2 r_f\right]}{\sqrt{\mathbf{S}}} w_0 \sigma_w \tag{7.18}$$

Thus, the capital goods value in the corporate portfolio will be:

$$\hat{v}_2 = \frac{1}{\sqrt{\mathbf{S}}}\left\{\frac{\sigma_3^2}{\sigma_2^2\sigma_3^2 - \sigma_{23}\sigma_{32}}\left[E(r_2) - r_f\right] - \frac{\sigma_{23}}{\sigma_2^2\sigma_3^2 - \sigma_{23}\sigma_{32}}\left[E(r_3) - r_f\right]\right\} \tag{7.19}$$

The result of this simplified model merely confirms, in a mathematically testable fashion, what can easily be guessed from the assumptions underlying the framework shown in Figure 7.1. Real investment is directly proportional to the difference between its expected rate of return and the expected rate of return on financial investment, but also to the risk of financial investment and the correlation between its risk and financial risk. It is inversely proportional to its specific risk, to the portfolio risk premium per unit of risk, and also to the risk-free interest rate.

Real investment in one country, therefore, can be crowded out by the rate of return on financial investments related to economic activities in other countries. This crowding out, of course, depends on the comparative riskiness of the two types of investment.

However, changes in risk-free rates managed by central banks do not change the relative attractiveness of real and financial investments. They can only change the relative attractiveness between risky and safe investments. Changes in the official interest rate can, therefore, only act on the portfolio share of liquidity because the final result on the real investment front will depend on comparison between its expected return and risk and the expected return and risk on foreign financial investment. In fact, when a portfolio consists of only one non-risky security and several risky securities, the set of risky assets behaves as if it were a single asset, i.e. the percentage composition in risky securities does not change in the same way as the proportion between non-risky security and risky assets does. Since changes in the risk-free interest rate only change the slope of the risk-return constraints, a change in the proportion between real and financial investments may only depend on peculiar assumptions regarding the shape and slope of the indifference surfaces of the decision-makers.

In our model, moreover, liquidity is a residual magnitude, as in all portfolio theories, given by:

$$\hat{v}_1 = w_1 - \hat{v}_2 - \hat{v}_3 \tag{7.20}$$

However, in our model, liquidity turns out to be directly proportional to the risk-free interest rate and risky asset volatility.

The first result depends on the fact that, as we have said, liquidity in this model consists of safe short-term money market debt securities. If we were to include token money in liquidity without a rate of return, as in Tobin's model (see Tobin, 1958), then the share of liquidity consisting of money should be inversely proportional to the risk-free interest rate, as might be expected. However, liquidity, understood as the mix of token money and short-term safe securities, turns out to be directly proportional to the risk-free interest rate managed by the central banks since changes in that rate change the risk premiums actually provided by risky assets, both real and financial, shifting the risk-return trade-off and altering the optimal choice of both real and financial investment levels. In fact, the rate of return on the real investment is none other than the rate of profit, whereas the rate of return on the financial investment is its *yield to maturity* – i.e. the interest rate that equates the present value of its expected future cash flows and its initial value. Both of these rates of return do not depend on the risk-free interest rate, but only on the initial value of the investment and the stream of expected future cash flows associated with it. Thus, risk being equal, an increase in the risk-free rate reduces the risk premiums of both types of risky investments and increases the demand for safe short-term securities.

By controlling the risk-free rate, the central banks effectively only control the borrowing capacity of governments. However, it is the terms of government debt that set the benchmark for the profitability of all other investments. If government bonds become more attractive, they crowd out other types of investment.

Increased volatility of risky assets, in turn, increases risk and promotes precautionary cash holding and vice versa and safe short-term securities, of course, could also include short-term securities provided by the shadow banking system, to the extent that, rightly or wrongly, they are considered safe. Thus, the increased volatility of risky assets in the early 2000s may explain not only the increase in corporate liquidity, but also the expansion of the shadow banking system.

The expected returns on foreign financial investment are obviously influenced by the higher profits in foreign productive activities, due to the lower cost of labour. Thus, the only chance for inside real investment to survive depends on the share of the risky component of portfolio and the difference between the inside and foreign systemic risk, which must be greater than its specific risk.

References

Allen, F. and Gale, D. (2000). *Comparing Financial Systems*. Cambridge, MA and London: The MIT Press.

Bernanke, B. S. (2015). "Why Are Interest Rates So Low?", http://www.brookings.edu/blogs/benbernanke/posts/2015/03/30-why-interest-rates-so-low.

Bloomfield, A. I. (1946). "Postwar Control of International Capital Movements". *The American Economic Review*, 36 (2): 687–709.

Bonifati, G. (2016). "Investimenti, consumi e occupazione. Capacità produttiva, domanda effettiva e distribuzione del reddito nel lungo periodo". *Economia & Lavoro*, 1: 77–107.

Brainard, W. C. and Tobin, J. (1968). "Pitfalls in Financial Model Building". *American Economic Review*, 58 (2): 99–122.

Branson, W. H. (1979). *Macroeconomic Theory and Policy*. New York: Harper and Row, Publishers.

Caballero, R. J. (1999). "Aggregate Investment". In: Taylor, J. B. and Woodford, M. (eds.), *Handbook of Macroeconomics*, Volume 1B. Amsterdam: Elsevier, pp. 813–62.

Clark, J.M. (1917). "Business Acceleration and the Law of Demand: A Technical Factor in Economic Cycles". *Journal of Political Economy*, 25 (3): 217–35.

Crotty, J. (1992). "Neoclassical and Keynesian Approaches to the Theory of Investment". *Journal of Post Keynesian Economics*, 14 (4): 483–97.

Eichengreen, B. (2007). *Global Imbalances and the Lessons of Bretton Woods*. Cambridge, MA and London: The MIT Press.

Fama, E. F. and Miller, M. H. (1972). *The Theory of Finance*. Hinsdale, IL: Dryden Press.

Foley, D. K. and Sidrauski, M. (1970). "Portfolio Choice, Investment, and Growth". *The American Economic Review*, 60 (1): 44–63.

Hall, R. E and Jorgenson, D. W. (1967). "Tax Policy and Investment Behaviour". *American Economic Review*, 57 (3): 391–414.

Hayashi, F. (1982). "Tobin's Marginal *q* and Average *q*: A Neoclassical Interpretation". *Econometrica*, 50 (1): 213–24.

Hirshleifer, J. (2008). "Investment Decision Criteria". In: Durlauf, S. N. and Blume, L. E. (eds.), *The New Palgrave Dictionary of Economics*, Volume 4. New York: Palgrave Macmillan, pp. 553–58.

Hobson, J. A. (1891/1992). "Can England Keep Her Trade?" In: Hobson, J. A., *Writings on Imperialism and Internationalism*. New York and London: Routledge, pp. 1–11.

Jorgenson, D. W. (1963). "Capital Theory and Investment Behaviour". *American Economic Review*, 53 (2): 247–59.

Keynes, J. M. (1937). "The General Theory of Employment". *Quarterly Journal of Economics*, 51 (2): 209–23.

Lamfalussy, A. (1968). *Les marchés financiers en Europe*. Paris: Presses Universitaires de France.

Mandel, E. (1990). "Introduction by Ernest Mandel". In: Marx, K., *Capital*. Volume I. London: Penguin Books, pp. 11–86.

Marx, K. (1885/1992). *Capital*. Volume II. London: Penguin Books.

Mayer, C. (1988). "New Issues in Corporate Finance". *European Economic Review*, 32 (5): 1167–89.

Mele, A. (2013). *Lectures on Financial Economics*, Lugano: Swiss Finance Institute, University of Lugano.

Meyer, J. R. and Kuh, E. (1957). *The Investment Decision: An Empirical Study*. Cambridge, MA: Harvard University Press.

Minsky, H. P. (1975). *John Maynard Keynes*. New York: McGraw-Hill.

OECD (2012a). "International Capital Mobility: Which Structural Policies Reduce Financial Fragility?" *OECD Economic Policy Papers*, 2.

OECD (2012b). "International Capital Mobility: Structural Policies to Reduce Financial Fragility?" *OECD Economics Department Policy Notes*, 13.

Pasinetti, L. (1966). "Changes in the Rate of Profit and Switches of Techniques". *Quarterly Journal of Economics*, 80 (4): 503–17.

Romer, D. (2012). *Advanced Macroeconomics*. New York: McGraw-Hill-Irwin.

Schumpeter, J. A. (1923/1939). *Business Cycle. A Theoretical, Historical and Statistical Analysis of the Capitalist Process*. New York and London: McGraw-Hill.

Shaikh, A. (2016). *Capitalism. Competition, Conflict, Crises*. New York: Oxford University Press.

Singh, A. (2007). "Capital Account Liberalization, Free Long-Term Capital Flows, Financial Crises, and Economic Development". In: Shaikh, A. (ed.), *Globalization and the Myths of Free Trade*. New York: Routledge, pp. 259–87.

Steindl, J. (1976). *Maturity and Stagnation in American Capitalism*. New York: Monthly Review Press.

Steindl, J. (1990). *Economic Papers. 1941–88*. New York: Palgrave Macmillan.

Stiglitz, J. (2002). *Globalization and Its Discontents*. New York and London: W. W. Norton & Company.

Stiglitz, J. (2004). "Capital-Market Liberalization, Globalization, and the IMF". *Oxford Review of Economic Policy*, 20 (1): 57–71.

Tinbergen, J. (1939). Statistical Testing of Business Cycle Theories. Volume 1. In: *A Method and Its Application to Investment Activity*. New York: Economic Intelligence Service, Agathon Press.

Tirole, J. (2006). *The Theory of Corporate Finance*. Princeton, NJ and Oxford: Princeton University Press.

Tobin, J. (1958). "Liquidity Preference as Behavior towards Risk". *The Review of Economic Studies*, 25 (2): 65–86.

Tobin, J. (1969). "A General Equilibrium Approach to Monetary Theory". *Journal of Money, Credit and Banking*, 1 (1): 15–29.

8 Conclusion

To sum up, today's financialisation is not an exogenous accident in the development of contemporary economic systems as some post-Keynesian economists seem to suggest. Nor is it a mere shift in the power relations between financial interests and other economic interests which is changing the way capitalism works.

Financialisation, in our view, is the result of a natural propensity of the capitalist mode of production, which is founded on the circuit of capital. This circuit, in fact, always starts from money capital which is financial capital in its own right and by its very nature. Money capital has to pass through the production process, in the form of productive capital, due to the fact that its apparent self-valorising ability is founded on the appropriation of the surplus value that results from this process. However, money capitalists are periodically seized by fits of giddiness in which they try to increase their capital with no commitment to production and the simplest way to do this is by transforming money capital into interest-bearing capital.

Expanding the financial sector and the financial markets simply creates a larger field of action for interest-bearing capital, on the one hand, and enhances the historical trend towards separation of capital ownership and corporate control – which burst onto the scene with the juridical form of the joint-stock enterprise itself – on the other.

The historical process of financialisation of capital was first hampered and slowed down by the events of the *Great Depression* and then masked and covered up by the exceptional upward phase of the *Golden Age*, but eventually re-emerged in all its power in the advanced countries as they began their decline as the core of the world economy.

Financialisation, of course, boosts a layer of financial rentiers with a *sui generis* psychology, more reminiscent of the ancient landed aristocracy than the modern capitalist class. Financial rentiers managing a large portion of the social surplus may even produce tendencies towards a slower accumulation of capital goods in the former core countries of the world economy, which, in turn, may promote new social problems. Capitalism, indeed, needs growth to avoid the accumulation of social conflicts. However, in our view, the rise

DOI: 10.4324/9781003223221-9

to power of finance and financiers in the Western countries has not radically changed the way capitalism works on a global scale.

After every profound economic crisis, followed by a more or less long period of slowdown of economic activities, economists suddenly begin to ask themselves whether things have definitively changed. This happened during the years following the Panic of 1873, known as the Long Depression, during the Great Depression of the 1930s, after the financial crisis of 1929, and is still the case today, after the financial crisis of 2007–2008, with the re-emergence of secular stagnation theories.

However, although there is probably a link between the financialisation of Western economies and their current structural crises, it would be a mistake to think that there is a one-way cause-and-effect relationship – i.e. the rise to dominance of interest-bearing capital has halted economic growth and generated stagnation. The reverse causal direction is also possible. It is the long-term trend towards stagnation of monopoly capitalism that has improved the primacy of finance in one part of the world. The latter, in turn, has acted on the cause, reinforcing the paralysis of Western economies, but we must not lose sight of the original causal sequence if the aim is to promote adequate political intervention.

The development of a financial system with many sophisticated debt instruments, backing each other through complex networks, could certainly be the cause of increasing macroeconomic instability and financial fragility, like any massive process of unregulated credit money supply. Financial speculation in the context of financial bubbles booming in secondary or derivatives markets can produce new interest-bearing forms of liquidity holdings for corporations, which may be viable alternatives to reinvesting profits in production plants and machinery in periods of high uncertainty. The expansion of consumer credit or public debt can also play the same role.

However, the rise of "money managers" is nothing but the full development of *money-dealing capital* already pointed out by Marx more than one and a half centuries ago.

Thus, in our view, neoliberalism and financialisation are a mere return to the original nature of capitalism after a 30-year interlude due to exceptional historical circumstances such as the events of the Great Depression and, above all, the successive establishment of a new world order, apparently bipolar in political and military terms, but truly characterised by the unchallenged dominance of a single hegemonic economic power – i.e. the "Pax Americana" highlighted by SSAA's early contributions.

Financialisation and increasing inequality are not in a cause-and-effect relationship, but are both results of the process of concentration and centralisation of capital as well as the resulting proletarisation.

However, if we maintain the view that the main problem of financialisation in advanced countries is the progressive shift from real to financial investments, then the main suspect is the financialisation of NFCs.

This process, in turn, is not the result of the "shareholder revolution" and changes in corporate governance imposed by the dominance of the financial markets, as many post-Keynesians hold. In point of fact, NFCs are not innocent victims of the rise to power of the financial markets, but are rather the main actors of their own financialisation process. What is today called the "pursuit of shareholder value" is, in fact, just another way of defining the traditional pursuit of capital owners' interests. This is not a perversion induced by finance, but the very nature of capitalism. It can only accidentally be non-respected when agency problems rise due to the complexity of the big bureaucratic forms of organisation of modern capitalist production. Indeed, the will to defend their own interests has always spurred capital owners to develop several corporate governance rules and managers' incentives to contrast the rise of possible agency problems.

The financialisation of NFCs is truly linked to their nature of forms of ownership based on financial instruments, on the one hand, and the new international context they are operating in today, on the other.

In point of fact, it is the very legal form of the joint-stock organisation, associated with large multinationals and multi-product scopes, that determines the financialisation of NFCs. The most evident proof of this is the rise of giant holding companies long before the current financialisation process.

As we saw in Chapter 3, today's large multinational NFCs can be considered to all intents and purposes an integral part of "finance capital" by their very nature and *finance capital*, according to Hilferding, overcomes the traditional distinction between industrial, commercial and financial capital. It is not the simple synonym for financial capital, but rather the fusion of the latter with every other forms of capital. It presents itself as capital in its own quintessence – i.e. "self-valorising value capable of increasing itself" in every field of human activity.

Joint-stock companies are a form of socialisation of means of production and communication that are so large that they tend to exclude all other forms of capitalistic organisation. The concentration and centralisation of capital have led to a situation in which a few dozen giant corporations dominate the economy of every advanced country and a few hundred multinationals concentrate much of the world's wealth in their hands. In other words, large amounts of capital, in its most abstract form – i.e. money capital – can use the joint-stock form of organisation to gain control of the money capital of many small capitalists and the savings of small savers, too.

Moreover, if financial crises can snowball on the savings glut and corporate saving, as we saw in Chapter 6, is a major cause of the latter, then it is possible to identify a new kind of mechanism which can connect business cycles and financial crises. Indeed, if the corporate savings glut is the consequence of corporate uncertainties deriving from a lasting downturn of a long-term cycle, then financial crises will continue to be sudden manifestations of the tensions which have been accumulating for a long time during this cyclical phase. If the dynamics of corporate saving are fundamental in determining and timing financial crises, then it becomes key to understanding their structural drivers, such as real investment profitability, and identifying the right fiscal policy instruments to control them.

However, it is the investment alternatives available to NFCs worldwide that play a key role in determining the growth rate of each national economic system. As we have seen, the possibilities for foreign investments, both direct and financial, may decrease the domestic accumulation rate.

Thus, as we saw in Chapter 2, in accordance with Arrighi and Braudel's views, current financialisation can be simply understood to be a symptom of the decline of capitalist countries that long occupied the core of the world economy, which is now moving from advanced Western countries towards the emerging Asian countries, pushing Western money capitalists to become the financial creditors of the new functioning capitalists in Asia. The withdrawal of capital from industry and its transformation into financial capital is in fact quite similar, as we saw in Chapter 2, to what some old capitalist oligarchies experienced in past centuries. When the capitalists' oligarchies decline, they initially try to turn themselves into the financial top layer in the hierarchy of the world economy, characterised by the flexibility to switch its investments continually from businesses with diminishing returns to those with growing returns.

When this happens, in the countries of the former core of the world economy, the main actor on the economic scene becomes *interest-bearing capital*, whether channelled by traditional banks or today's sophisticated forms of shadow banking. Yet, the circuit of interest-bearing capital – i.e. *M–M′* – always needs the circuit of productive capital to be implemented somewhere in the world. "Money breeding money" or "profits without production" are only possible in one part of the world if that money capital is transformed into productive capital somewhere else.

Thus, current forms of financialisation in the former core countries can only survive, thanks to globalisation, i.e. the free movement of financial capital around the world and the chances of survival of current financialisation frameworks are strictly dependent on the survival of the latter.

However, as we saw in Chapter 5, if it is theoretically possible to imagine societies composed predominantly of financial rentiers receiving income from their interest-bearing capital lent abroad, this implies a halt to capital accumulation within the country. Thus, in societies where only their top layers are made up of financial rentiers, all the rest of the population would find it difficult to find work and wages other than that as servants of the owning classes. This, on the one hand, implies a relative expansion of the sector of personal services in the country. However, as we have seen, under monopolistic competition, in capitalist societies without capital accumulation, a constant incentive to increase labour productivity survives, which, in a stationary state, cannot improve anything but increase unemployment. This is nothing other than what some sociologists today predict as the rise in "technological unemployment". As the subprime mortgage crisis in 2007 clearly demonstrated, it is not possible to imagine societies in which people without jobs, income and assets can survive for long on credit backed by financial and real estate bubbles. Yet, this means that fully financialised societies are indeed socially unsustainable in the long run.

If the general interest of the ruling class is to manage growing technological unemployment in order to maintain social harmony, new forms of income redistribution, such as basic income, are needed. The only solution to growing technological unemployment in stationary societies is to tax financial rent in order to subsidise the unemployed, promoting a fairer distribution of income.

Although they mainly represent the interests of the ruling classes, governments in advanced countries should therefore have as their main objective ensuring both the long-term conditions of reproduction of the system – i.e. the accumulation of capital – and the maintenance of social order and harmony. Therefore, to ensure the pursuit of the common interest of the ruling class itself, the particularisms of the various interest groups within it must be overcome. In doing so, governments should assume a partial autonomy of their own which does not make them an exclusive field of contention between the various dominant interest groups and leverage the interest of other social groups. This should be much easier insofar as other social interests turn out to be functional to the very long-term survival of the capitalist mode of production and, therefore, consistent with the common interest of the capitalist ruling class itself.

Unfortunately, the neoliberal development phase of contemporary capitalism has given new momentum to the particularism of the various sub-groups of capital owners and to market anarchy, weakening the role of nation states and their very ability to pursue the common interest of the ruling class.

Furthermore, although the present forms of financialisation can only survive, thanks to globalisation, the latter has unfortunately enhanced a worldwide spread of economic instability rather than growth, investment and prosperity. To avoid or limit financial instability, of course, there would theoretically be a need for capital controls and new mechanisms to regulate world finance. At the very least, short-term capital movements, which are the biggest contributor to financial instability, should be regulated with instruments such as the *Tobin Tax*. However, to avoid a decisive de-industrialisation of Western countries, controls on capital movements of a much more drastic nature would be necessary. Otherwise, financialisation could turn into the funeral monument of the historical decline of Western countries. However, once again, this would presuppose the rise of a political will that is above the short-term interests of the dominant economic power groups.

In any case, some recent events – such as Brexit, the re-emerging tendencies towards isolationism in the United States and the international political crisis produced by the Russian-Ukrainian conflict – seem to mark the end of globalisation. Financialisation itself, as we have known it since the 1990s, may also be coming to an end.

However, the possible end of globalisation will certainly give rise to new regional economic blocs. In this case, most future developments in international financial intermediation will depend on the greater or lesser economic homogeneity of these future blocs. Insofar as they are economically heterogeneous, in fact, new financial centres will be able to emerge in each bloc to transfer money capital from the richer areas to the areas with lower wages and higher returns on capital.

Unfortunately, the end of globalisation will also prompt new commercial wars, which the rising Sino-US tensions are a worrying sign. The failure of the alleged new global order that seemed to have emerged at the end of the Cold War is actually leading to a new multipolar contest between old and newly emerging economic powers. As we saw in Chapter 3, international competition between even larger conglomerates also tends to generate rivalries and tensions between the major states which are proud to promote the interests of their own corporations and can finally trigger wars – whether commercial or ultimately military. Thus, we can only hope that the re-emergence of the structural tendencies that capitalism displayed at the beginning of the 20th century will not also represent a return to the international conditions that triggered two catastrophic World Wars.

Index

Note: **Bold** page numbers refer to tables; *italic* page numbers refer to figures and page numbers followed by "n" denote endnotes.

[illegible] information please contact our EU [illegible]
[illegible] GPSR@[illegible] and Francis [illegible]
Verlag GmbH, Kaufingerstraße 24, 80331 München, Germany